DATE DUE

DEMCO 38-296

WELLESLEY STUDIES IN CRITICAL THEORY,
LITERARY HISTORY, AND CULTURE
VOL. 7

ALTERNATIVE
IDENTITIES

GARLAND REFERENCE LIBRARY
OF THE HUMANITIES
VOL. 1848

Wellesley Studies in Critical Theory, Literary History, and Culture

WILLIAM E. CAIN
General Editor

MAKING FEMINIST HISTORY
*The Literary Scholarship
of Sandra M. Gilbert
and Susan Gubar*
edited by William E. Cain

TEACHING THE CONFLICTS
*Gerald Graff, Curricular
Reform, and the Culture Wars*
edited by William E. Cain

**AMERICAN WOMEN
SHORT STORY WRITERS**
A Collection of Critical Essays
edited by Julie Brown

ALTERNATIVE IDENTITIES
*The Self in Literature,
History, Theory*
edited by Linda Marie Brooks

THE CANON IN THE CLASSROOM
*The Pedagogical Implications
of Canon Revision
in American Literature*
edited by John Alberti

GENETIC CODES OF CULTURE?
*The Deconstruction of
Tradition by Kuhn, Bloom,
and Derrida*
by William R. Schultz

**THE NEW CRITICISM AND
CONTEMPORARY
LITERARY THEORY**
Connections and Continuities
edited by William J. Spurlin
and Michael Fischer

**REGIONALISM
RECONSIDERED**
New Approaches to the Field
edited by David M. Jordan

REREADING MODERNISM
*New Directions
in Feminist Criticism*
edited by Lisa Rado

ALTERNATIVE IDENTITIES
The Self in Literature, History, Theory
edited by Linda Marie Brooks

ALTERNATIVE IDENTITIES

The Self in Literature, History, Theory

edited by
Linda Marie Brooks

GARLAND PUBLISHING, Inc.
New York & London / 1995

R

Library of Congress Cataloging-in-Publication Data

Alternative identities : the self in literature, history, theory / edited
by Linda Marie Brooks.
       p.   cm. — (Garland reference library of the humanities ; vol.
1848. Wellesley studies in critical theory, literary history, and culture ; vol. 7)
    Includes bibliographical references.
    ISBN 0-8153-1721-2
    1. Self in literature.   2. Identity (Psychology)   3. Self.   I. Brooks,
Linda Marie.   II. Series: Garland reference library of the humanities ;
vol. 1848.   III. Series: Garland reference library of the humanities.
Wellesley studies in critical theory, literary history, and culture ; vol.
7.
PN56.S46A47   1995
809'.93353—dc20   94-4895
                                                                            CIP

Printed on acid-free, 250-year-life paper
Manufactured in the United States of America

In memory of Marie Hoover Fisher
1889–1992

Contents

General Editor's Introduction

The volumes in this series, Wellesley Studies in Critical Theory, Literary History, and Culture, are designed to reflect, develop, and extend important trends and tendencies in contemporary criticism. The careful scrutiny of literary texts in their own right remains today a crucial part of the work that critics and teachers perform: this traditional task has not been devalued or neglected. But other types of interdisciplinary and contextual work are now being done, in large measure as a result of the emphasis on "theory" that began in the late 1960s and early 1970s and that has accelerated since that time. Critics and teachers now examine texts of all sorts—literary and non-literary alike—and, more generally, have taken the entire complex, multi-faceted field of culture as the object for their analytical attention. The discipline of literary studies has radically changed, and the scale and scope of this series is intended to illustrate this challenging fact.

Theory has signified many things, but one of the most crucial has been the insistent questioning of familiar categories and distinctions. As theory has grown in its scope and intensified in importance, it has reoriented the idea of the literary canon: there is no longer a single canon, but many canons. It has also opened up and complicated the meanings of history, and the materials and forms that constitute it. Literary history continues to be vigorously written, but now as a kind of history that intersects with other histories that involve politics, economics, race relations, the role of women in society, and many more. And the breadth of this historical inquiry has impelled many in literary studies to view themselves more as cultural critics and general intellectuals than as literary scholars.

Theory, history, culture: these are the formidable terms around which the volumes in this series have been organized. A number of these volumes will be the product of a single author or editor. But perhaps even more of them will be collaborative ventures, emerging from the joint enterprise of editors, essayists, and respondents or commentators. In each volume, and as a whole, the series will aim to highlight both distinctive contributions to knowledge and a process of exchange, discussion, and debate. It will make available new kinds of work, as well as fresh approaches to criticism's traditional tasks, and indicate new ways through which such work can be done.

William E. Cain
Wellesley College

Acknowledgments

With the exception of Bernard Dauenhauer's "The Human Way of Being and It's Political Implications," all the chapters in this volume were written or revised especially for *Alternative Identities*. Dauenhauer's article first appeared under a slightly different title in his *Elements of a Responsible Politics* (1991) and is reprinted here courtesy of Kluwer Academic Publishers. Victoria Davion's essay was prepared simultaneously in two separate versions for *Alternative Identities* and for the journal *Social Theory and Practice*. Since the journal version appeared first (19:2 [Summer 1993]: 161–82), the present version appears courtesy of *Social Theory and Practice*.

Preface

This collection grew out of a forum titled "The Self" that I organized in the Spring of 1992. My focus was on the notions of agency and social responsibility that underpin concepts of the self, a focus that seemed all the more pressing given the recent sociopolitical redefinitions of selfhood under the aegis of "Identity Politics." Because of the universal significance that attends such questions, I found that the problem was best approached through an appeal to a number of disciplines. The results are the views collected here, drawn from scholars in Cultural Studies, Comparative Literature, African American Studies, History, Philosophy, Political Science, English Literature, and Sociology.

When I commissioned the essays, Charles Taylor's *Sources of the Self: The Making of the Modern Identity* (1989) had recently appeared. One of the present contributors—Bernard Dauenhauer—was already teaching a seminar on Taylor's book, juxtaposing Taylor's arguments for the self's autonomy with Gilles Deleuze's claims for the self's dissolution. Within a few months, Seyla Benhabib's *Situating the Self: Gender, Community and Postmodernism in Contemporary Ethics* (1992) and two more books by Taylor, *The Ethics of Authenticity* (1992) and *Multiculturalism and "The Politics of Recognition"* (1992) had appeared, all of which addressed the problem of ethics and agency in the new reconfigurations of the self. It is in light of these recent studies, in light of the Winter 1992 seminar in which Dauenhauer thrashed out the issues between Taylor and Deleuze, and especially in light of the contributions by the participants of the Self Forum that this volume is conceived.

Woefully simplified, some of their questions were the following. Does the poststructuralist textualization of the subject affect emerging marginal identities? (James Winders). Did the "self" originate in institutional or vernacular literature? (Sarah Spence). How does African American autobiography transcend the historical script handed it by the U.S.? (R. Baxter Miller). What is history's role in the reconfiguration of the self? (David Roberts). What is education's role? (Lawrence Biskowski). How does an agent function ethically after poststructuralism? (Bernard Dauenhauer). Is the human fetus a self? (Bernard Dauenhauer). What effect does the replacement of a justice-based ethics by an ethics of care have on the self's moral integrity? (Victoria Davion). How is the maternal gaze of several modernist writers a model for postmodern identity? (Margaret Dickie). And finally, how autonomous is the postmodern self? (James Dowd).

The book has gathered too many friends to be mentioned individually, though special thanks should be given to Seyla Benhabib, Charles Taylor, and Nancy K. Miller. Their work on the self and their helpful conversations during participation in the Humanities Center conference on the self that I co-organized in 1993 most immediately influenced my assessment of the social and moral problems entailed in restructuring the self. Thanks also to Mette Hjort for her helpful suggestions during the conference, and to Susan Suleiman for her seminal work on the playfulness of the feminist self and for her involvement in my continuing work on personal identity. Thanks, too, to Henry Louis Gates for his own investigations of multicultural identity and for his suggestions and encouragement while he was here in 1993 as a Charter Lecturer. The volume has benefited stylistically from Joel Black's willingness to read a rough draft of my own essay, and technically from Bernard Dauenhauer's advice on the logistics of the book's production. My old student and friend Jim Tyrell deserves sincere thanks for his computer and indexing help, and even more gratitude for his humor in the long days of final assembly and preparation. Thanks are due to the Andrew W. Mellon Foundation and to the National Endowment for the Humanities whose financial support allowed me to do much of the reading that lead to this volume. I am grateful for the kindness and encouragement of Seyla Benhabib, Tony Brinkley, Eduardo Cadava, Alain Cohen, Elinore Fuchs, Josúe Harari, Richard Macksey, Kishin Moorjani, Wong Kam-ming and members of the UGA Women's Faculty Caucus—Linda Walters, Linda Grant and especially Susan Quinlan, without whose support during the political fracas accompanying every step of its publication this book would never have appeared. I'm also grateful to Garland's Senior Editor, Phyllis Korper, and Assistant Editor, Lynn Zelem, for their efficiency, and to General Editor William Cain for his interest and enthusiasm. Finally, thanks go to all the contributors for their patience with the tardiness of this volume's appearance, a delay due to the death of Marie Hoover Fisher—my oldest friend, my more than self, my grandmother, who felt that all this to-do about the self was just piffle. I dedicate this volume to her, if she'll have it.

Linda Marie Brooks

PART ONE

Introduction

Alternative Identities:
Stating the Problem

Linda Marie Brooks

> I would add something that remains required by. . . . the
> definitions of the . . . subject . . . , namely, a certain *respon-
> sibility*. The singularity of the 'who' is not the individuality
> of a thing . . . , it is not an atom. It is a singularity
> that . . . divides itself in gathering itself together to answer
> to the other, whose call somehow precedes its own identi-
> fication with itself, for to this call I can *only* answer, have
> already answered . . . Here, no doubt, begins the link with
> the larger questions of ethical, juridical, and political re-
> sponsibility around which the metaphysics of subjectivity
> is constituted.[1]
>
> — Derrida, 1991

> Nothing, not God, is greater to one's self than one's self.[2]
> — Whitman

Following its theoretical devaluation in the last decades,
the concept of the self is reemerging (again),[3] this time playing a
major role in the current sociopoliticized re-evaluation of society.
As Derrida's recent "answer to the other" indicates, vanguard
poststructuralists have themselves acknowledged the need for a
reappraisal of subjectivity in terms of "ethical, juridical, and political responsibility."[4] In the self's postmodern ascendancy,
multicultural models of the self have replaced individualist ones,
with gender, ethnic, and racial considerations influencing the
concept of personal identity as never before.

3

This collection is not intended as another manifesto of identity politics, an addition to what Laura Kipnis calls the "hypervisibility of the ideological category of the subject."[5] If anything, this volume aims to sidestep the internal inconsistencies currently associated with the issue. Certainly, the subject's current visibility is related to the emergence of global movements of liberation, with pressure by postcolonial and other marginalized groups for "more complex modulations of agency that can articulate the internal contradictions of subjectivity under 'late capitalism.'" But, as Nancy K. Miller writes: "This latter configuration has given rise, paradoxically both to 'identity politics'—the claims arising from a repertoire of often conflicting social inscriptions—and its repudiation (dunned internally by the antiessentialist discourses and externally exploded by geopolitical catastrophes)" (Miller 20). The present collection seeks what Miller calls "more complex modulations of agency," but in terms of the subject's ethical responsibility. For, in spite of the healthy questioning of hegemonous notions of individualism by these global movements, the new "relational"[6] views of human identity they produce (celebrated as "interactive," "situational," "embedded," "encumbered") have tended to leave the role of individual agency unclear. Even contemporary holistic models, which appear so crucial to ecological concerns have, as Mette Hjort observes in a recent study, tended to obscure the concepts of human agency and social responsibility.[7] The purpose of this collection is to address the question of the individual agent in current gender-, racial-, ethnic- and culturally-based models of selfhood. While the present essays offer various approaches, all reflect the multicultural project of replacing the static, unified self of traditional views with a notion of personal identity as evolving and multifaceted. And while the alternative self defined in these essays is sensitive to its own situatedness—to the situations in which it developed and which it functions throughout life—it is still chiefly characterized by a personal responsibility, a "presence" (for want of a better word) that stands accountable for its actions. Having suggested something of the currency and significance of these alternative notions of the self, I shall in what follows provide a brief characterization of each of the contributions.

I. Language and the Self

The Ambivalent Self

James Winders' study illustrates the strategic ambivalence underlying current redefinitions of the self. On one hand, the poststructuralist subversion of the self on the basis of its linguistic ground is both accurate and necessary. A grab bag of overdetermined tropes, the self-as-concept is easily undone by a flip through any dictionary. And like the tip of an iceberg, the self's conceptual inconsistencies reveal only a fraction of the more grievous problem attached to the Western penchant for individualism. Distorted by the ideology of self, Western thought has focused on the primacy of individual rights and freedom to the detriment of community life.[8] It has ignored the "real multiplicity" of human existence, for what moves history and defines ethical issues are not selves but "large social and economic forces." In the tradition of Mandel, Althusser and Mayhew,[9] Winders argues that to focus on the celebrities of an event—whether Robespierre in the French Revolution or the white policemen and Rodney King in the L.A. Riots—is to grossly distort that event. The logic of the recent L.A. riots has less to do with good or bad individuals, whether the selves who beat a relatively defenseless man or the selves who robbed defenseless store owners, than with a complex economic system that, equating material wealth and power with the good life, excludes racial minorities as participants. Excluding them from justice, Winders explains, is ancillary. Given this broader logic, an emphasis on the question of self is misguided and even pernicious.[10]

On the other hand, though Winders rejects the concept of self regarding societal events, he supports a concept of self regarding the emerging identities of marginal groups. The "contradictory" strategy behind this apparent reversal forms the crux of the essay. The "self" that Winders allows into section four of his essay—a section whose epigraph from Beckett's *Unnamable* reads, "The other advances full upon me"—is an alternative to the self of Western rationalism. It is an *evocation* rather than a concept and it is produced by the continually unresolved interplay of multiculturalism's two opposing projects—the rejection of hegemonic ideas of identity and the carving out of a space for minority selves.[11] To evoke this kinetic self, Winders assumes the dual strategy of the marginal groups he invokes, carving out the same conflicting spaces within his own essay. Like the nonrational tenor of postcolonial histories, the self produced by these conflicting spaces eludes rational boundaries: "The personal subjective histories of colonial Indian subjects," Winders writes, "defy interpretation according to the categories of private, bourgeois individualism." "[They] spoke with a 'voice of ambivalence' that Western historians have excluded from their assumptions about subjective human experience." Winders' own essay recreates this personal voice of ambivalence, a voice designed to subvert Western assumptions about the self.

Recent studies by Seyla Benhabib and Nancy K. Miller clarify the strategy behind Winders' personalized rhetoric.[12] The so-called "private" considerations of nurturance and care, Benhabib argues—considerations wrongly confined to the domestic sphere and excluded from the moral domain—are not only integral components of human identity, but complex sources of ethical behavior.[13] The nuanced and personal character of these relations guide Winders' writing. And because a programmatic ambivalence is inherently self-reflexive, Winders supplements this private quality with the project of self-questioning suggested by Dipesh Chakrabarty: "I ask for a history," Chakrabarty writes, "that deliberately makes visible, within the very structure of its narrative forms, its own repressive strategies and practices." Following Chakrabarty, Winders continually subverts the potentially repressive structure of his own essay, drawing in one instance on his own private meditations on the photographs of gay/lesbian poets that he discovered in an anthology:

> In 1990, the poet Joy Harjo gave a reading at a conference I attended in Oregon, and I attended a reception for her afterwards. I had been aware of her importance as a native American writer, but here was her photograph in the pages of this anthology. My first response to myself was the clumsy 'I didn't know she was a lesbian.' Why didn't I? Should I have been able to tell? Many people expect lesbians to have very short hair, but Harjo's is quite long. Is that in keeping with her native American identity? Should

> it remind me not to assume anything about a lesbian's
> hair?

Winders' diaristic and self-reflexive witnessing of his experience at the Oregon poetry reading and of his responses to the anthology photographs dramatize what Benhabib calls the situated, "concrete" other, the self unavailable to universal or substitutionalist concepts of identity. [14]

Winders' apparently contradictory response to questions of identity does not discard the concept of self but rather the grammar of the singular Western subject, the "subject" whose existence rests on positing and subsequently appropriating its objects. In its place, Winders posits a working alternative—interactive, relational, and endlessly referring, in which influence is regarded not as oppressive but as mutual and participatory. His conclusion of the essay with the "talking blues"—a form of communication that in its echo of the Derridean "pre-verbal,"[15] collapses the self/other distinction—is not accidental; having shown the inadequacy of rational language, Winders draws from nonrational, non "human" discourse to evoke the programmatic ambivalence of alternative identity.

The Vernacular Self

In her analysis of the vernacular literature of twelfth-century France, Sarah Spence demonstrates the medieval origin of the alternative self invoked by Winders. Yet, while Winders sees the linguistic base of Western identity as its dissolution, Spence argues that vernacular language constitutes, indeed embodies the self. Challenging Michel Foucault's claim that the self "begins" with the "desiring subject" of ancient Greece, Spence argues that the modern self surfaces in twelfth-century France, in a "complex interaction of body, language and space" produced by the vernacular literature that came to challenge the medieval Latin tradition. Spence demonstrates the interaction of this literature with human subjectivity and with the body by comparing it to Latin texts of the Augustinian tradition. [16]

Vernacular writers favored clear, concrete presentation of a topic, in contrast to the Church fathers' preference for "concealment" through religious interpretation or glossing.[17] The vernacular relation to the body and text was also crucially different. Drawing for illustration on the seven marks on Dante's brow in the *Purgatorio*, Spence shows that contrary to the Church fathers, the "good" reading or interpretation does not conceal the body but "incorporates [it] into the text in its engaged interaction with the work."[18] As a type of subjectification of the objective world in this sense, Dante's and vernacular literature's inter-weaving of body and text produced an intersection of subject and object that gave rise to the construction of an early self, an intersection of subject and object through the text. Through a comparison of Abelard, Marie de France, Raimbaut and others, Spence illustrates how the vernacular text provides a space of ac-tion that is related to the body while not being bound by it. As such, vernacular authors are able to create in and through their texts a model for the self.

Marking a crucial distinction between medieval and Carte-sian models of subjectivity, Spence uncovers one of the key ele-ments of current multicultural reconceptions of personal iden-tity. The medieval model of subjectivity, she writes, does *not* re-fer to the self that develops in response to a proto-Cartesian awareness of the subject/object split between self and world— that moment when the subjective becomes alienated from the objective and is re-allied to it through the mediation of language. Such mediation does not represent the origins of selfhood but simply "masculine efficacy in the world: the Oedipal stage, after all, doubles the male, not the female figure." Preceding the abso-lute, unified self of masculine efficacy is an earlier "ambivalent" self, allied not with power, alienation, and externalization but with appropriation and internalization—the subjectified object which later can be reobjectified, reified, reintroduced into the world.

It is not by chance that this earlier self in actual child de-velopment is pre-verbal, much as the Derridean alternative self invoked by Winders' "blues." There is, Spence writes, "at first nothing unified about this creation; a range of possibilities, rather, opens up which deny the necessity for an either/or choice. It is important to realize that at this stage there is no economy, only ambivalence and slippage." Ultimately, the self that emerges in the Renaissance and that comes forward as the definitive model of identity for Western culture is in fact derived from an earlier, more open and ambivalent stage of identity, the identity found in vernacular texts of medieval France. The very certainty of the "Cartesian subject"—the primary model with the Augustinian for the Western concept of self—rests on the uncertain, shifting ground of this earlier stage of selfhood, a stage that actually forms the basis for multicultural and indeed for postmodern reconfigurations of the self.

If language scatters the self in Winders, it concretizes the self in Spence.[19] What to Winders is the self's liability—the infinitely referring textuality referred to in poststructuralist criticism—is to Spence the self's strongest asset. Spence's argument reflects the central assumption of postmodernism: the fabricated, specifically the linguistically constructed, nature of ideas. Grounded in such an assumption, the self is admittedly a construct, not simply of language but of proliferating sociocultural systems and forces. But this fabricated and shifting nature does not impair the self's function as a guidepost for our understanding of the world and for the way we act within it. On the contrary, the capacity of the concept of personal identity to function as an ethical guide lies precisely in our understanding, and our continual awareness, of the self's constructed and evolving character.

Unscripting the Self

If we assume the constructedness or "narrativity" of the self, we can posit a working model of identity and of moral agency that can continually accommodate the multiplicity of ethnic and cultural groups that constitute a global culture. We can even judge the moral efficacy of various concepts of agency, as R. B. Miller shows, by gauging the universality of the ideals that underlie them. This approach to selfhood relies on the continuous re-performance of the scripts that make up world culture. A script, Miller observes, remains a living text only through repeated performances, repeated renewals, in time. America's Declaration of Independence, one of the most effective scripts of autonomous human agency, remains vital and effective only through its continuous accommodation to changing needs.

In a radical version of this accommodation and renewal process, African American autobiographers become, in their narratives, tellers, compelled by their survival to revise the limited historical scripts of American tradition that have been handed them. "What they want for their own narratives," Miller writes, "is to achieve the performance—the physical presence—within historical time and social space" that can vitalize and reinscribe such scripts. African American autobiographical narrative strategically calls for human theater, for the dynamic reliving and retelling of American history within human time. Only within the actual "telling of the story [can] the teller come to recognize the limitations of denotative language, of literal words." And only within a certain revisionary space can such telling occur. Repeating the "conflicting space" of the counter-narratives in Winders, and the preverbal and bodily space of the vernacular texts that challenge the Latin scripts in Spence, the social space of black American autobiography becomes the uncharted narrative territory "between the lines" of the script of American slavery.

Miller illustrates the transformation of this script and the creation of another mythic self in the autobiographies of Frederick Douglass, Linda Brent (Harriet Jacobs), W. E. B. Du Bois, and Langston Hughes. Much as the young Frederick Douglass writes "between the lines" of his young master's lesson book, transforming the dead slate with the living story of his self-creation, Douglass the autobiographer reinscribes his historical background with the story of his rebirth as timeless artist. As Miller explains, "Enslaved by the historical script, [Douglass] reads within this script the myth and metaphor of slavery as an idea and as a historical sign of human evil. Hence he revises for himself a romantically imaginative writing or art based on what he intuits as a divine design for his personal self."

A vivid instance of Douglass's reinscription of his historical identity occurs during the scene of his beating in Mr. Gardiner's shipyard, in which the historical events and characters are left behind in time while Douglass's mythic self, the self based on the transcendent ideal of racial equality, is lifted out of temporality and into the timeless realm of all future readers of his autobiography: Following the scene in which four white men beat him, Douglass writes:

> Dear Reader, you can hardly believe the statement, but it is true, and therefore I write it down. No fewer than fifty men stood by . . . and not a man of them all interposed . . . There were four against one. . . and no one said, 'that is enough'; but some cried out, 'kill him . . . . knock his brains out—he struck a white person.' I mention this inhuman outcry to show the character of the men, and the spirit of the time, at Gardiner's ship yard, and, in Baltimore generally, in 1836.

As Miller explains, the men who flail Douglass

> remain imprisoned within the historical script of their time but the rhetorical appeal of the artist . . . is to the reader in some future time when racism will be diminished . . . 'I already saw myself wielding my pen, as well as my voice, in the great work of renovating the public mind.'

The process works similarly in *Incidents in the Life of a Slave Girl*, the autobiography of "Linda Brent" or Harriet Jacobs, a nineteenth-century slave in North Carolina. Restaging the history of her own slavery, Brent transforms the "bill" recording her sale into a dead, commercial "script," transfiguring her autobiographical persona into a timeless narrator of American injustice.

Miller does not mean that the selves produced by these autobiographical apotheoses are otherworldly. The vibrancy with which they reenact their moribund scripts place them squarely within this world, as compelling in contemporary and future eras as they were during the period of American slavery that produced him. What fades, and what is exposed as insignificant because it fades, is the temporally local and thus static human identity within America's historical script. As Miller argues, the continual vitality of the autobiographical self stems from its continual re-performance through and within history, a process paralleling the vitalization of old stories by oral tradition. Like the strategic appropriation achieved by oral tradition, the art of African American autobiography continually reinscribes, and thus renews the vital presence obscured between the deadening lines of American racism.

II. Self and History

The Weak Self

The history that effects the self in David Roberts' essay is not
Miller's history; it is not a scripted set of events in a specific national past which the marginalized self must overcome. It is
rather an omnipresent phenomenon that grounds the identity of
all groups. When the meaning of history is metaphysically authorized, the self grounded by history is similarly meaningful; it
is "strong," autonomous, like the supposedly transcendent author in whose image the self is made; when history divests itself
of metaphysical authorization, the notion of the strong self dissolves. In its postmetaphysical period, Roberts argues, the period
that spans the late nineteenth century to the present, the sense of
history becomes the main element in the subversion of the strong
self. Postmodern thinkers such as Foucault posit "the dissolution
of 'man,' subjectivity, the self into history," so that, as Ian Hacking puts it, "'every way in which I can think of myself as a person and an agent is something that has been constituted within a
web of historical events . . . [T]he noumenal self is nothing.'"
      History on this view becomes suffocating. We feel bound,
trapped by the idea that "what we are" is a historical construct,
the "accidental result of a particular intersection of contingent
systems of power-knowledge." The self's dead-end relation to
history has as a result given rise in modernism to attempts to
remove the self from history, and in more recent theories to a
denial of the self altogether. To Roberts, however, a deepened
awareness of the role played by history in such theories can provide a way to salvage the self. There are, he observes, two conflicting responses to the dilemma of the postmetaphysical self:
the antihistorical and the historical. Antihistorical accounts argue
that human being is possible only by disrupting the mechanisms
of the historical world. A historical account, such as Roberts,
suggests a more constructive view of the modernist tension between self and the historical world. On this account, "the self becomes weak, provisional, historically specific, yet still coherent

enough for ongoing self-creation and world-creation through action."

Roberts' aim in the essay is to follow the strand of these two responses as they gather force in the late nineteenth century and then to compare that early development to current views of the subject, with a view of sorting the possibilities for a weak self. He first examines the early modernist preoccupations in the modern literary writers, Gide, Hoffmansthal, Musil, and Eliot, and then in the leading philosophers of the period, Nietzsche, Croce, and Heidegger. Nietzsche and Croce were alike in presenting a positive way of experiencing humanity's involvement with history. Nietzsche's *amor fati* and eternal recurrence allowed him to affirm a circular and hence completed history that does not overwhelm but permits humanity an innocent play. Croce, the early proponent of the weak self, posited an unfinished history in which the self's vocation and thus its coherence depended on its participation, however provisional, with the world as historical. Heidegger, by contrast, sought a mode of passive alienation from the world as history in order to "unthink" its technology.

Crucial to the modernist preoccupation with the post-metaphysical self was an assumption of its connection to history, an assumption that clarifies more recent theoretical views. Gadamer's hermeneutic approach to the self, in its focus on the truth and certainty of the outmoded strong self, overemphasizes the role of history and thus allies postmodern identity with a type of neo-authoritarianism. Poststructuralist thinkers, though offering premises that bode well for weak selfhood, subvert its possibility through their dismissals of history. Roberts finds Foucault mistakenly conflating history with the movement of power mechanisms, which leads him to reject history *and* the self as structures of dominance. Derrida, Roberts argues, overemphasizes the role of Hegel and thus of metaphysics in history, consigning history and the subject to the status of textual construct; this project, far from underwriting the intersubjectivity and communal history-making of the weak self, offers only subjectless strategies of disruption and play.[20] Rorty, whose neopragmatist leanings might support the weak self, nevertheless reduces history to an aesthetic activity through his

Bloomian emphasis on stronger and ever more novel misreadings of the historical.

Hence while hermeneutic approaches overemphasize history, poststructural attitudes toward the self are reducible to what Roberts calls a "premium on ritualistic disruption, on playing out of bounds, on autonomy—all defined in opposition to congruence with history." However, some sort of historical self would seem required for the successful continuation of life. While the transcendent principles authorizing the strong self are gone, evaluating goes on because, Roberts writes: "human being entails care for the happening of the world and human beings respond, if individually to the world on that basis."[21] Because we need to learn about this world from our need to act within it, we need the willingness to say "we," he argues, the willingness to admit to some sort of agential selfhood, regardless of how merely historical, how weak.

Re-Educating the Self

The human interaction that defines weak selfhood requires acceptance of and responsibility toward others, both qualities acquired through education. Yet, as Lawrence Biskowski notes, education has itself become suspect. Education has always been seen in terms of the self: we educate in a very large sense to *produce* "selves." But with the diminishment of the strong self, the meaning of education becomes problematic. What is there to educate, we might ask. More important, what do we mean, and *intend*, by the phrase "to educate"? How is the phrase "to educate" related to multicultural reconfigurations of the self? How should it be?

In exploring the assumptions of conventional education, Biskowski shows that education has always been at the service of one agenda or another, an agenda that envisions an ideal subject and that is designed to produce that subject by bracketing elements that threaten that agenda. To educate is to condition, and to condition is to exclude. Historically, projects of ethnic cleansing—whether in Armenia, Germany, or now in the former Yugoslavia—have always been the direct result of some form of exclusionary education.

Biskowski's answer to the insular selfhood produced by conventional eduation is in one sense to offer the solution given by Winders and Roberts—the reinsertion of the strong or noumenal self into a receptive interaction with the concrete world. Drawing on Hannah Arendt, Biskowski argues that Western philosophical tradition and the educational systems based on it have characteristically privileged values and human figures that (ostensibly) transcend situated human existence.[22] Educating the postmetaphysical self would entail instructing her not in the certainties and values of a single culture, but in the tentative and always evolving process of understanding the values of diverse cultures. The contextual emphasis of postmetaphysical education would be no mere relativism; it would rest on what Benhabib (also using Arendt) calls an "interactive universalism," in which universal principles, with their moral and epistemological blindess to "marginal" considerations, would at least partially give way to contextual responsibility. (Both Benhabib and Taylor admit that in questions of fundamental human rights—the right to life, for instance—universal principles must supersede the contextual.) The self "produced" by such an education, if one could still use that term, would not be the atomistic "individual"—the strong, autonomous, identity envisioned by Western education—but an alternative, "plural" figure—constantly receptive (even "weak"), responsive, and responsible.

This sense of self is grounded in a type of strategy, a type of play that underpins all human identity. To clarify such play, Biskowski summons an Arendtian/Heideggerian view of "world"—"world" as the complex web of human relationships and plurality—as the "one enduring point of reference" that is absolutely necessary to the self. There can be no subject or self without reference to its object, its "enduring point of reference." A gaming character thus emerges in the concept of selfhood, a sense of dialogic interplay or strategic interaction hailed in recent feminist theories (notably Susan Suleiman's),[23] in which one learns to assume another's perspective as one's own. To Biskowski, this strategy is epitomized in Arendt's praise of the presocratic Greek, who "learned to exchange his own viewpoint, his own 'opinion' . . . with those of his fellow citizens." Presocratic Greeks, Arendt wrote, "learned to *understand*—not to understand one another as individual persons, but to look upon the same world from one another's standpoint, to see the same in very different and frequently opposing aspects."

Biskowski's invocation of Arendt's "perspectival consciousness" repeats Benhabib's similar urging of Arendt's "enlarged thinking."[24] "Perspectival consciousness" in Arendt's terms, or "reversal of perspectives" in Benhabib's, is made possible by the kind of ironic play that grounds a situational sensibility. Such play, as Suleiman describes it, is the systematic willingness to engage self-reflexively and receptively with otherness. In "The Laughing Mother" Suleiman writes,

> Playing is an activity through which the human subject most freely and inventively constitutes herself or himself. To play is to affirm an 'I' . . . ; at the same time, and contrarily, it is in playing that the 'I' can experience itself in its most fluid and boundaryless state. Barthes speaks of being 'liberated from the binary prison, putting oneself in a state of infinite expansion.' Winnicot calls the play experience 'one of a non-purposive state, as one might say a sort of ticking over of the unintegrated personality' (Suleiman, *Subversive Intent*, 179–81).

To Biskowski, educating the postmetaphysical self entails instruction in the kind of play by which one constitutes one's personality as boundaryless and unintegrated; instruction in the ability to engage creatively and expansively with the not-self. The self such instruction creates reveals the nonpejorative sense of Roberts term "weak"—fluid, non-purposive, universal.

Arendt's teaching about selves, education and the "world," Biskowski writes, "is consistent with democracy, liberal concern for the individual, and postmodern anxiety about the autonomy of the self in the face of ubiquitous power and domination. It poses no direct threat to the private manifestations of other belief systems, modes of self-expression, or ways of being in the world. And it does so without recourse to metaphysical pretension, aesthetic expressivism, or transcendental ideals of selfhood." But it also has a two-fold effect: it outlines an educational philosophy that focuses on "enlarged thinking," on an ability to think with and as the other; and it creates the concept of the receptive self, the being who is guided by an acceptance of and a sense of responsibility for the "world." The question would seem to be, then, not what education should teach the self. It is rather whether education—as a process of self-cultivation envisioned by both the presocratic and by most (far older) Asian philosophies—should be geared not to *producing* a self but to promoting a capacity for selflessness.[25]

The Self En Route

Winders and Spence show how an awareness of the self's fabricated nature foregrounds its ability to accommodate the other. R. B. Miller shows how attention to the language underlying a model of selfhood can detect how the model has ceased to accommodate. Bernard Dauenhauer's argument for the self as a being *en route* shows how a narrative account of identity recasts static notions of autonomous selfhood in terms of a dynamic interaction of multiple forces. Like Roberts, Dauenhauer's aim is to reconstruct the concepts of human agency and responsibility in the wake of poststructural critiques of the subject. Using Heidegger's *Dasein*, or being in the world, and Merleau-Ponty's view of human being as "interrogatory," Dauenhauer suggests that being human "is to be in the world interrogatively," that is, to struggle in an interchange with the world which invites us to question. This interrogatory struggle "constitutes the human being as one who is always and essentially *en route*."

Though interrogation is basically open, however, it is not undetermined: "What calls forth my responses today includes not merely things ready for interrogation but also previous responses, both of my own and of other people. . . Thus when I think or act I am responding to a world already bearing the mark of prior human questioning." For Dauenhauer, poststructuralism's argument for boundless nonreferentiality and by extension for the denial of the subject, agency, and responsibility, actually affirms the possibility of the self. It clarifies the fact that as beings *en route*, we are embedded in an activity that is already established and irrevocably human:

> [T]o be *en route* is to find oneself always already linked to
> a route which is there to be trod and tended. Without
> route there is no human way of being. Without people
> there is no route . . . To be *en route* is to walk a path, to be a
> path dweller . . . All of our sayings and doings are inter-
> ventions in a game which is already under way before we
> arrive on the scene and which will continue after we die.

Hence while we are called upon to interrogate the world we are
determined by interrogations that have come before us. Being
determined in this sense is not to deny the self but to ensure the
self's responsibility.

The self *en route* is also constituted by the social reciprocity
and outcome of its actions. For Dauenhauer, this aspect of being
en route is epitomized by two of Hannah Arendt's notions of action. In the first, the self is both doer and sufferer: "Because the
actor always moves among and in relation to other acting beings,
he is never merely 'doer' but always and at the same time a sufferer . . . [T]he story that an act starts is composed of its consequent deeds and sufferings." In the second, action and the
historical accumulation of their consequences are the only
medium through which one *becomes* a self. Arendt again: "This
unpredictability of outcome is closely related to the revelatory
character of actions and speech, in which one discloses one's self
without ever . . . knowing . . . whom he reveals . . . This
unchangeable identity of the person . . . becomes tangible only in
the story of the actor's and speaker's life." The self is not only
linked with the other through its actions, in other words, but its
identity is generated only through the historical consequences of
these actions. The self becomes discernable through, not despite
its history.

A vital part of the idea that one's actions are self-constitu-
tive is the contribution that the self *en route* makes to the path she
or he treads. Dauenhauer writes:

> To walk a path is, of course, to follow it. But it is also to
> break it. Path walking both brings about something new
> and preserves something old . . . To be *en route* then is to
> struggle with and for the path. This struggle . . . is, of
> course, a struggle in which each person is inextricably in-
> volved with other people. It manifests itself in. . . .
> performances . . . The world elicits our interventions . . . It

> is through our interventions that [we discover] what the
> path is and what each of us is can come to be.

Dauenhauer's project is to reestablish the concepts of agency and of moral responsibility in light of recent critiques of the subject. By recasting poststructuralism's negative focus on the subjects' belatedness in terms of the dynamic interchange typical of "being *en route*," he makes significant inroads for both concepts.

The Potential Self

One of the most compelling aspects of Dauenhauer's contribution to the present discussion is its reflection, in his afterword "Self Questioning," of his own struggle with the question of the self. The developing nature of his view of identity becomes itself an illustration of the thinking self *en route*. Dauenhauer's concept of being *en route* stems from an essay that predates the present volume by several years. In the process of resubmitting the concept to the audience during the Forum that gave rise to this volume, Dauenhauer discovered a problem. The problem became the occasion of the essay "Self Questioning" and of the discovery of certain ethical implications underpinning the model of selfhood as being in time.

Dauenhauer's model of the being *en route* is an attractive one, for in it the self remains relatively unaffiliated and hence receptive to the multiplicity of ethnic and cultural perspectives with which one can interact. But the problem of such an understanding of the self is that it applies only to the healthy. As a being *en route*, one has or is a self only if one is physically and mentally capable of "journeying" on the path—of being actively influenced by its preestablished directions and of actively contributing to a change in those directions. Those who are not functional in the requisite sense, who cannot tread the path—persons on life support systems, the human embryo, the mentally impaired—do not, by Dauenhauer's earlier account, have or constitute selves.

The exclusion constitutes a serious omission. Yet its discovery permits Dauenhauer to develop in his Afterword a more fundamental quality of the nature of selfhood, specifically in relation to the question of the human fetus. The quality relies equally on the metaphor of the being in time. Yet, in this instance, the definition of selfhood focuses on the self's *potentiality* within a temporal progress, on the possibility of its coming into being.

Dauenhauer follows Paul Ricouer and the post-Cartesian consensus that all human beings have at some time had bodies, have at some time occupied a spatio/temporal site.[26] Possessed of bodies, we are implicated in the orders of physical and social causality. In the case of time, this translates as the idea that any instant of one's existence is related to all other instants of one's existence. This being the case, Dauenhauer argues, we can say that each of us is "geared into three . . . modes of temporality"— "one's own time," "social time," and "cosmic time"—all three of which are at least a sufficient condition for one to be a self.[27]

While being a self depends on our experiencing time in its full trimodality, the most important of these modes is one's own time, the *conscious* time: It is "the time in which I deliberate and choose, I evaluate what I have done and suffered, and make plans for what I will try to do in the future . . . It is the time in which I experience my own unattenuated individuality". Without this mode the other modes can have no meaning, or at least we cannot know whether they have meaning in the case of those who are not conscious. Those who are conscious, however, or who have the potential of becoming conscious can be said to lay claim to the status of selfhood, or at least to potential selfhood. Selfhood thus hinges on whether one can or cannot become conscious of one's trimodal existence; if one can come into consciousness of it, now or in the future, one has a self, or a potential self; if one cannot either now or in the future come into consciousness of it, one does not, and can not have a self.

Dauenhauer's treatment of the potential self is admittedly dependent on whether we accept the experience of time and/or bodiliness as relevant to the determination of selfhood. If we do, however, the concept of the potential self has two implications for the ethical propriety of abortion. The status of selfhood in the incurably comatose, the irreparably insane and in the brain damaged or fatally malformed embryo—in all those beings who cannot ever consciously experience the trimodality of their existence—is questionable at best, and denied at worst. But the self-hood of the curably comatose, of the curably insane, or of the healthy embryo would seem to be undeniable. If one argues, then, from the position of fundamental human rights—supposing that the right to life is chief among these rights—then Dauenhauer's definition of the self as a conscious or potentially conscious being in time clearly makes abortion morally wrong.

A rights-based concept of selfhood is only part of the question, however: communal interchange and situational context is the other. Where Dauenhauer's discussion leaves this aspect open-ended—he does not deal with the rights/responsibilities issue—Victoria Davion takes it up.

III. Self and/as Other

The Caring Self

The notion of the self as an autonomous individual with inherent rights superseding all other considerations appears antithetical to the alternative forms of identity presented here. Alternative identity would seem to make sense solely in terms of its context: it is not absolute but situational; it does not so much have "rights," as responsibilities. Unlike the strong, autonomous self based on justice and rights and operating on universal principles, alternative identity is weak in the sense that it is based on a perspective of care and operates on a contextual or situational basis.

Victoria Davion seeks to demonstrate the necessary interaction of these apparently incommensurable notions of identity, the strong and the weak, as they manifest themselves in human relationships. Davion's aim in the essay is twofold: to argue that our choice of "caring relationships" (the conventional province of the weak self) involves our "moral autonomy" (the province of the strong self), and is thus an ethical matter; and to discover how we maintain our moral autonomy in caring relationships. The apparent conflict between strong and weak notions of the self is foregrounded by the account of caring relationships given in Nel Noddings' radical version of Carol Gilligan's "care perspective."[28] It is not Gilligan's care perspective that exacerbates the "strong/weak self" debate, Davion argues, but Noddings' attempt to turn the care perspective into a full-fledged alternative to a rights-based, or justice-based, ethics.

Noddings' account of caring relationships involves significant moral risk. This is because her requirement that the caring person, or the "one-caring," undergo a "motivational displacement" and "engrossment" in the motives of the loved one can easily undermine the "one-caring's" moral autonomy. On Noddings' account, the one-caring is expected to forgo her/his most deeply held values and adopt those of the loved one in order to maintain the relationship. Thus Ms. A., in Noddings' example, whose closest friend Jim is an African American but whose husband belongs to the Ku Klux Klan is expected, according to Noddings' care ethic, not only to have his dinner on the table promptly at six so he can make a Klan meeting, and to buy him a gun, but to fight on the Klan's side against Jim and his friends. Though the example is extreme, Davion demonstrates convincingly that the "motivational displacement" and "engrossment" required by Noddings' care ethic subverts the moral autonomy of the one-caring.

Davion argues that an understanding of the problems of Noddings' theory serves two purposes: it demonstrates the ethical nature of choosing and evaluating our caring relationships, and it begins to indicate how a care perspective can help guide our evaluation of caring relationships. But such an understanding also uncovers in Davion's essay a more integrated form of alternative identity, a notion of self that possesses both weak *and* strong characteristics. According to Noddings' "relational ontology," the only absolute value is relationship: ethics are based on the type of beings people are—"we don't have connections; we *are* connections." However, Noddings makes two erroneous leaps from this ontology which uncovers the clue to evaluating caring relationships and also outlines the strong/weak self mentioned earlier. She first jumps from the idea that relationships are necessary to survival, to the idea that all relationships are good; she then infers that relationships are more valuable than the individuals relating.

This fusion of selves with relationships destroys the separateness necessary for genuine caring. As Davion quotes Sarah
Hoagland: "One who cares must perceive herself not just as both
separate and related, but as ethically both separate and related.
Otherwise, we cannot acknowledge difference." Davion uses
Hoagland's notion of the necessity of difference as a guide to the
choice and evaluation of caring relationships, and to the protection of one's moral autonomy with*in* a relationship. She writes:
"If one cannot acknowledge difference, one cannot evaluate the
projects of others, in order to have a responsible decision as to
whether to promote those projects oneself." But Hoagland's argument for the self's difference also illustrates the
"strong/weak" selfhood implied in Davion's argument.

Hoagland's insistence on the self's distinctness is borne out
by Seyla Benhabib and Charles Taylor, both of whom argue for
the importance of the self in multicultural considerations. To
Taylor, one cannot respect or "recognize" the projects, culture, or
identity of another unless one maintains one's own identity.
Without separateness, there would be no one to do the recognizing. (This ignores the insult of the mere lip-service "respect" we
give when we "recognize" another—particularly marginalized
others—without acknowledging our own values in that recognition.)[29] To Benhabib, recognizing the other requires constant
awareness of the distinction between "mere empathy"—a
"feeling with," which diffuses the recognizer's distinctness—and
an "enlarged mentality"—which allows the recognizer to genuinely take the other's standpoint.[30] A central requirement of the
care perspective is the ability to "reverse perspectives," or to take
the viewpoint of another. One cannot reverse perspectives, however, if she does not already have her own perspective.

What is missing in Noddings, Davion argues, is a focus on
the self, on "individuals within caring relationships as important
in themselves." The ethical ideal entails more than maintaining
relationships; it must also include one's vision of "one's best
self," a self that cannot be compromised.[31] To have moral integrity requires not simply caring for others, but for one's own
moral autonomy—"it requires that in each situation one pays
careful attention to what one is doing and who one is becoming
in doing it." The value of Davion's contribution to alternative

notions of the self is that by revealing the moral inconsistencies
of selflessness, she demonstrates the logical necessity of
including autonomy, integrity and distinctness—i.e. elements of
strong selfhood—in any multicultural reconfiguration of the self
as *weak*. She creates, in a sense, a strong/weak notion of identity.

By preserving the care perspective while questioning its
use as an absolute alternative ethics, Davion shows the *anti*-fem-
inist character of an ethics based solely on "care"—an ethics that
taken in Noddings' totalizing sense, becomes highly uncaring,
and unethical. The strength of the feminist challenge to the gender blindness of a rights-based ethics lies not in its capacity as a
replacement ethics, as another prescriptive code, but as an anti-
prescriptive, situational, and thus complementary activity.[32]

The Maternal Self

The maternal self might appear to be simply an extension of the
caring self; but in the work of the three Modernist women poets
whom Margaret Dickie treats it manifests itself in a poetics of
playful celebration. Moving from the ethical to the aesthetic,
Dickie focuses on the lyric "I" as the source of a completely different relationship to the other. In lyric poetry, the other is the
object of the speaker's gaze, and, in these women poets, it is
imagined as part of the self. Long restricted to the male gaze, the
lyric "I" takes on an entirely different project when it is identified with the woman speaker. The "maternal," despite its ideological baggage, is the best term to describe this project because
it is the metaphor that the poets themselves used.[33]

Although various male critics among their contemporaries
tried to absorb these women into the literary movements they
dominated (Stein into Cubism, H.D. into Imagism, Moore into
classicism, for example),[34] they remained independently experimental even in an age of experimentation. And part of their radical innovation had to do with their insistence on the maternal
gaze.[35] What has made their work so hard to describe is that it is

> not the work of a man looking at a woman. [It is] rather
> the work of a woman looking and sometimes looking at a
> man. And it is work. She does not assume the controlling

role and easily manipulative style of the speaker in
Eliot . . . who frames and limits the object of his vision.

The metaphors that these poets use for this gaze are maternal.
Stein claims, for instance, that she was trying for "'the rhythm of
anybody's personality,'" not to fix but to participate in the creativity of those she observed. In her portrait of Picasso, she describes the artist as "having something come out of himself," as
in childbirth.[36] For Dickie, Stein's deliberate effort to look, to
listen, and to describe the other resembles Julia Kristeva's
description of the maternal self in which the other and the self
are intricately linked. Unlike the controlling male gaze and the
traditional lyric "I" of men's poetry, Stein's speakers are
generative and celebratory. Dickie claims that Stein "saw herself,
as she saw others, powerfully significant not because she could
control and manipulate other people, but because she could
release their power by her own listening, observing and
describing."[37]

H.D. and Marianne Moore also use the maternal image to
describe their creative acts. For H.D., it is the "vision of the
womb." H.D.'s Hermes in "Hermes of the Ways" reflects the
same openness to experience that Stein's portrait painter displays. "'Dubious, facing three ways,' Hermes . . . is a crossroads
figure, split and yet optimistically awaiting." By contrast, Moore
finds the maternal self in a hovering octopus-glacier that is ob-
durate, threatening and yet "delicate, beautiful, durable, . . . and
'unegoistic.'"

The three poets differ in their representation of the maternal gaze. Stein's is a "mixture of inside and outside"; H.D.'s is a
"visionary consciousness"; and Moore's is "an insatiable curiosity." Nonetheless, Dickie concludes, "Poetic authority in both
[Stein and H.D.] derives from participation in the other, from a
suspension of control and a relaxation into an intuitive apprehension"—what H.D. calls a "jelly-fish consciousness which she
described . . . as an impulse to 'let go.'" "While Moore can never
be imagined as letting go," Dickie has remarked elsewhere, "she
gained poetic authority in the same manner—by giving it to
others."

Dickie is writing about a looking self. But she is also writing about a playing self, a ludic concept of agency in Stein, H.D.

and Moore that in its rejection of integrated, controlling models prefigures the programmatic elusiveness of feminist theory. Paul Smith clarifies this ludic sense of agency as it has emerged in feminism's recent "multiplication of its positions." "[S]ome of the most self-conscious of current feminist thinking," he writes,

> is concerned with actually theorizing this double strategy. [While the] subject is continually called upon to take on the marks of multifarious subject-positions[,] it is nonetheless incapable of colligating these positions without contradiction . . . This contradiction . . . and the negativity which underpin and produce [it] are what releases the 'subject' from perfect self-identity, homogeneity, and fixity. . . . It is negativity which also and simultaneously produces the human agent . . . It seems to me that the actual 'subject' that feminism is in a position now to discern is very much akin to what I have been calling the agent. At the junctures of feminism's various . . . propositions, a properly feminist agent can be discerned . . . Understood in this context, contemporary feminist theory could . . . be regarded as a project which recognizes that its aims would scarcely be met by either the positing of a fixed identity or the conjuring of some new and dispersed 'subject.' And in this respect it is almost unique—and thus salutary—among the various discourse of resistence.[38]

The maternal self in Stein, H.D and Moore parallels the ludic feminist agency celebrated by Smith as the only viable postmodern 'subject,' or self. It is, as Dickie shows, contradictory, heterogeneous and unfixed. In a provocative challenge to the normally "still" images of the maternal figure, Susan Suleiman invokes a playful, "laughing mother"—a protean, kinetic figure like H.D.'s Hermes of the Ways. In spite of the subversiveness of this figure to womens' already nebulous identity, Suleiman argues, we must still "admit the possibility of playing with the boundaries of the self, especially if . . . such play [is] a necessary part of artistic creativity" (Suleiman, *Subversive Intent*, 180). The maternal agency Dickie finds in the Modernists Stein, H.D. and Moore foreshadow this postmodern subversive play.

The Theatrical Self

To James Dowd, play, or theater, is the only "substance" of postmodern identity. The individual puts on a self, much as actors don costumes for the theater, wearing it only so long as it fits the scene. The emphasis in postmodern selfhood is not on depth but on surface, on image. Contemporary moral philosophers such as Alasdair MacIntyre and Charles Taylor condemn this view of identity as a cynical denial of the self's ethical ground. But, Dowd argues, the postmodernist eschews these grand narratives of human identity for a focus on difference, and on the smaller narratives of local groups. The substance of these smaller narratives of self is quite genuine, Dowd explains; it is simply not "at the core of one's real self" but on the surface. The test of its genuineness is in its effectiveness as performance. "The individual is expected to construct a convincing public self," Dowd writes, "and to remain true to this public self . . . by segregating one's audiences and not having them find oneself out of character." One assumes a self on the basis of whether it is "socially estimable" and "can withstand public scrutiny."

The growing tendency to see the self as a construction has become central to sociological studies. However, earlier theories such as Self Monitoring and Symbolic Interactionism could not account for the play that characterizes postmodern identity. Symbolic Interactionists tried to explain the self in terms of the internalization of role requirements, which lends the self its autonomy and social agency. Proponents of Self-Monitoring distinguished various levels at which people are aware of their effect on others. Most people are "low self monitors," content to "be themselves," Dowd writes. Actors—such as Hume Cronyn who wonders how to act at the funeral of his father—are "high self-monitors"; they practice extensive "impression management." As both Self-Monitoring and Symbolic Interaction theories declined in the 1960s, Erving Goffman's dramaturgical view of the self came to the fore. To Goffman, who coined the term "impression management," image and performance constitute the self. A precursor of postmodernism, Goffman's analysis contradicts the view of the "true self" and of the self given through social roles.

Postmodernism complements Goffman's dramaturgical view of self. The mass culture and mass media of postmodernity have removed the so-called "unique" factors that supposedly went into creating traditional understandings of the self. They have transformed the notion of personal identity from the congeries of lived experience to identity as a form of style given through TV, film, and computerized virtual reality. We have *all*—at least most inhabitants of "developed" societies—become adept impression managers, watching ourselves on video camcorders, perfectly content in knowing that what we see is not a representation of our "true Self" but of our socially fashioned image. Still, Dowd argues, this self-fashioning is motivated by values of dignity and self-esteem: "[S]ocial interaction . . . is an arena in which the very important, but fragile, qualities of reputation and social honor are at stake. Dignity and self-esteem are the weighty concerns that remain even in [postmodernism] the primary motivation for impression management." The frequent charge, therefore, that the rise of theatrical identity represents the decline of self as moral agent has no real evidence.

What is not clear is whether Dowd's account of the theatricality of the postmodern self could be said to represent the playful self-reflexivity described by Suleiman and Paul Smith. For Dowd, the predominance of the mass media has taken a toll on the self's autonomy—strong or weak: commercial advertising images combined with sophisticated electronic communication remove the need for the concrete self; institutional surveillance technology subverts the privacy required for self-integration. The need simply to construct a self often takes precedence over the content of the construction, undermining the choice of moral integrity as one of the self's components. At its best, the counterstrategy of postmodern selfhood should be that of healthy, self-reflexive humor. In *The Critique of Cynical Reason*, a study challenging postmodern malaise with the sensuality and loud satiric laughter of Diogenes, Peter Sloterdijk writes:

> Are we agents of the state and of institutions? Or agents of enlightenment? Or agents of monopoly capital? Or agents of our own vital interests that secretly cooperate in constantly changing double binds with the state, institutions, enlightenment, counterenlightenment, monopoly capital,

> socialism, etc., and in so doing, we forget more and more
> what our 'selves' sought in the whole business?[39]

Unlike Dowd, Sloterdijk invites us to transform the double binds of postindustrial cynicism into the *kynicism* of self-satire.[40] Dowd does argue that the theatrical self retains a vestige of moral agency, inasmuch as its concern with image is a concern for dignity and reputation. But whether such moral agency is accomplished through self-satire, or through the feminist self-irony described by Suleiman and Smith, is uncertain.

NOTES

1. Jacques Derrida, "Eating Well," in *Who Comes After the Subject*, eds. Eduardo Cadava, Peter Conner & Jean-Luc Nancy (New York: 1991), 100.

2. I have said that the soul is not more than the body,
   And I have said that the body is not more than the
   soul,
   And nothing, not God, is greater to one's self than
   one's self is.

   Walt Whitman, *Song of Myself*, st. 48, ll. 1269–1271, in Whitman *Leaves of Grass*, New York: 1992), 224.

3. Michel Foucault argued that the concept of the self, or the "desiring subject" emerged in ancient Greece, was diminished during the self-denial of the early Christian period, and reemerged during the humanist celebration of the renaissance. Cf. Michel Foucault, *The History of Sexuality: Volume I: An Introduction*, (New York, 1980); *The History of Sexuality: Volume II: The Use of Pleasure*, (New York, 1986); *The History of Sexuality: Volume III: The Care of the Self*, (New York, 1988); Stephen Greenblatt, *Renaissance Self-Fashioning: From More to Shakespeare* (Chicago: 1980).

4. Derrida is the most visible in a growing list of poststructuralist thinkers who are reconsidering the deconstructionist stance on the issue of the subject and its social implications. The recent edition, *Who Comes After the Subject?* collects a significant group of "French" thinkers (so termed by editor Jean-Luc Nancy) on the subject, including among oth-

ers, Blanchot, Deleuze, Derrida, Descombes, Irigaray, Kofman, Lacoue-Labarthe, Levinas, and Lyotard. Cf. *Who Comes After the Subject?* eds. Eduardo Cadava, Peter Conner and Jean-Luc Nancy (New York: 1991).

5. Cf. Nancy K. Miller, *Getting Personal: Feminist Occasions and Other Autobiographical Acts* (New York: 1991); Laura Kipnis, "Feminism: The Political Conscience of Postmodernism?" in *Universal Abandon? The Politics of Postmodernism*, ed. Andrew Ross (Minneapolis: 1988).

6. Cf. Nancy Julia Chodorow, "Toward a Relational Individualism," in *Reconstructing Individualism: Autonomy, Individuality, and the Self in Western Thought.* eds. T.V. Heller, M. Sosna & D.E. Wellbery (Stanford, 1986) 197–208.

7. Mette Hjort, *The Strategy of Letters* (Cambridge, MA: 1993), 3.

8. On the Communitarian challenge to the Liberal, specifically the American, Liberal concept of Individualism as the basis for human ethics, see Alasdair MacIntyre, *Whose Justice? Which Rationality?* (Notre Dame: 1988); Seyla Benhabib, *Situating the Self: Gender, Community and Postmodernism in Contemporary Ethics* (New York: 1992); and Benhabib, "Liberal Dialogue Versus a Discursive Theory of Legitimation," in Nancy Rosenblum, ed., *Liberalism and the Moral Life* (Cambridge, MA: 1989), 143–157; Charles Taylor, *Sources of the Self* (Cambridge, MA: 1989); Charles Taylor, *The Ethics of Authenticity* (Cambridge, MA: 1992); Charles Taylor, *Multiculturalism and "The Politics of Recognition"* (Princeton, NJ: 1992); Charles Taylor, "Cross-Purposes: The Liberal-Communitarian Debate" in Rosenblum, *Liberalism and the Moral Life*, 159–183.

9. Cf. Louis Althusser, *For Marx*, B. Brewster (London: 1969); Ernst Mandel, "The Role of the Individual in History: The Case of WW II," *New Left Review* 157 (1986): 61–77; Bruce Mayhew, "Structuralism versus Individualism: Pt. 1. Shadowboxing in the Dark." *Social Forces* 59 (1980): 335–75.

10. Winders' distinction illustrates the distortion inherent in the media aestheticization of social events, whether of ethnic and religious wars, as in Yugoslavia, or of more openly commercial ventures, as the computer-presented Persian Gulf campaign. As Winders quotes: "National advertising, more systematically and pervasively than any other institution, has produced the dominant ideals of human subjectivity." Cf. Jackson Lears, "The Ad Man and the Grand Inquisitor: Intimacy, Publicity and the Managed Self in America, 1880–1940," in *Constructions of the Self*, ed. George Levine (New Brunswick, 1992).

11. Winders writes: "Feminism, understood as plural and multiple in its effects, seems bound simultaneously to expose the masculinist as-

sumptions. . . . of 'the subject' *as well as* to advocate the need for new feminine/feminist selves to emerge" (emph. his). Postcolonialism, he notes further, exhibits the same duality, exposing "the racist and ethnocentric ground of the majority culture's advocacy of self while carving out a cultural space for the expression of minority 'selves.'"

12. Benhabib writes: "One of the chief contributions of feminist thought to political theory in the western tradition is to have questioned the line dividing the public and the private. Feminists have argued that the 'privacy' of the private sphere, which has always included the relations of the male head of the household to his spouse and children, has [rendered] women and their traditional spheres of activity . . . . beyond the pale of justice. The norms of freedom, equality, and reciprocity have stopped at the household door . . . Women's absence [from these norms] is not just a political omission and a moral blind spot but . . . .an epistemological deficit as well." Cf. Benhabib, *Situating the Self* (New York, 1992), 12–13; see also Miller, *Getting Personal* (New York, 1991).

13. Arguing for the situated nature of human identity, Benhabib queries:

> Can I describe a situation as one of arrogance or hurt pride without knowing something about you as a concrete other? Can I know how to distinguish between a breach of confidence and a harmless slip of the tongue, without knowing your history and your character? . . . When we morally disagree . . . we do not only disagree about the principles involved; very often we disagree because what I see as a lack of generosity on your part you construe as your legitimate right not to do something; we disagree because what you see as jealousy on my part I view as my desire to have more of your attention. *Situating the Self*, 160.

14. In another part of the same meditation on what he calls "a type of being, or self, that is definitively *un*definable," Winders' parallel of the gay poet "Antler" to Walt Whitman, and of Richard Howard to Baudelaire opens into the question of whether writers who must lug the baggage of "precursor poets" have endlessly referring identities. Are writers, as Foucault argues, an abyssal montage of literary influences? Is this montage different from a writer's "personal" self?

15. Cf. Derrida, "'Eating Well.'"

16. According to Spence, Augustine associates the text with the naked or wounded body, which requires the concealment or glossing of the Church fathers. The obscuring character of such interpretation was

itself virtuous, for in covering the naked text or body, one kept vice at bay.

17. To vernacular author Marie de France, heard tales that were openly presented offered a prevention of vice that was superior to the concealment provided by theological interpretation.

18. Dante, she argues, proposes "not the creation of an internal subjective landscape through a recognition of the wholly external quality of the world—a recognition that ultimately leads to a sense of isolation and alienation (and autonomy). Rather, what this process demands in the embodiment of the word is the subjectification of the objective world."

19. Spence's argument for the constitutive role of language in human identity parallels Benhabib's exploration of Habermasian "discourse ethics as a conversational model of enlarged mentality." Cf. *Situating the Self*, 182.

20. Mette Hjort's suggestion that strategies imply strategists is useful in this regard. Cf. *The Strategy of Letters* (Cambridge, MA, 1993).

21. As Roberts writes: "Care and the resulting moral response are not 'rational' in the sense of affording an a priori grasp, so that we *know* what to do, but neither are they irrational, warranting license, play, or weightless innocence. To care is to discipline moral response with a rational element, not by invoking 'Reason' or claiming enlightened status, but simply by asking historical questions."

22. For Arendt, Biskowski writes, "post-Socratic philosophy is itself a form of world alienation, a turning away from appearance, perspective and opinion and towards contemplation, theoria, and a much more secure (enduring and wholly unperspectival) Truth. [Similarly], Western science seeks to penetrate behind opinion and the mere appearance of phenomena to the reality of the causal mechanisms . . . The test of truth becomes precisely its lack of contextuality . . . We seek an Archimedean point, a perspective on the world that is no longer in it, nor in history or a particular context, nor embodied in a particular person in a particular place and time. We attempt through science and theoria to transcend entirely the world and its relativism, our own situatedness and selfhood."

23. Cf. Susan Rubin Suleiman, "Feminist Intertextuality and the Laugh of the Mother," in Suleiman, *Subversive Intent: Gender, Politics and the Avant-Garde* (Cambridge, MA: 1990, 141–81; Madelon Sprengnether, *The Spectral Mother: Freud, Feminism and Psychoanalysis* (Ithaca: 1990); Paul Smith, "Feminism," in Smith, *Discerning the Subject* (Minneapolis: 1988), 113–53.

24. Benhabib quotes Arendt: ". . . the thinking process which is active in judging something, is not, like the thought process of pure reasoning, a dialogue between me and myself, but finds itself always and primarily, even if I am quite alone in making up my mind, in an anticipated communication with others with whom I know I must finally come to an agreement. And this enlarged way of thinking, which as judgement knows how to transcend its individual limitations, cannot function in strict isolation or solitude; it needs the presence of others 'in whose place' it must think, whose perspective it must take into consideration, and without whom it never has the opportunity to operate at all." Cf. Benhabib, *Situating the Self*, 8–9.

25. Cf. Tu Wei-ming, *Confucian Thought: Selfhood as Creative Transformation* (NY: 1991); Robt. E. Hegel & Richard C. Hessney, *Expressions of the Self in Chinese Literature* (New York: 1985).

26. According to this position, "it is essential that persons have at least some of the time, physical attributes," i.e., they have at some point occupied a place or point on the spatio-temporal continuum. Dauenhauer focuses on the temporal element of this set, using Heidegger on time and Ricouer on time and narrative. Cf. Bernard Williams, "Are Persons Bodies?" in *Problems of the Self* (Cambridge, 1991), 64–82; 72.

27. Dauenhauer adds later: "How one deals with these three modes amounts to making an interpretation of what it is to be a self."

28. To use Davion's summary of Gilligan:

> The care perspective in ethics involves seeing oneself as connected to others. . . . [F]rom within [this] perspective . . . relationship becomes the figure, defining self and others.
>
> Within the context of the relationship, the self as a moral agent perceives and responds to the perception of need. The shift in moral perspective is manifested by a shift in the moral question, from 'What is just?' to 'How do I respond?'

Cf. Carol Gilligan, *In a Different Voice* (Cambridge, MA: 1982); and Gilligan, "Remapping the Moral Domain: New Images of the Self in Relationship," in *Reconstructing Individualism* (Stanford, 1986), 237–53.

29. Cf. Benhabib, *Situating the Self*, 162; Taylor, "The Politics of Recognition," in Taylor, *Multiculturalism and the "Politics of Recognition"* (Princeton, 1992), 1–25; Taylor, *Sources of the Self* (Cambridge, MA: 1989), 49; Taylor, *The Ethics of Authenticity* (Cambridge, MA: 1992), 48–49.

30. Benhabib, *Situating the Self*, 168.

31. Here, again, Davion reflects Taylor's notion of the "inner voice" of one's "authentic self." Cf. Taylor, *The Ethics of Authenticity*.

32. Like Benhabib, Davion displaces the care perspective in a situation involving universal rights; in the latter case, Kantian universalism or an ethics of justice must be reinstated. To Benhabib, a "coherent sense of self is acquired by the right mixture of justice and care." Cf. *Situating the Self*, 197, 187.

33. While it is true that Davion warns that using a maternal metaphor in an ethics of care confines one to an ethics of luck (you can't choose your relationships with your children), Dickie uses "maternal" more in terms of the beneficial social category advocated by Suleiman. See Sara Ruddick's "Maternal Thinking," *Feminist Studies* 6, no. 2 (1980), 342–67 (*Maternal Thinking: Toward a Politics of Peace* [Boston: 1989]). According to Suleiman, Ruddick's argument for the "*social category* of the 'maternal' (which can be occupied by men as well as women, although in fact it is most occupied by women) carries with it certain specific, largely beneficial ways of thinking" (Suleiman, *Subversive Intent*, 207n).

34. Alfred Stieglitz publicizing Cubism hailed Stein as a Cubist; Imagist Ezra Pound introduced H.D. as an Imagist; and classicist T. S. Eliot praised Moore for her classicism. Suleiman similarly explores the epistemological skewing of the concept of the avant-garde that results from its exclusion of female artists. Cf. Suleiman, "A Double Margin: Women Writers and the Avant-Garde in France," in *Subversive Intent*, 11–33.

35. The fact that only one of these poets bore a child demonstrates that the poems' maternal presence has nothing to do with physical mothering.

36. "'It was a long tormenting process,'" Stein recalls in her autobiography, "'she looked, listened, and described.'"

37. To Dickie, the effort to recognize the other without imposing one's own voice characterizes maternal selfhood, regardless of gender. David Michael Levin discusses the same capacity in some detail in *The Listening Self: Personal Growth, Social Change and the Closure of Metaphysics* (New York: 1989). Tony Brinkley argues for a similar capacity in his analysis of Claude Lanzmann's Holocaust masterpiece, *Shoah* stressing its value in uncovering and preserving historical evidence. To Brinkley, Lanzmann's technique of "witnessing" or listening intently, instead of "interpreting" or imposing one's own perspective on what one hears is itself an enactment of the self-effacement and sensitivity required not only to recognize the evidence of the other *as* other but to preserve the evidence of crucial historical events against the distortions of partisan

revisionism. Cf. Tony Brinkley and Joseph Arsenault, "The Shoah, Annihilation, with Respect to the Sublime," *Centennial Review*, 35; 3 (Fall, 1991), 479–500; Tony Brinkley and Steven Youra. "Tracing the Shoah." n.p. n.d., Unpublished MSS.

38. Cf. Smith, *Discerning the Subject* (Minneapolis: 1988), 148–51.

39. Cf. *Critique of Cynical Reason* (Minneapolis: 1987), 114.

40. Sloterdijk proposes to "turn the disillusionment with enlightened modernity away from melancholy and cynicism and to make illusions productive for an enlightened thought on another level. He wants to achieve this goal by reclaiming . . . the tradition of kynicism, embodied in Diogenes, whose privileged satiric laughter, sensuality, the politics of the body, and a pleasure-oriented life are forms of resistance to the master narratives of Platonic idealism." Cf. Andreas Huyssen, Foreword, *Critique of Cynical Reason*, xv.

PART TWO

Language and the Self

The Ambivalent Self

Individ, You All: Constructions and Deconstructions of Self

James A. Winders

> There are always selves—a sense of personal order, a characteristic mode of address to the world, a structure of bounded desires . . . What is central is the perception—as old in academic writing as Burckhardt and Michelet—that there is in the early modern period a change in the intellectual, social, psychological, and aesthetic structures that govern the generation of identities.
>
> —Stephen Greenblatt, *Renaissance Self-Fashioning: From More to Shakespeare* (1980)

> National advertising, more systematically and pervasively than any other institution, has produced the dominant ideals of human subjectivity under advanced capitalism.
>
> —Jackson Lears, "The Ad Man and the Grand Inquisitor: Intimacy, Publicity, and the Managed Self in America, 1880–1940," in *Constructions of the Self*, ed. George Levine (1992)

> I was trying so hard to be myself,
> I was turning into somebody else.
>
> —The The, "Out of the Blue (And Into the Fire)," *Infected* (Epic, 1986)

I. Losing Yourself in a Crowd?:
Premodern and Postmodern

"Mindless violence." "Irrational behavior." "Insanity." Phrases like these echo around us in the aftermath of the L.A. riots, usually uttered by those who have been looking the other way during the last decade, as incidents of police, Klan, and neo-Nazi violence against African Americans have increased alarmingly. Inner city neighborhoods have been allowed to deteriorate as middle class whites and blacks alike have fled to suburbs. The urban "hoods" have been beset by crime, most of it associated with drugs. Television, by far the most powerfully addictive drug at large in our culture, proffers visions of contentment and self-worth believed attainable through headlong participation in consumerism. Most families now need several members in the work force to support their consuming habits.

The controversial home video documenting the Los Angeles police beating of Rodney King aired to an inner-city audience already reeling from both abuse and neglect. Even if they don't live in inner-city war zones, experience has taught black Americans to regard the police warily. In spite of this, blacks as well as most Americans not seated on the Simi Valley jury assumed that the video footage proved beyond a reasonable doubt that the four police officers had used excessive force. When the acquittal was announced, Los Angeles, and eventually other American cities, exploded in incredulous rage.

Was it senseless? Not to citizens bitterly convinced anew that the judicial system exists to protect and preserve the material status quo, its police force resembling the private security guards of a luxury resort. What about the looting? However one may wish to judge the behavior, the looters went right for the very commodities that define the good life: VCRs and other high-tech appliances, luxury furniture, expensive clothing and jewelry.

As Roland Barthes once observed about professional wrestling, the signs generated by television broadcasts (and why distinguish "programs" from commercials?) are easy to read. Fatalistic attitudes and cultural despair make the tantalizing advertised images of big ticket consumer goods unbearable. How can those excluded from the very suburban communities founded on this principle of consumerism ever hope to get in the game? As Ice-T expresses it in "Escape From the Killing Fields," "The man's got a sure-fire system: an economic prison."[1] Given an extraordinary opportunity to get their hands on the tokens of the good life as defined by our consumer culture, hundreds of residents of South Central decided to take advantage of it.

The behavior of crowds fascinates even as it alarms and terrifies us. It is a subject that has long held the interest of historians. Recent social historians have provided fresh examples of dramatic episodes of collective actions that, among other things, can serve to illuminate our contemporary preoccupation with the relation of self to society—to "others." Natalie Zemon Davis, to cite one prominent example, has pursued this task with considerable energy. In her analysis of *charivari* and related types of early modern European communal rituals, Davis has demonstrated convincingly the logic behind these popular manifestations, challenging the traditional interpretation that insisted on seeing them as supportive, for all their unruly character, of the social order. According to the traditionally accepted historical viewpoint, the excesses of carnival were permitted in order to function as some kind of social safety valve, providing the periodic release that made a rigidly hierarchical society tolerable during the rest of the year. But "the comic and festive inversion,"[2] as Davis puts it, of what Mikhail Bakhtin called *carnivalesque* practices, could also serve to *undermine* the very systems that regulated and sanctioned these periodic festivals and rites of transgression. [3]

The value of Davis's contribution to cultural history stems in large part from her refusal to impose an anachronistic sense of "self" on a period of European history in which that concept was barely emerging. The logic of early modern popular uprisings will escape any historian inclined to understand society as merely the sum total of its individual components. This is equally true of our present social reality. Encumbered by an ideology of self (designated as "the autonomous subject," the "free individual," or whatever one wishes), we cannot help but be baffled by those simultaneously terrifying and exhilarating historical moments when individual agendas become indistinguishable from collective purpose. Since citizens of the contemporary U.S. are arguably the least politically sophisticated in the world, and since ours is the society that has pushed the ideology of self to its greatest extremes, we may have little to offer in response to violent popular actions beyond observing that "nice people" wouldn't behave in such a way.

Indeed, that is just how enormous numbers of our fellow citizens see it: society consists for them of fully-formed individual characters, for good or ill. Some people are decent types, and others are just bad people. According to modernist literary legend, the French writer Jean Genet was nine years old when a relative said accusingly "Tu es un voleur !" ("You are a thief!") Apparently Genet, who experienced this as a kind of epiphany, was glad to have the mystery of self-identity cleared up at such an early age. At least he knew what he was. Once one has accepted a firm definition and description of self, there is no small pleasure in being able to say, as Popeye would put it, "I yam what I yam."

This Popeye syndrome, if I may call it that, shapes an outlook that cannot help but render the actions of a crowd incomprehensible. Evidence continues to accumulate that premodern habits of thought precluded such assumptions, and the proliferation of new historical texts that render this cultural category of self problematic could be seen to demonstrate the tendency of postmodern culture to revive and incorporate selected aspects of the premodern. Just as historians of early modern Europe must distance themselves from all that we have learned to assume about "self," that same lens of self distorts our view of collective cultural manifestations of today. Current historiography of early modern Europe (c. 1500–1800), informed by new theoretical perspectives on gender, sexuality, the body, and language, seeks to make sense of *collective* actions and social practices at a time when the so-called self was just emerging as a cultural construction.

The flood of new scholarship on the French Revolution of 1789–99, so late within this period, takes us far beyond the attention lavished by previous generations of historians on such towering individual figures as Robespierre or Danton. Studies that focus on the *sans-culottes* (the most populist of the radical revolutionaries), the revolutionary artisans, and on the early industrial workers now probe the *collective* logic of a revolutionary climate more traditionally celebrated for its promotion of individual liberties. To invoke the famous motto of the revolution, the words *liberté* and *egalité* have to be balanced out by the word *fraternité*. Linking themselves to forms of collective identity derived from secret fraternal societies[4] and, further back, from craft guilds, revolutionary workers expressed their demands in terms of what one historian has called a "language of labor," understood as a "discourse" in Michel Foucault's sense of the term.[5]

When Natalie Davis interprets the unruly festivals of 16th-century French peasants,[6] or when Robert Darnton seeks to decode the signifying practices of 18th-century journeymen printers and apprentices as they slaughter the neighborhood cats,[7] they focus not on the motives or ideas of individual participants, but on the narrative, so to speak, that unfolded in group action. Much like their "new historicist" counterparts in literary criticism, these new cultural historians borrow from the cultural anthropology of, among others, Clifford Geertz to interpret elaborate rites, festivals, and uprisings as tales or stories cultures tell themselves.[8] There could be no individual author of such a polyphonic narrative.

Are we living at a time when the self is losing some of its force as a cultural category, even, we may say, as a cultural tendency? Michel Foucault, one of the first thinkers to imply that an examination of the self's historical emergence might help us to delineate the lines of force it exerts on our present culture, painstakingly charted the genealogy of the discourses of "self" as far back as Hellenistic antiquity. By doing this in order to demonstrate the strategies and "technologies" of self that allow for the production of complex webs of power relations throughout our history, Foucault, largely through the spell his own powerful discourse casts, may have had the effect of arguing for the inescapability of these relentless productive power relations of self.

Yet this same Foucault, in the book that first catapulted him to real prominence in France, crafted a powerful metaphor of the disappearance of "man" as a Western cultural preoccupa-

tion. He was assailing humanism, and the critics who have described the "gleeful" tone of this neo-Nietzschean pronounce-
ment (symptomatic of poststructuralism) are legion. Foucault's
vertiginous prose is worth quoting at length:

> One thing in any case is certain: man is neither the oldest
> nor the most constant problem that has been posed for
> human knowledge. Taking a relatively short chronological
> sample within a restricted geographical area—European
> culture since the sixteenth century—one can be certain that
> man is a recent invention within it . . . it was the effect of a
> change in the fundamental arrangements of knowledge.
> As the archaeology of our thought shows, man is an in-
> vention of recent date. And one perhaps nearing its end.

If those arrangements were to disappear as they appeared,
if some event of which we can at the moment do no more than
sense the possibility—without knowing either what its form will
be or what it promises—were to cause them to crumble, as the
ground of Classical thought did, at the end of the eighteenth
century, then one can certainly wager that man would be erased,
like a face drawn in sand at the edge of the sea. [9]

Can we wager that "self" will be erased in a similar manner by the incoming tides of postmodern culture? However one
wants to decide this, it is tempting to blur the lines between
"man" and "self," since Western humanism appears to have invested heavily in both, and to read the early Foucault against the
late genealogist of self.

Both in humanist discourse and in the new theoretical discourses that proclaim its limits, terms like "self" and "man" are
continually displacing each other. It is therefore frequently necessary and helpful to pause to consider definitions carefully, and
we possess no better example than the meticulous attention Foucault brought to problems of language.

II. The Self in Other Words

"There are always selves," writes Stephen Greenblatt at the beginning of a book that painstakingly shows how fragile and

gradually constructed self was as a social category in Renaissance England. Of course "the self" exists. There is even a widely-circulating magazine called *Self*. However easy it may be to dismiss the magazine, its very title flatters the notion that this thing we call self equals "the total, essential, or particular being of one person," to quote a standard dictionary definition.[10] Needless to say, it wouldn't be "widely circulating" if not for advertisers eager to appeal to our fervent desire to see ourselves as unique in a consumer culture that in practice cannot afford to allow us to be anything of the kind.

Now, just imagine you had never heard of something called "self," and were struggling to grasp the concept by attending to the clues provided by the magazine's cover. I will describe the cover of the May, 1992 issue: it is dominated by the smiling face of a model with stylishly long blonde hair, but her picture is cropped so that it appears off-center and to the right. She inclines her head somewhat, her chin resting on her hand. The large yellow letters across the bottom of her photo proclaim "great legs! Who's got them—how to get them." Forming an L-shape perpendicular to this message is a column of four brief titles or captions meant to give the reader additional reasons for opening the magazine. In descending order, they read:

> Go Golden !
> 31 safe new self-tanners
>
> Happy Moods
> How to catch one
>
> Your man can have multiple orgasms
>
> The truth about sugar

From this evidence "self" would seem to have something to do with appearance, emotions, pleasure, and diet. Those of us already initiated into the cult of self might observe admiringly that these few visual clues encapsulate a great deal, but if we had no previous experience of the concept of self, wouldn't we be somewhat confused? To use the very specific postmodern terminology of Gilles Deleuze and Félix Guattari, we might be more inclined to view those cover titles as a catalog of just so many

Cover, *Self* Magazine, September, 1994. Courtesy *Self*. Copyright 1994 by the Condé Nast Publications Inc.

"desiring machines."[11] "Self" to us would appear to be a term for designating a related group of preoccupations or concerns rather than a carefully circumscribed entity or state of things.

Meanwhile, we've only considered the first dictionary definition listed for "self." In the second definition, self is related to the "qualities ("individuality/personality") that allow us to distinguish one person from another. Note that appearance is not one of these. The third definition ("one's *own* consciousness"), relies heavily on the notion of property. Does self then refer to those aspects of consciousness that you yourself own? If your consciousness was a library, would it be like the New York Public Library or more like the Pierpont Morgan Library? How do you get access to the on-line catalog? Is there an interlibrary loan system? Does your "self" belong only to you? If "selves" constitute some kind of cultural capital, then the simultaneous emergence of the modern concept of self and the modern capitalist economy is no mere coincidence.

The fourth definition of self ("one's interests, advantages") confronts us with the demands of a political economy based on accumulation and maximizing profit. That kind of economy produces the very phenomena that serve to define the next word I want to consider: "individual." *The American Heritage Dictionary* defines "individual" in rapid succession as "singleness," "distinctiveness," and "separateness," as if to say with shrill urgency: *Please* make no mistake about this! There is also a rigidly absolute quality to the Latin root meaning "indivisible." The concept of the individual, then, is a radically atomistic one. From Democritus through Newtonian physics, atoms were regarded as indivisible, but such a definition no longer qualifies as acceptable physical theory. And, after Freud and Lacan, notwithstanding the Ego Psychology school, it is no longer tenable to view the human psyche as "indivisible." Lacan's reading of Freud was one that enlarged considerably upon those points in Freud's text that seem to suggest fragmentation and "splitting" (*Spaltung*), [12] and Lacan's own contributions to psychoanalytic theory emphasize the permanent divisions produced in the psyche through the mirror stage and the eventual acquisition of language. Lover of puns, Lacan, had he been an English speaker, may well have coined the term "dividual" to substitute for "individual."

Still, "individual" is a term we want to be able to apply to ourselves, all the more urgently in a world that threatens to overwhelm it as a possibility. Young people, subject to enormous pressure to conform and not having lived long enough to cultivate and enrich their most eccentric tendencies, desperately avow their individuality. The middle-aged professor surveys the classroom bright with young faces. With their voices and, sometimes, with their pens, they swear to him "we're all individuals. We're all different. We're all unique." This they chorus in similar accents, dressed remarkably alike, demographically rather homogeneous. In this situation, the professor's abiding fantasy summons up the intervention of the one true subversive and master ironist who would dare to blurt out: "I'm not!"

Since one of the working assumptions here is that these several terms for our subjective existence all serve mutually to support each other, what have we come up with so far? Self: total and essential being, individual qualities, personality, one's own consciousness, and one's unassailable separateness. Taken together, this would constitute the ground of possibilities for all that postmodern theorists have meant by "subject," defined first of all as "under someone's power."[13] To be subjected to power, to be a subject in that sense, is a condition that suggests the repressive aspect of power.

In Foucault's thought, however, power must also be understood as productive and enabling for the subject; "subject" in turn being understood as an intersecting point in a grid or network of relations of what Foucault calls power-knowledge. Thus human beings are subjects in the sense of a subject in language, a position named by pronouns or other linguistic "shifters" from which certain enunciations may emanate. As Beckett's "Unnamable" says, "It's the fault of the pronouns,"[14] on which the influential French feminist writer Monique Wittig performs radical surgery in her book *The Lesbian Body*. A complementary theoretical insight was provided by Louis Althusser, who viewed the subject as an ideological construction "hailed" or "interpellated" through language, what we might want to call the "Hey, You!" effect. In addition to its linguistic role, the subject, according to Foucault, provides a strategic apparatus for the deployment of knowledge in relation to power, all "human sciences" being understood by Foucault as discourses that produce "the subject" as knower as well as the known—the object (subject as object) of discipline in all senses of that word.[16]

Finally, we must confront that troublesome term "identity," something we have become accustomed to regard as being in "crisis." Predictably enough, the dictionary offers five different definitions. The first word in the first definition given is *collective*: "collective aspect of the set of characteristics by which a thing is definitively recognizable or known." Just what might this mean in terms of the self? Do all my characteristics need to arrive at one particular collective aspect I and others can be pleased to call my "identity"? If someone becomes familiar with several of my characteristics, but remains oblivious to others, has that person failed to be initiated into the secrets of my identity?

The word "identity" provides another example of the construction in language of the exaggeratedly atomistic ideology of self in our culture. We become different selves or assume differing identities depending on our social interactions. Which one of these many manifestations represents the *true* identity? As long as we persist in our habit of distinguishing sharply between an intensely intimate private sphere of social life and a grudgingly tolerated impersonal public one, a binary opposition that has become a major target of feminist critique, we might be quick to assume that our "real" identities are revealed to those who know us most intimately. Historians of the early modern family have produced enough evidence of a profoundly different set of expectations about the relationship between family and socal life in general to suggest that what Lawrence Stone has labeled "affective individualism"[17] has a very limited history, producing cultural effects that by no means encompass the full range of human social life. For a long time we have assumed that the public poses we must adopt mask a deep and abiding essence that can only be discovered though intimate acquaintance. It was this obsession with probing the deeper meanings always believed to lie beneath surface appearance that led Roland Barthes to find welcome relief in what he took to be the Japanese cultural advantage of providing meanings readily on the surface: signifiers without signifieds inconveniently hidden from view.[18]

Even the first definition of "identity" presents major problems and inconsistencies which multiply as we range through the remaining four definitions. These take us from the behavioral or personal characteristics that allow an individual to be recognized as a member of a group, to qualities of sameness or resemblance, to the condition of remaining the same, and finally (and here we seem to have returned at last to "self") "the personality of an individual regarded as a persisting entity." If all this puts Humpty Dumpty back together again, we cannot avoid noticing the many cracks fissuring the fragile shell. In any case, let's not put Humpty back together. As chefs trained in the culinary school of Freud and Lacan, let's make omelettes instead.

The terms whose definitions we have been considering occasionally contradict one another but in other ways all fit back within the overriding social and ideological category of self. I wouldn't say that they fit therein as neatly as Russian dolls. The resulting construction more nearly resembles that of a precariously patched together Humpty.

III. The Loss of Self and the World Within Us

Culturally, we have invested an enormous amount in our belief in the category of the autonomous subject, for which "self" may sometimes serve as a shorthand, and at other times as a larger subsuming category. I hope so far to have demonstrated that the very terms by which we seek to designate aspects of self and individual existence are inhabited by contradictions and strains that show this central cultural zone to be a strongly contested site, especially if we understand ourselves to be in a transitional cultural stage in which these definitions are being renegotiated. Individual personality as a "persisting entity"? Self as "total" or "essential" being? How fervently can we believe in these possibilities? These definitions are haunted historically by the traces of what has been lost. How much of what we call "self" is but the residue of what earlier generations experienced as vitally communal public life? Rainer Maria Rilke's seventh *Duino Elegie* contains lines which may be read with that thought in mind. I'll first read the German, followed by Stephen Mitchell's incomparable translation:

> Nirgends, Geliebte, wird Welt sein, als innen. Unser Leben
> geht hin mit Verwandlung. Und immer geringer
> schwindet das Aussen. Wo einmal ein dauerndes Haus
> war, schlägt sich erdachtes Gebild vor, quer, zu Erden-
> klichem völlig gehörig, als stand es noch ganz im Gehirne.
> (lines 50–55)

> Nowhere, Beloved, will world be but within us. Our life
> passes in transformation. And the external shrinks into
> less and less. Where once an enduring house was, now a
> cerebral structure crosses our path, completely belonging
> to the realm of concepts, as though it still stood in the
> brain.[19]

In his book *Sources of the Self: The Making of the Modern Identity*, Charles Taylor, imbued with the kinds of concerns Robert Bellah and others have expressed regarding the modern loss of community,[20] reads Rilke's lines as a lament for a lost spiritual vitality.[21] For my purposes, I prefer to read them as a commentary on the excessively interior direction of our personal interactions with an outside world bereft of all value save the tokens and mementos deposited within our private mental vaults.

As *subject*, Rilke uncovers unexpected levels beneath the current reexaminations of the self. Feminist theory has much to teach about the relation of gender to the category of the subject. While reminding us of the multiplicity contained within the word "woman," feminist theory implicitly cautions us against a one-dimensional reading of the word "man."[22] As awareness of the sexual and the textual politics of gender lead to projects of rereading, Rilke is but one of many masculine authors who can be read *differently* in the wake of feminist criticism. Rainer *Maria* Rilke, who was dressed as a girl into adolescence and then, shorn of his long locks, was packed off to a military school. From what "subject" position does Rilke write? What gender? Read this way, Rilke takes us from the insight that "the subject" has traditionally been a masculinist concept, to a consideration of the complexities of gender and language found in his verse, to a recognition of the "feminine" in any writer.

It should be easy to see that Rilke's lines quoted above drive home a theme of loss. A sense of loss and longing informs both postmodern cultural debates and the historiography of early modern Europe. Peter Laslett's *The World We Have Lost* remains one of the classics of English social history.[23] In his approach to postmodernism as a collection of symptoms of "late capitalism," Fredric Jameson sets up a kind of Hobson's choice between the belief that (1) an authentic "self" or "subject" existed in the preindustrial era and (2) that the self or subject has always been at most a necessary fiction, a skeleton on which to drape the ill-fitting garb of pronouns.[24] Opposed to Marx's classic account of the qualities divested from subjects under capitalism by processes of alienation, Foucault has provided a chilling scenario of subjects *invested* with the fragmenting, criss-crossing circuitry of discourses coursing with the contradictory energies of power-knowledge.[25]

Those historians engaged in applying a theoretical synthesis of *Annales* school-style investigations of *mentalités*,[26] literary theory, and cultural anthropology to early modern European society do not seem to claim that "what was lost" in the transition to modernity was a fully-formed, organically whole and communally rooted self in the usual sense of that word. They are more specific in their descriptions of processes and activities that contributed to the formation of selfhood in the modern sense. Natalie Zemon Davis, in her retelling of the story of Martin Guerre, focuses on specific aspects of French Protestantism, in particular on the Basque peasants, to show how the marriage of Bertrande de Rols and Martin Guerre was informed by newly emergent concepts of self, especially in the case of the wife's role in the marriage.[27] In her earlier study of urban French Protestant women of the sixteenth century, she describes some of the key gestures of defiance through which these women supported their cause while calling attention to their stubborn independence, including refusing to participate in Catholic feast days, studying the Bible alone or with family and Protestant friends, using their houses for illegal assemblies, wearing the somber black clothing of a dissenter, smashing baptismal fonts, and so on.[28]

The theme of Protestant insistence on individual biblical interpretation and the solitary (for the literate few) act of reading is crucial to Stephen Greenblatt's inquiry into what he has called "Renaissance self-fashioning" in the celebrated cases of More, Tyndale, Wyatt, Spenser, Marlowe, and Shakespeare. Robert Darnton, having announced his intention to develop a sub-field of cultural study tentatively titled a "history of reading," has argued that the shift from reading aloud in groups (the illiterate many eagerly attending the privileged literate one in their midst) to silent reading "might have involved a greater mental adjustment than the shift to the printed text," since it "made reading an individual, interior experience."[29] Darnton's insight may help to trace one of the steps in the formation of Lawrence Stone's "affective individualism," whereby persons came more and more to dwell within themselves, tending the "cerebral structures" of which Rilke speaks. We might also say that the rediscovery of "the reader" in postmodern criticism has its parallel in the emergence of premodern reading practices. The latter attended the birth of the modern self, while the former might be said to testify to the postmodern self's embattled character.

Perhaps far too much of postmodern cultural criticism expresses a nostalgic lament for lost essences. At first, the theory of Jean Baudrillard seems to decry the disappearance of a viable political culture that might have resisted the hyperreality of simulation, though it becomes increasingly clear that his is a profoundly aristocratic lament disdainful of the culture of the masses (not to mention mass culture). As Baudrillard's most thoroughly misogynist book *De la séduction* suggests, postmodern antihumanism is more than the joyous affirmation of a scattering or dissemination of the unified ego.[30] It is also a recognition of how closely wedded the notion of the subject has been to masculinity.

IV. Self, Other, and Difference

The other advances full upon me.
—Samuel Beckett, *The Unnamable*

Upon first reflection, one possible implication of the work of Nancy Chodorow and Carol Gilligan on the sociology of gender and human psychological development would seem to be that men have a greater stake in advocating "the self" as an autonomous subject. Women, we are told, learn a means of self-definition formed through intimacy and relation to others.[31] Separate self=fortress self=macho self. Culturally, whatever lies outside the isolated conscious subject has always, Alice Jardine tells us, been coded as "feminine."[32] But all this theorizing by no means suggests that women have everything to celebrate in the demise of "self," any more than the complacent acceptance of the stereotypes outlined by Gilligan's different "voices" can be seen as an inherently "feminist" stand. No matter how much feminist theory may encourage a critique of the subject, it must always proceed from affirmation of the personal, what Nancy Miller calls "the witnessing 'I' of subjective experience."[33]

Feminism, understood as plural and multiple in its effects, seems bound simultaneously to expose the masculinist assumptions at work in the cultural practices that encourage the unquestioning acceptance of "the subject" *as well as* to advocate the need for new feminine/feminist selves to emerge. This pluralist impulse is reflected as well by what we have come to call "identity politics." I would describe this as a process whereby previously excluded or despised groups seek to oppose all that has worked culturally to denounce and despise their difference, even as they affirm (their) difference, transforming stigmatizing labels into proud standards.

One result of this dual strategy is the unlearning of "history" in the singular sense (as *His* story) and the ambitious project of teaching new, collective histories. One of the best ways to see this at work is in the *Subaltern* and related schools of "Third World" historiography. In a recent article in a special issue of *Representations* devoted to postcolonial cultural perspectives, historian Dipesh Chakrabarty explains that the personal subjective histories of colonial Indian subjects defy interpretation according to the categories of private, bourgeois individualization imposed by the British colonizers. The colonial Indian subject, he argues, spoke with a "voice of ambivalence" that Western historians have excluded from their assumptions about subjective human experience.[34]

The colonizer contents himself with a few superficial and general observations about the mass of colonized subjects. The "other" comes to be viewed as a type; a syndrome or symptom. The contemporary black American cultural critic Cornel West has commented bitingly on the "homogenizing" impulse through which white Americans represent all black people as being alike.[35] At its most subtle, his analysis suggests that the Western WASP sense of self depends totally on the otherness of minorities within the cultures it has dominated. Chakrabarty issues an urgent call for a new self-critical honesty in historical studies:

> I ask for a history that deliberately makes visible, within the very structure of its narrative forms, its own repressive strategies and practices, the part it plays in collusion with the narratives of citizenships in assimilating to the projects of the modern state all other possibilities of human solidarity.[36]

The twofold task of scholars such as West and Chakrabarty is to continue to expose the racist and ethnocentric underpinnings of the majority culture's advocacy of self while carving out a cultural space for the expression of minority "selves." It is not an either/or proposition.

It works in much the same way from the perspective of gender, which in its most radical advocacy of "other" kinds of subjects, takes us beyond the binary masculine/feminine opposition assumed by a heterosexist culture. An exemplary work from this perspective is Carl Morse's and Joan Larkin's 1988 anthology of gay and lesbian poetry, whose provocative use of photographs produces unexpected and useful effects.[37] As with other aspects of cultural criticism that interrogate the category of the subject, the critical study of sexuality including sexual preference helps us to understand the degree to which "compulsory heterosexuality," as Adrienne Rich terms it, has distorted our understanding of "individual" experience. In the wake of historical investigations by such authors as Michel Foucault, John Boswell, and Jeffrey Weeks, we are beginning to understand the historically specific and arbitrary manner through which sexuality came to be equated with "identity."[38]

We might thus be tempted to view gay sexuality as that which "deconstructs" heterosexual ideology, even as it assists in the deconstruction of "the subject." And yet nevertheless, there is the Morse/Larkin anthology with its photographs of happy, confident, proud, defiantly "different" poets: visual evidence of alternative identities. Though some of the poets are photographed in profile, many gaze boldly at the viewer as if to say, "Here I am: a poet, gay, and content with myself—but don't assume that you can know what I am really like." This implied caveat hints at a type of being, or self, that is perhaps definitively *un*definable. Roland Barthes, discussing his own discomfort at being photographed, referred bemusedly to the unnaturally contrived *photographic* face he was aware of putting on for the occasion.[39] Whether or not this implies a "true" photograph obtainable of a human face, frequently photographed celebrity faces proliferate to the point that it becomes increasingly difficult to discern an "original." Cindy Sherman's art, in which she photographs herself in multiple "disguises," pushes this undecidable tendency to its postmodern zenith.

A number of the Morse/Larkin photographs embody this very ambivalence. I will begin with James Baldwin, because I was conscious when viewing his portrait of what Barthes described as the *punctum* or detail within the photograph that motivated the viewer's response.[40] Gazing at Baldwin's picture, I couldn't decide whether it was his sad baggy eyes, the excessively thick necktie knot, or his oddly askew collar that arrested my attention.[41] Paul Mariah, whose work I had not known, is presented in dual superimposed images: profile and a frontal view. Does this express the impossibility of subjective definition, or the real multiplicity that the term "self" masks? Muriel Rukeyser's face is bold, honest, no nonsense. Very much a New York face. Do I see a poet named Rukeyser, or do I superimpose my filter for all that "New York" entails for me?

I see the face of Gloria Anzaldua, known to me through her editing of the important book *This Bridge Called My Back: Writings by Radical Women of Color*. It is a soft, laughing, pleasant face. I'm not sure if I am surprised. In 1990, the poet Joy Harjo gave a reading at a conference I attended in Oregon, and I attended a reception for her afterwards. I had been aware of her importance as a Native American writer, but here was her photograph in the pages of this anthology. My first response to myself was the clumsy "I didn't know she was a lesbian." Why didn't I? Should I have been able to tell? Many people expect lesbians to have very short hair, but Harjo's is quite long. Is that in keeping with her Native American identity? Should it remind me not to assume anything about a lesbian's hair? That there are really no clues appearance can give about sexuality?

The more I look at these photographs, the more I feel caught up in a dialectic of repetition and difference. I see variety yet a limited number of possible poses and facial expressions. Here is a photograph of a certain "Antler"—his only name, it seems—that would conform to the popular stereotype of "aging hippie." The face belongs at a Grateful Dead concert. But I focus on the slouch hat, and I see: Walt Whitman as a young man (the Whitman of my photographic imaginary being the venerable white-haired, white-bearded elder statesman of poetry). Richard Howard, brilliant translator of so many of my favorite French writers, appears to recline in leisured contentment. Despite Whitman's line about "leaning and loafing" and "observing a spear of summer grass," I assume in my response to Howard's photograph that he is thinking of one of the Baudelaire poems he translated, *L' invitation au voyage* from *Les Fleurs du mal*. His pose makes me think of Baudelaire's refrain *luxe, calme et volupté* and of the line *aimer à loisir*, which he translates rather freely as "with all the time in the world for loving each other."[42]

I therefore see "Antler" and Richard Howard in relation to celebrated poets of their respective literary traditions, and perhaps they see themselves that way. Even the artists who most loudly proclaim his or her disdain of influences or models from the past can usually be shown to have incorporated them. Writers never escape the shadow of their precursors. Moreover, when we view photographs of writers, we are looking at examples of a particular kind of photographic convention. There is a limited repertoire of possible poses, and the photographic credits listed on dust jackets of commercially published fiction and poetry are composed of a limited number of names, many of them frequently repeated. Our "photographic selves," to return to Barthes's phrase, like our selves in general, are composites formed through a multitude of associations and influences.

I set aside these meditations on photographic portraiture, sexuality, and identity in a spirit of unavoidable ambivalence. I suppose learning to tolerate one's own ambivalence is basic to a postmodern sensibility. But, within our cultural heritage, there is a simpler, more direct way of voicing frustration with life's maddening complexities. The word for it, "children," is *Blues*. I know of no more eloquent commentary on ambivalence, aporia, or undecidability than the lines in Mississippi Delta blues classic "Louise McGhee" by Son House:

> I gets up in the mornin'
> With the blues three different ways.
> I have two minds to leave here,
> I didn't have but one say "Stay."[43]

I have two minds that say to leave this essay now, not but one that says "stay." So I'm leaving you with these blues. Bob Dylan was famous for long, rambling talking blues performances in his early career. As his career enters its third decade, he has become more than a little notorious for reinventing his own persona every few years. I'll leave you with some lines from a Dylan "talking blues" called "I Shall Be Free—No. 10" that speak to the complexities of self and subjectivity I have sought to dramatize:

> I'm just average and common too,
> I'm just like me and the same as you,
> I'm everybody's brother and son,
> I'm not different than anyone
> Ain't no use in talkin' to me,
> It's just the same as talkin' to you! [44]

NOTES

1. Ice-T, "Escape From the Killing Fields," *O.G./Original Gangster* (Sire Records, 1991).

2. Natalie Zemon Davis, "Women On Top," *Society and Culture in Early Modern France* (Stanford: 1975), 131.

3. In his groundbreaking study *Rabelais and His World*, trans. Helen Iswolsky (Cambridge: 1968), Mikhail Bakhtin described an early modern European peasant culture of subversive irreverence, scorning the authority of the ruling class with which it was nevertheless engaged in continual dialogue. An obvious contemporary American example of this phenomenon is the controversial cultural role of Rap music, known for its deliberately violent, coarse language and hostility to the police and related symbols of authority.

Bakhtin's "dialogic" concept of culture as well as his demonstration of the *carnivalesque* aspects of peasant culture have been enormously influential among cultural historians of modern Europe. Davis emphasizes the theme of the *carnivalesque* most thoroughly in her chapter "The Reasons of Misrule," *Society and Culture . . .* , 97–123. See also Dominick LaCapra,\ *"Madame Bovary" On Trial* (Ithaca: 1982) and Arthur Mitzman, "Roads, Vulgarity, Rebellion, and Pure Art: The Inner Space in Flaubert and French Culture," *Journal of Modern History* 51, no. 3 (September, 1979): 504–24.

4. Cf. Margaret C. Jacob, *Living the Enlightenment: Freemasonry and Politics in 18th-Century Europe* (New York: 1991).

5. Cf. William H. Sewell, Jr., *Work and Revolution in France: The Language of Labor From the Old Regime to 1848* (Cambridge: 1980).

6. Cf. Natalie Zemon Davis, "Reasons of Misrule."

7. Robert Darnton, "Workers Revolt: The Great Cat Massacre of the Rue Saint-Severin," *The Great Cat Massacre and Other Episodes in French Cultural History* (New York: 1984), 75–104.

8. Geertz demonstrates this best in "Deep Play: Notes on the Balinese Cockfight," *The Interpretation of Cultures: Selected Essays* (New York: 1973), 412–453.

9. Michel Foucault, *The Order of Things* (New York: 1970), 386–7.

10. All definitions quoted in this section are from *The American Heritage Dictionary of the English Language*, ed. William Morris (Boston: 1976).

11. Cf. Gilles Deleuze and Felix Guattari, *Anti-Oedipus: Capitalism and Schizophrenia*, (Minneapolis: 1983).

12. Jean Laplanche et J.-B. Pontalis, *Vocabulaire de la psychanalyse* (Paris: 1967), 67–70.

13. In Lacanian theory, to be a "subject" is to be in thrall to language, "subject" to the signifier. Cf. Paul Smith, *Discerning the Subject* (Minneapolis: 1988), 71.

14. Samuel Beckett, *The Unnamable* (New York: 1958), 164.

15. Monique Wittig, *The Lesbian Body*, (Boston: 1986), 10–11, where Wittig explains and demonstrates her strategy most forcefully:

> *J/e* is the symbol of the lived, rending experience which is m/y writing, of this cutting in two which throughout literature is the exercise of a language which does not constitute m/e as subject.

16. Whether there is actually room in Foucault's thought for the fourth listed dictionary definition of subject as "basis or cause of action" is a matter of fervent debate. Cf. *Foucault: A Critical Reader*, ed. David Couzzens Hoy (Oxford: 1986). It seems clear that, for Foucault, self, subject, and "the individual" are primarily to be understood *critically* as products or effects of power. See Alessandro Pizzorno, "Foucault and the Liberal View of the Individual," in *Michel Foucault: Philosopher*, ed. and trans. Timothy J. Armstrong (New York: 1992), 204–11.

17. Lawrence Stone, "The Growth of Affective Individualism," *The Family, Sex and Marriage in England 1500–1800* (New York: 1979), 149–80.

18. Roland Barthes, *The Empire of Signs*, tr. Richard Howard (New York: 1982). Barthes even locates this tendency in the shape of Japanese eyelids.

19. Rainer Maria Rilke, *The Selected Poetry of Rainer Maria Rilke*, ed. and Stephen Mitchell (New York: 1984), 188–9.

20. Cf. Robert N. Bellah et al., *Habits of the Heart: Individualism and Commitment in American Life* (New York: 1986).

21. Charles Taylor, *Sources of the Self: The Making of the Modern Identity* (Cambridge: 1989), 501.

22. Elizabeth Kamarck Minnich, "From Ivory Tower to Tower of Babel?," *South Atlantic Quarterly* 89, no. 1 (Winter, 1990), 184.

23. Cf. Peter Laslett, *The World We Have Lost: England Before the Industrial Age*, Second Edition (New York: 1973).

24. Cf. Fredric Jameson, "Postmodernism, or the Cultural Logic of Late Capitalism," *New Left Review* 146 (1984), 53–92.

25. James A. Winders, "The Persistence of the Gendered Subject in Marx's *Economic and Philosophic Manuscripts of 1844*," *Gender, Theory, and the Canon* (Madison: 1991), 68.

26. The "school's" name derives from the influential review *Annales: Economies, Societes, Civilisations* founded in 1929 by Marc Bloch and Lucien Febvre. The *annalistes* have offered the concept of *mentalites* to replace the narrow elitism of traditional intellectual history. Robert Darnton (see Note 7) is a leading proponent of *l'histoire des mentalites*.

27. Cf. Natalie Zemon Davis, *The Return of Martin Guerre* (Cambridge: 1983).

28. Davis, "City Women and Religious Change," *Society and Culture . . .* , 92.

29. Darnton, "First Steps Toward a History of Reading," *The Kiss of Lamourette: Reflections in Cultural History* (New York: 1990), 185.

30. Cf. Jean Baudrillard, *De la seduction* (Paris: 1979) and James A. Winders, "Baudrillard, the Masses and Hyperreality: The Limits of Postmodern French Cultural Theory," *Proceedings of the Annual Meeting of the Western Society for French History* 18 (1991).

31. Kathleen B. Jones, "On Authority: Or, Why Women Are Not Entitled to Speak," in *Foucault & Feminism: Reflections on Resistance*, ed. Irene Diamond and Lee Quinby (Boston: 1988), 125.

32. Alice A. Jardine, *Gynesis: Configurations of Woman and Modernity* (Ithaca: 1985), 114.

33. Nancy K. Miller, "Getting Personal: Autobiography as Cultural Criticism," *Getting Personal: Feminist Occasions and Other Autobiographical Acts* (New York: 1991), 14.

34. Dipesh Chakrabarty, "Postcoloniality and the Artifice of History: Who Speaks for 'Indian' Pasts?," *Representations* 37 (Winter, 1992), 17.

35. Cornel West, "The New Cultural Politics of Difference," *October* 53 (Summer, 1990), 103.

36. Chakrabarty, 23.

37. I was particularly struck by the successful use of the photographs since I recently spent several years at work on an anthology that includes a number of writings by gay and lesbian authors. It is called *Reading for Difference: Texts on Gender, Race, and Class* (Fort Worth: 1993). Largely for reasons of cost, I and my co-editors decided to forego the use of photographs. My one reservation about their use in anthologies intended for student readers is that any eccentricity in these portraits might allow students to vent their own homophobia, thus prejudicing their readings.

38. Cf. Michel Foucault, *The History of Sexuality, Volume One: Introduction* (New York: 1980), John Boswell, *Christianity, Homosexuality, and*

Social Tolerance: Gay People in the Western World from Classical Antiquity to the Fourteenth Century (Chicago: 1980), and Jeffrey Weeks, *Sexuality and Its Discontents: Modern Meanings, Myths, Sexualities* (London: 1985).

39.   Cf. Roland Barthes, *Camera Lucida: Reflections on Photography*, trans. Richard Howard (New York: 1981).

40.   Ibid.

41.   All photographs described in this section are from *Gay & Lesbian Poetry in Our Time*, ed. Carl Morse and Joan Larkin (New York: 1988).

42.   Charles Baudelaire, *Les Fleurs du mal*, trans. Richard Howard (Boston: 1982), 58.

43.   Son House, "Louise McGhee," *Father of the Delta Blues: The Complete 1965 Sessions* (Columbia/Legacy, 1992).

44.   Bob Dylan, "I Shall Be Free—No. 10," *Another Side of Bob Dylan* (Columbia Records, 1964).

The Vernacular Self

Origins of the Self: Vernacular Identity in 12th-Century France

Sarah Spence

No sooner was the self proclaimed dead than it was proven to have always existed. The poststructuralist scrutiny which asserted that the self was, at best, little other than text, did more to inscribe than erase it; the tremendous resistance raised to such proclamations spoke to the existence of a self whose definition and origin could be speculated upon, hypothesized about, if not determined precisely.[1]

There are, of course, two questions, two types of origin that can be considered: the one of the individual, be it in the womb, or the brain in the vat; the other, and it is this I wish to address here, as it is historically situated. For as much as Foucault's argument pushes the existence of a self back to ancient Greece by defining it as the desiring subject, his argument rests on the submergence of self in the other-focused ideology of early Christianity. To approach the self in these terms, as Foucault does in the *History of Sexuality*, is to suggest, however, that the self merely goes underground until the world finally rights itself again, turns back to the logocentric vantage point rediscovered in the Renaissance.[2]

Such a definition of the self is, ultimately, circular. It is difficult to swallow the "underground river" approach to the historical continuity of the self, especially if the self is perceived as a quasi-organic entity with an origin and perhaps a demise. If the self has an origin it should be determined by its definition and constitution as recently eulogized: not just as desiring subject but

as a complex interaction of body, language and space. The desiring subject of ancient Greece is not the one which defines itself as
language, as text, and which uses language to differentiate and
mediate between body and world. This phenomenon owes more,
ironically, to the seemingly self-denying language of Early
Christianity, and owes as much to a distancing from, not assimi-
lation of the classical Latin tradition as well. It is, in short, my
thesis that the self we now vigorously defend indeed has an origin, but that origin is not to be located in ancient Greece, or in
the Renaissance, but in the twelfth century. And that origin has
more to do with the complex interaction of language and body
brought about by the rise of a competing vernacular tradition
than with the concept of a desiring subject, pure and simple.

I.

In the 56-line Prologue to her stories, or *Lais*, the twelfth-century
author Marie de France draws a distinction between her own
approach, which is to dispense with silence and secrecy
("Whoever has received knowledge/ and eloquence in speech
from God/ should not be silent or secretive/ but demonstrate it
willingly"), and that of the ancients who, as "Priscian" testifies,
speak obscurely (*oscurement*), requiring the reader to "gloss the
text and supply interpretation" ("gloser la lettre e de lur sen la
surplus mettre"). Marie provides justifications for both sides.
The process of glossing was intended, evidently, to "keep vice at
a distance" ("de vice se voeult defendre"); Marie feels, by contrast, that this is no longer true, that what keeps vice at bay for
her—what keeps her "veillié," vigilant—is the recording of lais
she has heard; not obscurity, then, but arguably its opposite: the
open and clear presentation of heard tales.

That glossing is a virtuous activity can be found not only
in Priscian but even earlier in Augustine. In the passage of the *De
Doctrina Christiana* which D.W. Robertson, Jr. has rightly made
famous, Augustine states that "Scripture teaches nothing but
charity, nor condemns anything except cupidity." He clarifies
this by saying that "charity [is] the motion of the soul toward the
enjoyment of God for His own sake, and the enjoyment of one's

self and of one's neighbor for the sake of God; [while] cupidity is a motion of the soul toward the enjoyment of one's self, one's neighbor, or any corporal thing for the sake of something other than God. That which uncontrolled cupidity does to corrupt the soul and its body is called a vice." (DDC III, 10,16)

Since it is scripture that teaches charity, reading correctly, charitably, becomes, in Augustine's hands, not only *a* virtuous activity but *the* most virtuous one. The very process of charitable interpretation is the model on which virtuous activity is patterned. Moreover, this charitable activity is, elsewhere in the same text, specifically related to the act of healing: "just as physicians when they bind up wounds do not do so haphazardly but neatly . . . so the medicine of Wisdom . . . is accommodated to our wounds, healing some by contraries and some by similar things . . . The . . . principle of contraries is illustrated in the fact that the example of His virtues cures our vices . . . [while] similar bandages . . . [include the example of] born of a woman he freed those deceived by a woman." (DDC I.14)

It is the bandaging of a wound that constitutes this virtuous activity; the very process of reading and interpreting is virtue, charity, itself, while its opposite, cupidity, is the action of focusing on the unglossed text as it is; and that unglossed object, which is called by Augustine "any corporal thing," is also perceived as a body that is wounded.

What these passages from Augustine hand down to the medieval tradition is, first, an association between the covered body and the text and, second, the idea that the text is two very different things, given that charity is a reading that bandages: it is both the wounded body and, in the glossing, it is the concealment of that body.[3] As paradoxical as this sounds, it nonetheless is supported by Augustine's language. Troublesome text—that which does not of itself offer a charitable reading—is like a naked, wounded body; the charitable act of glossing both sees the body in its wounded state and seeks to cover it up, to conceal it. Text serves to correct and to heal by glossing, covering and revising. Text as a concept, then, is both wounded body and the suppression of body while glossing provides the paradigm for dealing with the corporeal, material world.

The linking of text with body and its suppression is a commonplace in early medieval thought. Beryl Smalley cites numerous examples in which the same Latin word, *corpus*, refers specifically to both body and text at the same time.[4] Text links with body, sacred text with sacred body; through the process of accommodation, reading and glossing become a sacramental act and what glossing trains us to do is to see the body as a "not-body."

Marie de France's disagreement with this type of glossing speaks to a larger questioning of the assumptions that underlie such a reading. In asserting that it is her moral duty not to conceal but to speak out through her texts she is suggesting that her reading strategy—and her interaction with the world—has changed. For her, obscuring the text through glossing can no longer keep vice at bay.

II.

A comparison with the following passage from Dante's *Purgatory* proves instructive:

> Sette "P" nella fronte mi descrisse col punton della spada,
> et "Fa che lavi, quando se'dentro, queste piaghe" disse.
> (Purg. IX: 112–114)

> (He inscribed seven "P"'s on my forehead with the point
> of his sword, and said "Wash these wounds off when you
> have entered inside.")

The incised letters that mark the contrite Dante's forehead at the entrance to Purgatory draw on the same Augustinian tradition which asserts an alliance between body and text as well as between sin and the wounded, naked body. For Dante, as for Augustine, the body-text association derives from a belief that reading correctly is a key to living correctly. The semiotics of the flesh that fascinates each author lies at the heart of both their text and their theology. But Dante's understanding of the relationship between text and body is quite different from that of Augustine. While the 7 "P"s function much as the wounded text does for Augustine—requiring a charitable interpretation—the goal of the reading is quite other. The wounds are to be "washed away" when Dante enters "inside" Purgatory. The gradual acquisition of virtue and hence of charity serves to erase the marks from the body, not to cover them over, and so to return the body to its initially pure state, to reveal, in fine, not to suppress. The way the "P"s are addressed is, as with Augustine, through learning to interpret, yet it is an interpretation that, as the passage suggests, turns towards, not away from the body.

This good, virtuous reading is taught to Dante in the first terrace of Purgatory through bas reliefs depicting scenes of humility where the model at work is that of the Annunciation in which the words of the archangel Gabriel are heard and accepted by Mary and, as a result, produce Christ, the word made flesh. Here then we have a second instance of the intersection of text and body, or, as Dante himself refers to it, *visibile parlare*, visible speech, the process of making visible by the taking on of the flesh. But even as Mary incorporates and makes visible the words of Gabriel, so Dante's true reading of the picture, which seems to speak to him, incorporates and embodies the true meaning as it becomes visible in him.

For Dante, in short, the good reading is one that literally incorporates, that turns his very body into a part of the text in its engaged interaction with the work. Where Augustine turns away from the body Dante turns toward it; even the seven "P"s which are the text of vice, will in their erasure reveal the body when he moves further inside Purgatory. The body is thus not hidden but foregrounded, and that body is not distanced in any way from him but is, instead, his own.

Ironically, the annunciatory hermeneutics represented by Dante's progress through Purgatory both foregrounds the body and emphasizes the need for internalization. The type of interpretation, of understanding being proposed is one that depends upon a simultaneous appreciation of two opposed things: what we might call the internal and the external or the subjective and the objective. Yet what becomes clear in a careful reading of the text is that what Dante is proposing is not the creation of an internal subjective landscape through a recognition of the wholly external quality of the world—a recognition that ultimately leads to a sense of isolation and alienation (and autonomy). Rather, what this process demands in the embodiment of the word is the subjectification of the objective world, that is, the possibility of creating an interior landscape that exists at the juncture of the objective and subjective, that defines the subjective as the mark of objective difference.

Here again a comparison with Augustine is instructive. While he too aims ostensibly to turn inward, his methods, as the example from the *De Doctrina Christiana* makes clear, consist of a progressive externalization. More and more layers of reading and glossing are added to the text as bandages to the body, and meaning and interpretation reside, ultimately, on the outside, not within.

The foregrounding of the body and the internal would suggest that, at best, we are in what both Freudians and Lacanians would term a pre-Oedipal, pre-self understanding of the subject/object relationship. Yet Madelon Sprengnether's rereading of psychological development opens the door for a reformulation that is useful to us here. [5] To call either Marie's or Dante's hermeneutics pre-anything is to treat it anachronistically. Rather, with Sprengnether, I would suggest that it represents the construction of an early self from the subjectification of the objective world. In other words, Dante's treatment of body and Marie's approach to glossing both suggest the formulation of a self out of the intersection of subject and object through text. But this construction is not the result of an epistemological rupture, and the mediation of that rupture through language. The association of text and body, in other words, does not, at least at first, result in an equation between text and self in the Lacanian sense; language does not for Dante or Marie serve to mediate between inner and outer. Rather, it appropriates, takes in, feeds on, and introjects the external world.

Nowhere is this clearer than in the earlier *Lais* of Marie. Marie's new form of tale-telling, her reading that speaks to the formulation of a new relationship between text and self is motivated not, as in Augustine, by the virtue of charity, or even the vice of cupidity but, rather, by a new category, that of the one being harmed by vice. In the prologue which precedes the first lai, Guigemar, she writes: "But anywhere there is a man or a woman of great worth, people who envy their good fortune

Marie de France. Courtesy of the Picture Collection, New York Public
Library.

often say evil things about them . . . I don't propose to give up because of that."

The emphasis on envy is crucial, since, as with Dante, envy focuses on foregrounding the visual. As important, however, is Marie's self-representation as the victim of this vice. She does not reject the idea that virtuous activity is still associated with, or at least comparable to, textual activity; she merely suggests that Priscian's view, which to her mind is obscuring, is not the way to handle her concern. Covering over, bandaging, healing, even turning from, the text is not the way to deal with being envied, she implies. It is, I would suggest, the purpose of the *Lais* to expose the proper approach, the new reading strategy, which will deal effectively both with the vice of envy and with the new category of being vice's victim.

But before looking at the response that surfaces it would perhaps be useful to look at a contemporary text that likewise recognizes this role of vice's victim yet is unable to respond to this redefinition. The *Historia Calamitatum* of Abelard, which is as much a biography of his culture as an autobiography of the author, is, I would suggest, such a transitional work. In many ways it echoes Augustine in its association of text and body, and in its demonstration of how that body, when not suppressed, is dependent, imperfect, wounded and powerless.

There are few other texts in which the body, particularly and explicitly the wounded body, is so closely linked with the text as Abelard's *Historia*. His love for Heloise is described in terms of reading ("Love brought us to gaze into each other's eyes more than reading kept them on the text"); his castration is specifically paralleled by the public humiliation of having his book burnt. Yet precisely what is missing is the interpretative motion, the process of turning body into not-body, the hermeneutic act. The text Abelard writes about his life, the text that could in fact gloss and conceal, specifically reveals. His opening remarks make this clear: "I have decided," he says to his friend and protege Walther, "to write you a letter of further encouragement based upon the experience of my own misfortunes so that when you compare your trials with mine you may consider them of little or no account and be stronger to endure them." All subsequent remarks, both philosophical and self-reflexive, are equally focused on tearing away the veils of inherited commonplace, such as the assumption that St. Denis, the patron saint of France, is Pseudo-Dionysius the Areopagite; or that words acquire meaning by virtue of a transcendental signifier. Even as his nominalist argument is grounded in the rejection of the common existence of universals, so his understanding of reading and text is not based on suppression. Text for him is not both body and the suppression of body. It is, instead, only body.

In rejecting the interpretative turn Abelard is acknowledging the growing emphasis on the visual and the spatial. Like Marie, he too aims not to conceal but to reveal, to bring to light rather than to obscure. Like Marie as well his nemesis is envy: "From this my troubles began and have plagued me to this day; and the more widespread my fame has become, the more has the envy of others been enkindled against me." (Hinc calamitatum mearum, que nunc usque perseverant, ceperunt exordia, et quo amplius fama extendebatur nostra, aliena in me succensa est invidia.) Yet while Abelard seems to have rejected the Augustinian understanding of a charitable reading, he has not yet landed on a new strategy. The identification of text with only body, and of reading with looking at that body, is ultimately only frustrating. The problem and its solution hinge on the fact that, given the patristic identification of text with wounded body and its concealment, removing the veil of hermeneutic gloss can only reveal a taboo, physical, "corporal thing." In context this thing is always perceived as partial, as imperfect. What is needed is a way to present that "corporal thing" as an entity of its own, a body that, when not obscured, is complete and autonomous.

Such a view of body is, indeed, possible. In the Old Occitan lyric "En aital rimeta prima" the troubadour Raimbaut d'Aurenga, a rough contemporary of Marie de France, offers a poem about the autonomous body that acknowledges the existence and power of envy, as well as a way to deal with being a victim of the vice. "In a rhyme similar to the first/ Direct and apt words please me,/ for building without rule or line": "bastir ses regl' e ses linha." The architectural metaphor here is clearly intended to link this lyric to Raimbaut's first poem, the much discussed "Cars, douz, e fenhz"[6] whose opening strophe reads as follows:

"The low song of the wren, on account of which I am ex-
alted, is dear, sweet, and fictitious to me, for it spreads
abroad, exists and grows with joy at the time when the
crickets, near the cork tree, sing in the wall under the block
of stone; so that their voices, which are lighter than cork,
are aligned and squared; and let no one exalt himself so
high except the cricket and the female wren."[7]

The architectonic cast of this strophe makes the audible visible;
the songs of the wren and the cricket are visualized and used to
flesh out the scene.

But while the rhyme patterns of Raimbaut's two poems are
indeed similar, the underlying approach is directly opposed:
there the primary metaphor is explicitly architectural, here the
poem will be built without rule or line; there the language is
darkly shaded, here direct and apt.

These lines also suggest that the lyric will be breaking
away from more than its own immediate predecessor. "Bastir ses
regl'e ses linha" can also refer to rules and lines of another sort:
regla has as secondary meaning monastic rule; *linha*, genealogical
lines. Laura Kendrick's argument that troubadour lyric was opposing the univocality of the church and Howard Bloch's thesis
that troubadour lyric was part of a larger movement that turned
away from a system of thought restricted by genealogy are both
supported by this line suggesting that Raimbaut, like Abelard, is
engaged in the action of breaking free from established systems
of thought and action.[8]

There is more, though, in these lines when they are coupled with the ones which immediately follow:

Pos mos volers s'i apila;
E atozat ai mon linh
Lai on ai cor qe m'apil
Per totz temps, e qi.n grondilha
No tem'auzir mon grondilh.

Since my will is fixed on it;
Although my line has been weakened
There where I would be firm
Always, and if anyone grouses about it
May he not fear my grousing.

Again *linha* appears, this time in conjunction with the verb *atozar*. This verb, Raimbaut's editor Walter Pattison notes, "is not recorded in the dictionaries, but since *toza*, "maiden," *tozet*, "child," and other words on the same stem exist, we can postulate a meaning "to rejuvenate." He goes on: "The idea of rejuvenating oneself through love is common enough . . . and by hyperbole the joy of love can be extended to one's associates or one's family."[9] But love is not mentioned anywhere in these lines and Pattison's hypothesized meaning for *atozar* depends upon its inclusion. I would propose instead that *atozat*, linked as indeed it is with the words meaning maiden and child, could be translated as emasculate or, if that is too strong, weaken. Placed back in context this produces the following: "Since my will is fixed on it, though my line is weakened there where I would be firm," *linh* now being literally lineage and, metonymically, phallus.[10]

In other words, Raimbaut is busy rejecting his monastic and genealogical inheritance, both of which deny the needs and the strengths of the body. The first strophe ends with "e qi.n grondilha/ No tem'auzir mon grondilh,": "and if anyone grumbles, let him not fear my grumbling," translates Pattison. But *grondilh* carries connotations of animal noises, such as growling, which again underscores the reading given here to the first six lines: rejecting the systems which suppress bodily needs Raimbaut now runs the risk of being treated like an animal; this is a risk he is willing to take.

Throughout the poem, in fact, Raimbaut aligns himself with animals rather than other people. He describes his *joi* as *frainh* and *esfila*, reined in and broken, thus implicitly likening it to a horse. The birds *chant* and *qil* in the third strophe, the poet likewise *chant*s and *qil*s. He *sailh fort* and *grim*, bounds up and leaps, like an animal, causing him to be held in contempt by his lady, all, I would suggest, as demonstration of what he can do by himself, free from the restrictions of rule and line.

For Raimbaut's identification with the animals is a polemical statement which asserts his acceptance not only of his body but of the world as a whole: *linh* appears one other time, in the combined form *relinh*, in the third strophe: "Qan vei rengat en la cima/ Man vert-madur frug pel cim,/ e qecs auzelletz relinha/ . . . per cui vas Joi relinh": "When I see many firm-ripe fruits in the treetops and each little bird realigns toward love . . . I realign toward joy." It is the sight of the firm-ripe fruits—again, strikingly suggestive in this form (even more so if translated as vert mas dur: vigorous but hard)—and the birds which cause him to refocus his attentions, to discover his new alignment which is toward *Joi*, that same *Joi* likened in the second strophe to the horse.

It is, in short, Raimbaut's use of his body as point of reference not point of departure which sets him apart from the ways of line and rule. He knows what he knows because of, not despite, his body. He is presented throughout as like the animals because, like them, he is anchored in a body which perceives the world through its senses. This approach, however, while liberating in many respects, also has its limiting side which is spelled out in the second strophe of this poem: "About the false men who file and declare and speak because of which I file each one of them, and constrain and point out and stare . . . wherefore I wither and pant and stare." (De la falsa genz qe lima/ E dech'e ditz (don quec lim)/ Ez estreinh e mostr'e guinha . . . Per q'ieu sec e pols e guinh.) He not only sees, he is seen, and he withers up because of the glance of the *falsa genz*; it seems clear that he is here presenting himself as envy's victim.[11]

But Raimbaut, unlike Abelard, is not destroyed by envy. What Raimbaut's poem shows us is that while he is aware of his body and sight he does not define himself solely in terms of the body or its suppression. His body may wither and pant and stare but he does not die or become impotent. Quite the opposite: inspired by the sight of "firm-ripe fruits and singing birds" he turns to Joy, about which he sings and cries, and the nightingale arouses itself and wounds him "in that part of the body so wounded by love" to paraphrase Pattison's gloss.

In other words, although Raimbaut shares with Abelard an orientation toward the world that is anchored in the body and the visual, he does not identify his text with his body.[12] Rather, he suggests that he is both visible and invisible—never wholly exteriorized—and that a poem can show the world subjectively while playing out the objective in its tangible textual elements, such as rhyme and form. Pure reflection is rejected, passed by; the poet never appears fully in his own poem; other texts are always altered. The rhyme scheme reflects the parameters of the subjective vision: the frame. Within that, Raimbaut places the view he sees. He thus uses his poems to reflect the world, but to reflect it selectively and in so doing, he contains absence as he organizes the poem around his view of the world.

What Raimbaut creates in "En aital rimeta prima" acknowledges a departure from univocal authority, from deferral and toward the objects of this world and this life. Such a change involves a shift in perspective from linear to volumetric, from temporal to spatial, as the voices involved shift from two—those of now versus those of then—to three—those of this world, those of the next, and those that can sing of both. Most importantly, that self is created by rejoining God and the world, by viewing God as existing because of, not despite, the world.

Raimbaut's poetics are best expressed by the Narcissus image provided in a later text, *The Roman de la Rose* .[13] Here, after a version of the Narcissus tale is rehearsed, the Lover looks into the Fountain himself. Through the water he sees two crystals which reflect the garden behind him, and the rose from which the rest of the story is generated. All other considerations aside— and there are many—this story would seem an exemplum of Raimbaut's poetics. Reflection occurs, but it is reflection from within and it is reflection that does not include the observer. What the lover sees is everything but himself. It is reflexive, mimetic, yet mediated. This is exactly what Raimbaut aims to do throughout his lyrics. While the poem is made more visual, symmetrical and spatial through the elaborate rhyme schemes, word play, and the thematic of sight, it is never wholly visual or corporal; it is at once spatial, closed and yet removed from the physical world. It has dimension but it is not bound by the laws that usually govern physical objects; it includes but is not closed in by the physical world.

III.

Marie's criticism of Priscian's approach to texts speaks of a similarly changed relation to both body and world. Her lais focus on discovering a way to acknowledge the visual without granting it

full power; to translate victimization into strength. The super-
natural element in her lais all inhabit even as they constitute
such a space of mediation. Her heroes, many of them at least,
leave the confines of the envy-ridden court to explore a more
open, less defined space without. In each case the visually-ori-
ented vice of envy is countered by a new reading strategy, a new
caritas, that is based on the visual but is not limited to what can
be seen. As Guigemar is told, in words that echo the opening
lines of the Prologue: "You're in love; take care not to hide it too
well" ("Gardez que trop ne vus celez" 446). Love, for Marie, like
Raimbaut's text, often breaks rules and transgresses lines. It neither turns from the body, nor does it cover it over, as Augustine's *caritas* did. But neither is it locked into pure exteriority.
Rather, inspired by the visual (Andreas Capellanus tells us that
blind men cannot love) it thrives when allowed to exist in the in-
termediate state of being both visible and invisible, private and
public.

The question that remains, however, is why Abelard never
found such a strategy. He had all the right elements, it would
seem, he was just not able to valorize them. The dead ends that
become increasingly prevalent in his text, and the impotence
which they imply, are potentially undone by the process of writing about love. Although not acknowledged explicitly in his text,
it is clear that his love for Heloise is an answer to being envied,
even as his writing creates a textual self which can escape from
the traps set by his detractors, the prototypical enviers. Abelard
does not get to this point, in part perhaps because of the inherited limits of the Latin tradition to which he belongs, a tradition
which asserts that body and text are one. Raimbaut, Marie, and
Dante, who all write in the vernacular, however, are able to
break free from this assertion. While the text for Abelard, in
other words, remains conceptually associated with a body which
can only be concealed or revealed, the vernacular text carves out
a new space of poetic action that is more independent, more
powerful. For Abelard the visual only serves to verify imperfec-
tion. For Marie de France, the troubadours and Dante it becomes
the means to mediation and love.

What I am suggesting is that the vernacular text has the
capacity to offer up a new strategy for reading in that it provides

a space of action that is related to the body while not being
bound by it. In its unique relationship to Latin, the vernacular as
literary language is able to suggest an alternative approach to the
body and the world, one that does not censor but rather medi-
ates. As such, the vernacular authors are able to create in and
through their texts a model for the self.

The vernacular is capable of this only because it is equally
able to partake of inner and outer worlds simultaneously. The
body surfaces, as in Raimbaut, first in its claim to true exteriority,
as the signifier that is genuinely objective, a fact subverted by
Augustinian semiotics in its repeated attempt to hide the body
through glossing. But in its objectivity the signifier also becomes
that which can mark difference, and it is that difference which
can then be introjected and form the basis of subjectivity. Its very
exteriority is the cause of its interiorization; its objectivity the
cause of its subjectification.

What I hope to have shown is the development of subjectivity in 12th-c. France that arose in conjunction with—and at
least partially as a result of—the development of the written vernacular text. Yet what is crucial to my argument is the observation that I am not talking about a self that develops first in response to a proto-Cartesian awareness of the subject/object split
between self and world—that moment when the subjective becomes alienated from the objective and is reallied to it through
the mediation of language. Such an argument speaks not of the
origins of self but of masculine efficacy in the world: the Oedipal
stage, after all, doubles the male, not the female figure. Yet this
argument—and the self so constructed—is founded on an earlier
self, as Sprengnether argues, allied not with power, alienation,
and externalization but with appropriation and internalization—
the subjectified object which later can be reobjectified, reified,
reintroduced into the world.

With actual child development this earlier self is pre-verbal. When repeated, either later in life or in the larger ideological
framework I am considering here, neither stage is without its
language. Rather, language is shown to function in two entirely
different ways, both of which relate to the body: first as an object
that can be appropriated and internalized, then as a source of
mediation which *precisely because of its earlier introjection* is able to

bridge the gap between subject and world while belonging wholly to neither. The later mediating power of language—of text—is derived from its earlier ability to be embodied and internalized. While both are powers that belong to the category of ambivalence, the one emphasizes difference, the other unity. Language's ability to be introjected comes from the perception that it belongs first to the world—that it is already an object in the world just like the body that it is about to join while, at the same time, remaining distinct from that bodily object. The very fact that the Latin tradition of letters had for so long been associated with both the body and its suppression established a context which linked text and body in the cultural mind. Yet Latin was never an ambivalent body, a subjectifiable object. Rather, it remained wholly external, an image of the unified signified from which difference must be marked. The body which could be internalized was one which was like Latin, yet could also be subjectified, mark difference and be personalized: was like the body but different from it.

The vernacular, in short, becomes the vehicle of the self. It exists in both the objective and subjective realms and so can adequately represent the sign and the self. It is neither wholly external nor wholly internal; through its derivation from Latin it is allied with the body, yet it, unlike Latin, allows for difference. The initial role of vernacular text, then, is not mediating but differentiating, as male from female, as body from not-body, as an object that is like the other objects in the world yet also different enough, ambiguous enough to be internalized.

There is at first nothing unified about this creation; a range of possibilities, rather, open up which deny the necessity for an either/or choice. It is important to realize that at this stage there is no economy, only ambivalence and slippage. That is, differentiation is not being marked through exchange; the text is not a third party, rather, the text marks difference by its ability to be both subject and object, internal and external. It is only when the text becomes the means to another end—when its efficacy in the world becomes important—that economy per se enters in. It is when the purpose of the text becomes rhetorical, turns to objectifying the subjective will of the poet to its audience, the text then becomes associated neither with woman or man, not with internal and external self but with the mediation of self and world. The text then becomes localized in an object and fixed in the external world.

Here is where discussion of the self usually starts; here is where I intend to end, for the objectified subject is but the last of a series of selves, as post-structuralist denial of the self makes even clearer. The self that is fashioned in the Renaissance is a self that is derived from an earlier, more open, more ambivalent stage. The certainty of the Cartesian subject is built on very uncertain, shifting grounds, grounds that nonetheless carry the seeds of possibility and the roots of subjectivity. Subjectivity is indeed created out of the world, and it is created out of an awareness of difference. But it is not founded on, or dependent on alienation or rupture. Text is essential to subjectivity, but not because of its ability to belong fully nowhere, to mediate only, but rather because it belongs initially everywhere and transforms fluidly. Self, and the vernacular language that creates it is, at least in 12th c. France, a food that sustains, enables, and ultimately reproduces. But first it is part of an enclosed and appealing awareness of the world, the body and difference.

For even as the vernacular literary tradition defines itself in terms of the Latin one, so the self is defined by an awareness, acceptance and distancing from the autonomous body; writing in the vernacular provides a new model for appropriating the body, one that is defined not by censorship, as it was for Augustine, but by a simultaneous acceptance and denial of the Latin *corpus*.

NOTES

1.   The alignment of text and self with spatial differentiation is accepted by Jonathan Culler, *Structuralist Poetics* (Ithaca: 1972); J. Derrida, "Living on Borderlines," *Deconstruction and Criticism* (New York, NY: 1979), 75–176; and, by negation, by William V. Spanos, "Breaking the Circle: Hermeneutics as Dis-Closure," *Boundary* 2 (1977), 5:421–457. On the interconnection between self and text see S. Corngold, *The Fate of the*

Self: German Writers and French Theory. (New York, NY: 1986) who draws on the fact that both Freud and Lacan encourage us to "attain ... that ... which creates our being" (p. 3) and then posits that literature opens the way into being: "poetic activity ... is privileged evidence of the self" (p. 3), and J. Mehlman, who claims that "fiction ... figures as constituting—rather than constituted by—the self" (cited by Corngold, 226). In this context it is also worth noting the striking similarity that exists between definitions of the self and those of the fictional text, e.g., Wolfgang Iser, who speaks of fiction as the overstepping of boundaries, "virtual space" (*The Implied Reader*, 1974). In a lecture presented at the University of Georgia in April 1990 Iser spoke of fiction as "defamiliarized reality ... overstepped ... not discarded." He also noted that fiction is "incontestable... inaccessible ... cannot be reified," and emphasized its visible/invisible qualities, as well as its ability to conceal and reveal at the same time: "simultaneity of what is mutually exclusive." In addition, Paul Ricoeur, "The Hermeneutical Function of Distanciation," *Hermeneutics and the Human Sciences*, (Cambridge: 1981), speaks of similarities between human relationships and texts.

2.   Michel Foucault, *The History of Sexuality* (New York, NY: 1986).

3.   Here I would have to disagree with Beryl Smalley, who argues that body is likened to text because it veils meaning. *The Study of the Bible in the Middle Ages* (Notre Dame: 1964), Chap. 1.

4.   Ibid.

5.   *The Spectral Mother: Freud, Feminism and Psychoanalysis*. (Ithaca: 1989).

6.   On the relationship between space and time in troubadour lyric see P. Bec, "Espace poétique" *Cahiers de Civilisation Médiévale* 29 (1986), 9–14.

7.   Cars, douz e fenhz del bederesc
     M'es sos bas chanz, per cui m'aerc;
     C'ab joi s'espan viue noire
     El tems que'lh grill pres del siure
     Chantan el mur jos lo caire;
     Que's compassa e s'escaira
     Sa vos, qu'a plus leu de siura
     E ja uns non s'i aderga
     Mas grils e la bederesca.

This poem has been edited three times, by Walter T. Pattison, *The Life and Works of the Troubadour Raimbaut D'Orange* (Minneapolis: 1952) 65–72; J.H. Marshall, "On the text and the interpretation of a poem of Raimbaut d'Orange (*Cars, douz*; ed. Pattison, I)" *Medium Aevum* 37

(1968), 12–36; and Marc Vijlstecke, "*Cars, Douz e Fenhz* de Raimbaud d'Orange," *Etudes de philologie romane e d'histoire litteraire offertes a Jules Horrent* (Liege, 1980), pp. 509–16. Vijlstecke, reacting against much of what Marshall has proposed, returns in large part to Pattison's rendering.

8.   Laura Kendrick, *The Game of Love: Troubadour Wordplay.* (Berkeley: 1988); R. Howard Bloch, *Genealogies and Etymologies: A Literary Anthropology of the French Middle Ages.* (Chicago: 1983).

9.   Pattison, p. 74.

10.   William Burgwinkle's 1988 Stanford University dissertation, *The Troubadour as Subject: Biography, Erotics and Culture* (DAI 49/12A, p. 3743) includes similar new readings of several poems.

11.   That envy is a vice based on vision is made clear by its Latin etymology: as Cicero and others point out, to envy (*invidere*) is to look at closely (*in-videre*). That this etymology was still active in medieval usage is evidenced by a sermon of St. Bernard in which he speaks of envy in precisely these terms (PL 183, cols 235–238).

12.   The form of that poem serves to underscore this point. *Coblas unissonans,* the order of the rhymes is a, a', b, c, b', c', d, d'. Symmetrical in one sense, couplet, chiastic pair, couplet, the form still evades perfect symmetry since the couplets employ different rhymes: within each couplet the rhymes are not exact but are grammatical variations; variations, in other words, that alter the sense precisely in relation to the particular person or action being described. While they relate two figures through their similarity they also distinguish them through their person or voice. The form thus defines itself through a repeated process of similarity and difference. This dialectic of identity and difference is, I feel, at the base of this lyric of Raimbaut's. He distinguishes his first poem from his second; he separates himself from the *falsa genz,* and is separated from his lady, yet in the end these distinctions are only proof of common ground.

13.   While I disagree with Kay's conclusions, her observation about the role of the *Roman de la Rose* in Bernart's poem seems right on target. "Love in a Mirror," *Medium Aevum* 52 (1983), 272–285.

Unscripting the Self

The Rewritten Self in African American Autobiography[1]

R. Baxter Miller

> But, of course, no idea is perfect and forever valid. Always
> to be living and apposite and timely, it must be modified
> and adapted to changing facts . . . [T]his process must deal
> not only with conscious rational action, but with irra-
> tional and unconscious habit, long buried in folkways and
> custom.[2]
>
> —W. E. B. Du Bois

> I congratulate you also on the power of language . . . I
> know that some people think that an artist is a man who
> has nothing to say and who writes in order to prove it. The
> great writers of the world have not so conceived their task
> and neither have you.[3]
>
> —Joel Spingarn

Literally, a script is a text performed by actors with gestures and movements, giving shape to what was previously ab-
straction. A script, with designs for sound and movement, sets
detailed instructions for those prescribed to follow it. Consider
the U.S. Constitution. For more than two hundred years since its
origin in 1787, imaginative Native Americans, Hispanics,
women, and Blacks have looked for it to vindicate their personal
freedom. They have envisioned it as a living script for acts of
human liberation. To the Founding Fathers, the script was the
blueprint for a democratic republic. Yet like the American Declaration of Independence, which preceded the Constitution by

over ten years, the earlier document still provides an interpretive opportunity for innovators and free thinkers.

The last thirty-seven years or so of American history have reenacted the drama between those who call for the performance—the presence—of American democracy on behalf of all citizens, and those who ask only for a return to accepted lines. While some people insist on the letter of the constitution, others ask for its spirit. Indeed, many of the current disagreements over issues of textual interpretation rest on ideological preferences. Though most governments would like naive audiences to believe that scripts exist without tellers, even the most well-meaning narrators have agendas. In 1954, the Supreme Court of the United States, then under the leadership of Chief Justice Earl Warren, outlawed racial segregation in the public schools of the States. Those on the Warren court understood in principle the brilliance of W. E. B. Du Bois's ideas, probably without ever having read his theory of narrative.

For the most part, the narrative theory of Black American autobiography sides with the Warren Court, proposing that a democratic and legal script lives only through the ennobling performance of enlightened citizens. Linda Brent, Du Bois, and Langston Hughes all inherit the historical script of American tradition, but all become in their narratives tellers, compelled by their survival to revise the limited scripts handed them. What they want for their own narratives is to achieve the performance or the physical presence of real space and time. What African American autobiographical narrative calls for is human theater. For, in the telling of the story, the teller comes to recognize the limitations of denotative language, of words. Even words cannot say some things. But the conscientious awareness of resaying them demonstrates the superiority of great narrative over even great law. The distinction is what makes the potential story of America greater than America is at any established point in time and space. To Frederick Douglass and Linda Brent, the performers of the slave narrative will eventually vindicate themselves as creative artists who recount moments of enlightenment within slave experiences. To Du Bois, the performers of his autobiographical narrative will reveal the Euro-American script of cultural hegemony. His taboo work must reveal the silence enforced

upon the abused messenger who reveals the ideological sordid-
ness that even the democratic script conceals. And to Langston
Hughes, the brilliant performers of African American narrative
are yet unborn.

For the sake of clarity, I will take "narrator" to mean the
fictionalized teller of the autobiographies. The "author" will de-
note the historical writer of the text and connote the encrypted
voice of authority that determines viewpoint as well as tone. Of
the two roles, the narrator tends to be more of a developed character and a definable personality. While the narrator is almost a
fictionalized person in the text, the author becomes the mythic
voice within it. The author includes the more limited narrator,
who can only signify the author. The "scriptor," by contrast,
writes more out of the cultural prescription than out of any self-
generating vision. And though authors distinguish themselves
by writing their way to artistic freedom, scriptors remain within
bounds of formal conventions.[4] By "script" I mean the literary
protocols dictated by cultural power brokers. Indeed, script suggests the mandatory grounds for any canonization of texts.
Artistic narrative involves the degree of accomplishment
through which a writing self proves at once to be enlightened
about all of the conventional parameters of traditional script. But
the greatness of the autobiographical self is to transform the
rules so as to preserve the authentic expression, the performance
of history as reconstituted by personal imagination.
"Performance" I take to be the communal level of symbolic action through which a text not only enlightens the reader but becomes itself a material force for vision and change. Performance
takes shape as the theatrical dimension through which active
readers restore dead scripts to living forms.

Of the narrators who seek to recover the text of self from
an imposed script of history, none surpasses the autobiographical art of Frederick Douglass. Douglass helps restore slavery
from the dispassionate recital of sociological fact to the compelling drama of personal story. Since 1980, there has been a tendency to appropriate the revolutionary art of Frederick Douglass
to the more textually prescribed ideology of American tradition.
Douglass is, according to this view, like the folk heroes of the
American nation itself. Toiling hard and aided by moral vision,

he resembles David Crockett, the legendary frontiersman and racist nemesis of Native Americans. Douglass is, in other words, quintessentially "American" because he represents a "valiant struggle for achievement and respectability."[5] Douglass becomes a forced "exemplar" of British Romanticism as well, though his complex affinity with the romantic sensibility is in fact suggestive, if virtually unexplored. The Douglass autobiographer demonstrates, one critic says, the most significant features of the Wordsworthian child who is father of the heroic man. While such statements indicate the almost desperately integrationist tendency of recent scholarship, Douglass does show an extraordinary insight and prescience. With a kind of divine aura and favor, he sets a tone for heroic effort and for useful accomplishment. As with Langston Hughes, Richard Wright, Malcolm X, Maya Angelou, and so many others after him (my own extrapolation of cultural tradition), Douglass adapts a narrative strategy for reading wisdom back into the consciousness of the child.

I would simply offer a different reading of Douglass's auctorial purpose. Enslaved by the historical script, Douglass reads within this script the myth and metaphor of slavery as an idea and as a historical sign of human evil. He thus revises for himself a romantically imaginative writing or art based on what he intuits as a divine design for his personal identity. Ultimately, he advances from the mere copyist of eighteenth-century thought to the romantic rebel of nineteenth century thinking. He becomes both guardian of a traditional past and creative rewriter of an agenda for a living future. To restate the observation in Coleridgean terms, Frederick Douglass is a writer not of the primary imagination—or of the one that most of us are born with and therefore the one we take—but of the secondary imagination, by which we reconstitute what is still humanly possible. His mission is to rewrite the spirit of the U.S. Constitution back into the letter of the law and into American history.[6]

Critics have misread Douglass as being a mere copyist of the recorded facts, taking at face value his original Preface to *My Bondage and My Freedom* (1855) in which he writes: "The reader is, therefore, assured, with all due promptitude, that his attention is not invited to a work of ART, but to a work of FACTS— FACTS terrible and almost incredible, it may be—yet FACTS, nevertheless" (3). But the narrator proves consistently ambivalent toward such an emphasis, as when he writes a mythic appeal during the beating of his Aunt Hester: "When the motives of this brutal castigation are considered, language has no power to convey a just sense of its awful criminality" (59). In addition to the mythic art that is both an extrapolation of the meaning (yet a rereading of history), Douglass suspects some kind of divine plan. He says that his personal removal from Eastern Shore Maryland to Baltimore may well have been more than an interesting and fortunate moment in his life. Had the event never happened, his will to freedom may never have developed along the same line, and he may have remained a slave: "I have sometimes felt, however, that there was something more than circumstance." By the publication of *Life and Times* in 1892, the tone suggesting divine intervention might have disappeared. But Douglass had advanced from his limited role as an American copyist to that of an African American artist. Clearly, his own written language has become a means to bridge the gap rhetorically between history and divine law. As he says of Mrs. Hugh Auld, the slave mistress, "it was SLAVERY not its mere INCIDENTS THAT I hated. I saw through the attempt to keep me in ignorance; I saw that slaveholders would have gladly made me believe that they were merely acting under the authority of God, . . . in making slaves of others; and I treated them as robbers and deceivers."

In the eras of structuralism and poststructuralism, a thoughtful oversimplification[7] may well mislead us to narrow our critical inquiry to the question of literacy in the Douglass autobiographies, or to only the dialectic there between slavery and literacy. In the shipyard of Master Hugh Auld and of Durgan & Bailey, for instance, Douglass begins to learn the skill (not the art) of writing. He observes that the carpenters mark the location for the prepared timber, inscribing an "S" for the starboard side, an "S.F." for the starboard forward side, and so on. Here, at least, Douglass seems true to his early promise, now bolstered perhaps by his historicist editors, to "let others philosophize; it is my province here to relate and describe; only allowing myself a word or two, occasionally, to assist the reader in the proper understanding of the facts narrated."

And it is certainly true that Douglass takes advantage of his playtime with white boys to practice his alphabets. Indeed, Douglass uses opportunities of comradeship with boys near the Bethel church and elsewhere to challenge them to write better than he so that he can learn what they know. When early on he is left as the sole keeper of the Master's house, he writes between the lines of young Tommy's copy books, imitating the son's writing as closely as possible. Later, he copies on a flour barrel words taken from the Bible and the Methodist hymn book as well as from other sources. Often he imitates the words in his own hand late at night when others are asleep. Hence, McDowell's assertion has merit when he writes that "This hand-to-hand combat between black and white men for physical, then narrative, control over bodies and texts raises the question of who is on whose side? For, in its allegiance to the dialectics of dominance and subordination, Douglass' narrative is, and not surprisingly so, a by-product of Master Tommy's copybook, especially of its gender division of power relations."[8] Indeed, McDowell's statement means to women studies what Houston Baker's famous statement[9] means to black studies: "The voice of the unwritten self, once it is subjected to the linguistic codes, literary conventions, and audience expectations of a literate population, is perhaps never again the authentic voice of black American slavery."[10]

But it is possible to reread between the narrative lines of the Auld copybooks as Douglass himself writes there. Thus, the reader, as well as the writer, subverts the script that only white boys and men have the right to literacy. Douglass undermines the white patriarchal tradition far more than he shows any complicity with it: he is more a relative of Aunt Hester than of Mrs. Auld, who sides with her white husband against Black American literacy. "When left thus, I used to spend the time in writing *in the spaces* [my italics] left in Master Thomas's copybook, copying what he had written. I continued to do this until I could write a hand very similar to that of Master Thomas. Thus, after a long, tedious effort for years, I finally succeeded in learning how to write [*for myself*]" (281). The emphasis that Douglass writes "for himself" is important. Of two of the stronger scenes edited from the original text (the other being Colonel Lloyd's forbidden garden) the narration of Captain Auld's assessment of Tommy Auld proves instructive:

> He was not even a good imitator. He possessed all the disposition to deceive, but wanted the power. Having no resources within himself, he was compelled to be the copyist of many, and being such, he was forever the victim of inconsistency; and of consequence he was an object of contempt, and was held as such even by his slaves.

Tommy Auld posed no role model for Frederick Douglass, who was seeking to recover himself as a Black man rather than to grow into a white one. Frederick Douglass writes his way from being a copyist of the white Patriarchal script into a literary artist of African American truth.

An even more striking passage exemplifies the performance of the emerging autobiographical self as it grapples with the slave's destiny. For a brief period during Douglass' work in Mr. Gardiner's Baltimore shipyard, black and white carpenters had labored side by side, each race represented by skilled workers. Suddenly, the white carpenters go on strike, refusing to work with Blacks. Because war vessels for Mexico must be launched in July, it is difficult to hire during summer, though the whites insist that the employer discharge all of the "free" colored workmen. The white workers' racist hatred takes shape against Douglass. When Edward North, one of the most aggressive workers, strikes Douglass, Douglass retaliates. Though Douglass could manage any of the white workers singly, four of them attack him at once, one approaching from the front with a brick while others flank him from each direction. Closing in from all sides, they deal him stunning blows to the head, even placing a boot in his left eye as he falls among the timbers. When he recovers through sheer will, rushing at the cowards with a carpenter's spike, workers finally intervene, saying that it is impossible to "stand against so many." Douglass' comment on the attack is telling:

> Dear reader, you can hardly believe the statement, but it is true, and, therefore, I write it down. No fewer than fifty white men stood by . . . and not a man of them all interposed . . . There were four against one . . . and no one said, 'that is enough'; but some cried out, 'kill him—kill

Frederick Douglass (younger). Courtesy of W. W. Norton & Company, Publishers. Reproduced from William S. McFeely, *Frederick Douglass.* New York: W. W. Norton & Co., 1991.

> him—the d----- nigger! he struck a white person.' I men-
> tion this inhuman outcry, to show the character of the
> men, and the spirit of the time, at Gardiner's ship yard,
> and, in Baltimore generally, in 1836 (*Bondage*, 191).

Douglass the autobiographer wins the dramatic encounter through a narrative sleight-of-hand. The brutes who flail him remain imprisoned within the historical script of their time, but the artist appeals rhetorically to the reader in some future time when racism will be diminished. While the ruffians are bound by the temporal script of history, the man of imagination freely asserts his eternal claims before a future court of readers. And it is certainly from within this self-constituting imagination that he judges the unjust script of history:

> I already saw myself wielding my pen, as well as my
> voice, in the great work of renovating the public mind and
> building up a public sentiment which should, at least,
> send slavery and oppression to the grave, and restore to
> "liberty and the pursuit of happiness" the people with
> whom I had suffered, both as a slave and as a freeman
> (*Bondage*, 240).

Literary power derives from the recreation through words of an African American self that inhabits both space and time. The pen of Douglass exists in historical space just as the voice takes place in the historical period of the nineteenth century. But the value or myth of the voice persists into our own time and beyond. Its literary purpose is to "renovate," to rewrite the script of the "public mind." What the rewriting facilitates is a new "public sentiment" or symbolic vision to displace the slave script.

By now most readers of American autobiography recognize Linda Brent as the slightly fictionalized representation of Harriet Jacobs, a nineteenth-century slave in eastern North Carolina. Brent recounts her story as a twenty-one-year-old slave who hides from the sexual advances of a Dr. Flint, whose name reveals his "cold heart." For seven years she conceals herself in the overhead den of her grandmother who lives nearby, eventually escaping to New York where she finds kindness from the Bruces for whom she works as a domestic. Despite the rather stock plot of slavery and escape, the tale's structure is loosely decentered. Emerging from her "cell," her unexercised limbs atro-

Frederick Douglass. Courtesy of the National Portrait Gallery, Smithsonian Institution.

phied, Brent transforms the ignoble script given her by the Southern Planters: "I had not lived fourteen years in slavery for nothing," she writes. "I had felt, seen, and heard enough, to read the characters, and question the motives, of those around me. The war of my life had begun; and though one of God's most powerless creatures, I resolved never to be conquered" (19)[11].

Near the end of her narrative Brent calls for the performance of her written design:

> 'The bill of sale!' Those words struck me like a blow. So I was *sold* at last! a human being *sold* in the free city of New York, late in the nineteenth century of the Christian religion. It may hereafter prove a useful document to antiquaries, who are seeking to measure the progress of civilization in the United States (200).

The commercial script recurs with the repetitions "sale!" "*sold* . . . sold." Narrating historical record, Brent recognizes that her report, like all scripts, can become a dead language. Why write out "the nineteeth century of the Christian religion" unless to ironize the fact that the Western world measures time by the clock of its faith. Though the West hides the moral claims of its language, its structure belies the religious and political interests that ground it.

More important, Brent knows that her own rewriting of the Western script will be fulfilled only through staged performance: "The bill of sale is on record [script] and future generations [interpreters] will learn from it . . . It may hereafter prove a useful document [script] to antiquaries [tellers], who are seeking to measure [and perform] the progress of civilization in the United States." Brent envisions the transformation of period-bound narratives as ethical milestones for the American future. Her text is at once structural, self-contained, and phenomenological. It marks a continuing, if sometimes deferred, pattern forging the historical consciousness of her race. What makes her narrative world more than a mere script is that it resists interiority, a presumptive arrogance of linear and textual closure. It avoids, in other words, the limits of formally reduced time and space. For even these last two are signs, fragments, of a scriptor's imagined and recreated voice.

Though W. E. B. Du Bois proves in many ways to be the least dramatic of the autobiographers considered, he was, in part like Brecht and Artaud, the most theatrical of them in revising a text for the times. His fifteenth trip abroad frames his 1958 autobiography, allowing for a unity of text that spans his birth in Great Barrington, Massachusetts in 1868 to his unnarrated death in Ghana in 1963. In *Soliloquy* (1968), a draft completed at ninety, he writes:

> Autobiographies do not form indisputable authorities. They are always incomplete, and often unreliable. Eager as I am to put down the truth, there are difficulties; memory fails especially in small details, so that it becomes finally but a theory of my life, with much forgotten and misconceived, with valuable testimony but often less than absolutely true, despite my intention to be frank and fair.

The passage deserves its fame, for it proposes that narrative theory divorce itself from any detailed presentation of narrative. But like narrative, even this theory is a product of economic history, just as the text in part has become the subjective product of Du Bois. By contrast, theory separates itself from racial memory. What limits the narrative in theoretical precision enhances its human depth and complexity.

Du Bois emphasized the "narrator's" mortality. He writes of the way that *Darkwater* (1920), his first autobiography, provided at fifty many particulars that are either missing from the later text or are strange by current standards. To him, *Dusk of Dawn* (1940) presents life as he read it at the age of seventy, twenty years before his current revision of the text in *Soliloquy*. What he finds in all the drafts of his life is a disjointed series of contradictions: "[T]his book," he writes, "is the Soliloquy of an old man on what he dreams his life has been as he sees it slowly drifting away; and what he would like others to believe." Does the narrator transcend the narrative? He mentions some "fixed documents" in life such as a memorandum on his twenty-fifth birthday; some letters from his mother; his accusation to President Hayes that he had suggested that no Black thinkers existed or that none preferred to better themselves if they did.

Scripts give an illusion of permanence, for they ultimately lack the mythic power that would enable them to transcend the limits of their times. But while texts can have formal beginnings and ends, narrators are humanly incoherent, as Du Bois's narrative shows: "The century in which it was mine to live is now in its last decade," he writes. "In all probability I shall not finish it, since life seldom goes by logical completeness, but I shall be near enough its end to speak with a certain sense of unity. In all my plans and dreaming, I do not remember ever thinking of a long life" (12–13). Even the life of the teller cannot be engineered precisely. In recalling trips to France in 1892 and 1950, Du Bois retraces his own unpredictable development from the American pragmatism of William James to his own communism in old age. From 1892 to 1910, he had challenged the philosophy of Booker T. Washington, who had been so willing to accommodate racism in America in order to secure a few practical utilities for Tuskegee Institute. In his later, more radical years, such silence had spurred him to thoughts of rare dramatic intensity as he sat in a November 8, 1951 Washington courtroom, unjustly accused of being a political criminal. Despite the innocence of himself and of the others who were accused, DuBois writes,

> most Americans of education and stature did not say a word or move a hand. This is the most astonishing and frightening result of this trial. We five are free but America is not. The absence of moral courage and intellectual integrity which our prosecution revealed still stands to frighten our own nation and the better world. It is clear still today, that freedom of speech and of thinking can be attacked in the United States without the intellectual and moral leaders of this land raising a hand or saying a word in protest or defense, except in the case of the Saving Few. Their ranks did not include the heads of the great universities, the leaders of religion, or most of the great names in science. Than this fateful silence there is on earth no greater menace to present civilization (389).

While the literary is rooted firmly within history, it is precisely the flux of history, the unpredictable intensity, the illogical silences, that make the narrator distrust it. Though scripts are, in other words, limited by time, gifted narrators inevitably expose the "assigned" scripts for the enslaving documents of tradition that they are. African American narrative seeks to expose the

ideological agenda behind scripts, thus clearing a field for the
self to evolve. Du Bois distrusts even his own exposures, his own
narrative that seeks to expose historical script: "Probably, looking back after the event," he writes, "I have rationalized my life
into a planned, coherent unity which was not as true to fact as it
now seems; probably there were hesitancies, gropings, and half-
essayed bypaths, now forgotten or unconsciously ignored" (191).

Contemporary theory would suggest at least two different
methods for reading African American narratives. Structuralism
asserts, as in the instance of a fine lecture by Jean Ricardou, the
way that the stature of the novel *Madam Bovary* derives from the
way that the image of the hunter transforms himself into that of
the doctor.[12] Hence the privileged elite displaces the workman
through a presumably redemptive act of literary imagination.
But while the experience of this structural reading is admirably
political, its politics are evident only to a community of privileged readers who share the encoded values. Indeed, some question whether *Madam Bovary* is political at all, commending the
novel instead as an apolitical whole. In the midst of this exchange, many African Americans would ask,

> What's a song if it does not inspire?
> If it has no message to bring?
> If a song does not lift you higher?
> It's not good enough to sing.

These lines, from the lyric "I Heard That" (1975) by Quincy
Jones, frame the historical narrative of Black music in the African
Diaspora.[13] Though the song suggests a narrative theory, it does
not comment directly on aesthetic. But it clearly implies a material existence that transcends the words on the page, words that
to many stucturalist and poststructuralist scholars constitute the
sole concern. Whatever the claims of formalism and structuralism, great art—and by induction great narrative—creates a lyric
wherein teller speaks to hearer. The bond may be rhetorical, but
the artistic moment proves intensely real, indeed irreducible.
Thus while the structuralist reduces broadly human stories to
textual space—just as a few Black aestheticians of the early six-
ties and seventies sought to reduce African American art to
political acts[14]—the autobiographer seeks the motivation behind
his narrative history. I am suggesting a need for an aesthetic of

the self in African American autobiography that accounts for both the self's placement in space *and* time and its participation in a communal and political consciousness, encrypted in autobiography, that transcends time.

In the first of two reflections in *Soliloquy* Du Bois suggests that narrative theories must be revised in the future for scientific accuracy (205–206). From 1894 to 1910, he had been primarily a teacher of social science, working two years at Wilberforce University in Ohio, and then at the University of Pennsylvania for more than a year. During this time he had emphasized scientific methods. At Fisk University in Nashville he had already learned something about natural science and later, at Harvard, had taken up chemistry and geology. Slowly his theory of technology became his theory of art. "I began to conceive of the world as a continuing growth rather than a finished product," he wrote. Having his earlier religious training rejected during his study in Germany, he emphasized the biological law of his growth.

Thus while his tale in *Soliloquy* takes root in the past, the vision within his story points to the future. In 1895, Wilhelm Roentgen (1845–1923), a German physicist, had invented the X-Ray. Three years later the French chemist Pierre Curie (1859–1906) and his wife, Marie Marja (Manya Skiodowskie) Curie (1867–1934) would discover radium. By the turn of the century Guglielmo Marconi, a relatively unknown Italian of twenty-two, would help develop radio. In 1903 the first powered airplane flight would occur. Raised "in the shadow of modern science," he proposed a logical explanation for all things. He had joked with others about the human failures at flight; but he flew unhesitatingly from Paris to London. In 1921, somewhat astonished to see automobiles on the streets there in 1900, he lived to see "automobiles fill the streets and cover the nations." He was genuinely surprised to see an American city lit by electricity, and when people crossed the Atlantic Ocean in gas-filled Zeppelins, his customary arrogance gave way to awe. The constant rewriting of historical consciousness—the learned awareness by which we continue to reassess scripts—was a gift of Du Bois's recreative imagination. It is a human power vindicated by science.

Yet, science was simply a superficial form of a deeper myth contained within that power. To Du Bois, Christian ritual prepared the way for systematic spectacle. Nearly two hundred pages after the reflection, Du Bois begins to close (he never really closes—only defers) his text with the spiritual authority of St. Paul: "I have lived a good and full life. I have finished my course" (413).[15] Indeed, his declaration of "delights" and "pleasures" echoes the great poetry of the Psalms. When he names those "souls" who will "follow" him, he assumes the role of a Messiah. To a great grandson "born Christmas day before last," he leaves the rites of death and rebirth. If the seasons pass, he bequeaths to others his creative powers. And though he wishes to narrate his world empirically, and thus claims that the miracles in his life are not those of Christianity, he always invokes what he believes to be the code of Christian morality. Though historical time binds his narrative, his story becomes part of a myth, both scientific and Christian, that lifts a script beyond time.

The performance theory in the work of Langston Hughes performs a similar function. In *The Big Sea* (1940), Hughes recounts his 1923 trip to New York in order to attend a performance of Ibsen's *Lady from the Sea* by the famous Italian actress, Elenora Duse (1859–1924). He had frequently heard about "the hands of Duse, the eyes of Duse," a woman whose very presence alone was said to stir the human spirit. He had read of Duse in Gabrielle D'Annunzio's *The Flame of Life* (1906), a virginal Juliet on the "dusty roads of Italy" (130–31). A serious illness in 1909 had dulled Duse's powers, however, and as she entered the stage to huge applause, Hughes saw that her magical presence had dwindled to a mere voice. What was missing in Duse, the living performance, became integral to the work of Hughes, who broadened the distinction between formal narrative and performance in order to resurrect the truths of racial equality.

His exchange with a reknown Lincoln University alumnus is exemplary. As a Lincoln student, Hughes had completed a campus sociology project which showed that 63% of the nearly all-black student body preferred an all-white faculty. When the young Hughes encountered the alumnus walking on the campus and had related his findings, the information had offended the older man: "He walked away," Hughes writes. "I looked at him crossing the campus, famous, well-to-do, the kind of man the graduation speakers told us to look up to" (309–310).

While the elderly professor speaks with the racial subservience of Booker T. Washington—"Young man, suppose I told the truth to white folks"—Hughes reads the language of the great abolitionists. Within this telling of history the speaker writes himself down as a Hunger Artist whose purpose is to restore heroic ideals to history. For a second, the disagreement between elder and youth suspends the narrative. The teller recognizes intuitively that a story is marked by a profound moment of displacement: "I began to think back to Nat Turner, Harriet Tubman, Sojourner Truth, John Brown, Fred Douglass—folks who left no buildings behind them—only a wind of words fanning the bright flame of the spirit down the dark lanes of time." The moment is one in which all assigned scripts are disrupted. Into the space vacated by prescribed ideology the storyteller writes his freed text. The professor's "walk" suggests an internal journey that the storyteller must inscribe. The narrator ("crossing") must finish a rite of purgation.

Hughes had displaced a narrative theory of architecture with one of the human spirit, methodically inverting one of the most splendid traditions in English poetry. From the captivating house poems of Ben Jonson, through the detailed conceits of George Herbert's temples, images of edifices extend at least to the house poems by William Butler Yeats. Hughes' narrator deliberately imbues the old man with this architectural poetic tradition, connecting him with the myopic desire to erect the beautiful culture on a cornerstone of injustice: "The old grad has his buildings, just as Booker T. Washington had Tuskegee." While the elder has taken to heart the traditional script, he lacks the genius to pass it on. In the teller's brief hesitation comes a painful silence. And into the puzzled moment of pause, of epiphany, the reader will rewrite the autobiographical text.

In *I Wonder as I Wander: An Autobiographical Journey* (1956), both the performer and the teller share the epiphany. Nowhere else in Hughes' narrative world do the roles of decoder and performer blend more clearly into a triumphant whole. During the Spanish Civil War in 1937 the famous flamenco singer *La*

Langston Hughes. *Later That Day* (1949). Photo by Griffith J. Davis.

Niña de los Peines, Pastora Pavón, was a brilliant entertainer. As her bluesy art resisted both war and death, she, like the story-teller, was an artist who signified human courage. When Hughes heard that she had refused to leave Madrid, he prepared himself to enter the besieged city. There he saw her at eleven o'clock one morning when she appeared on a bare stage among guitarists who clapped their hands and tapped their heels. Sitting straight in a chair, this old woman began slowly to dominate the perfor-mance with her half-spoken and half-sung solea. As the guitars played behind her, the poet listened only to that wild, harsh, lonely, and bittersweet voice. Hughes, who would hear La Niña sing many times, compared her flamenco to Black southern blues because, despite the heartbreak implied, it signified the triumph of a people.

African American autobiography lifts literature into the complementary languages of narrative and theater. Frederick Douglass and Linda Brent suggest that African American narra-tive calls for a redefined performance of civilization; Du Bois in-sists on the imperative of the enlightened storyteller to rewrite the text for the times; Langston Hughes hints that the true per-formers of it have yet to sing. While Brent implies that a stan-dard for reading the American future must be moral, Du Bois says that the measure of narrative must ultimately be scientific. Hughes profits from all of them, from the moral vision of Brent and the technological sweep of Du Bois. He privileges the mythic and spiritual power of the text—the imaginative impetus through which it is "built"—over even its material form.[16] All of the autobiographers, in the last analysis, redeem mere scripts from history; each champions art over immutable law.

NOTES

1. This article is an expanded version of a paper delivered at the International Conference on Narrative Theory in Nice, France, June 15, 1991.

2. W.E.B. Du Bois, *A Soliloquy* (New York: 1968), 295. Hereafter, Du Bois.

3. In Du Bois, 288.

4. Although most authors combine scriptor with artist and narrator, scriptors are often neoclassical in formal preference as well as in academic privilege, while outstanding writers tend toward the romantic rebelliousness.

5. Waldo E. Martin, *The Mind of Frederick Douglass* (Chapel Hill: 1984), 271–3. Hereafter, Martin.

6. For the most part, Douglass writes from outside of the traditional mythology and ideology to readers still enslaved within it. His authentic voice as outsider ensures that others can retrace the mental steps in a personal cognition of freedom. Ironically, Douglass' own completion of the venture remained hindered by his need for acceptance by whites. His frantic search through the Philadelphia streets for Mrs. Sears, the daughter of his former master, is exemplary. Cf. *Life and Times*.

7. Cf. R. Stepto, Jr. *From Behind the Veil: A Study of Afro-American Narrative* (Urbana: 1979); T. Ziolkowski, "Antithesis: The Dialectic of Violence and Literacy in Frederick Douglass' Narrative of 1845," in *Critical Essays on Frederick Douglass*, W.L. Andrews, ed. (Boston: 1990), 148–165. Hereafter, Stepto and Ziolkowski.

8. Deborah E. McDowell, "In the First Place: Making Frederick Douglass and the Afro-American Narrative Tradition," in *Critical Essays on Frederick Douglass*, W.L. Andrews, ed. 192–213; 206. Hereafter, McDowell.

9. Cf. Eric Sundquist, "Frederick Douglass' Literacy and Paternalism," in *Critical Essays on Frederick Douglass*, 120–132: 121; Ziolkowski, 150–151.

10. Houston A. Baker, Jr., *The Journey Back: Issues in Black Literature* (Chicago: 1980), 338–9.

11. Her consciousness separates her from the silent tellers of many modern plays, and points toward works such as Amari Baraka's *The Slave*, which uses a Black Tiresias figure to frame the dramatic action.

12. Lecture, International Conference on Narrative Theory, Nice, France, June 13, 1991.

13. The song, was commissioned for a historical narrative of African American music at the African American Museum of History in Wilberforce, Ohio.

14. Maulana Karenga, for example, had asserted during the Black Arts Movement in the United States that black art had to be functional, committed, and relevant. Cf. Karenga, "Black Cultural Nationalism," in *The Black*, Addison Gayle, Jr. ed. (New York: 1971), 31–37.

15. Cf. Timothy 2: 4:7: "I have fought a good fight, I have finished *my* course, I have kept the faith."

16. Consider how Melville's narrator privileges Billy Budd over his own tale: "But the form of Billy Budd was heroic." Cf. Herman Melville, *Billy Budd and Other Stories* (New York: 1924; 1961), 39.

PART THREE

Self and History

The Weak Self

Suffocation and Vocation: History, Anti-History, and the Self

David D. Roberts

Selfhood and the Historical World

The sovereign ego or transcendent self has apparently suc-cumbed, a victim of the wider assault on our metaphysical tradi-tion. While it is not clear what possibilities open once that strong, "modern" notion of selfhood falls away, there may remain scope for a weaker self, a weaker inner space. What might go on there, however, and how that inner space might relate to the world, is uncertain.

Recognition of the self's historicity has helped undermine its sovereignty; the transcendent and enduring subject dissolves into impersonal systems that are historically specific. Thus, for example, Michel Foucault posits the dissolution of "man," sub-jectivity, and the self into history, so that "what we are" is a his-torical construct, the result of a particular intersection of contin-gent systems of power-knowledge. As Ian Hacking puts it: "It is a Foucaultian thesis that every way in which I can think of my-self as a person and an agent is something that has been consti-tuted within a web of historical events. Here is one more step in the destruction of Kant: the noumenal self is nothing."[1]

Any attempt to reconceive the self must consequently probe the relationship between selfhood and the world as histor-ical. The experience of selfhood entails a sense of relationship with the world's historical progression, a sense of one's place in its totality, understood as a sequence of past, present and future. This relationship contains an inherent tension, however, between the self's being fully autonomous and fully at one with the changing, historical world.[2]

To stress the finitude and historical specificity of the self overcomes an ambiguity in the "modern" tradition, making it clearer that selfhood is not to be conflated with subjectivity or mind in general, or with some universal human attribute like reason or language.[3] Rather, selfhood entails individuation and finitude. A measure of the historicity of the world is that all individuals are caught up in the provisional, unstable totality differently. And to reconceive selfhood requires a deeper consideration of the forms of interaction among finite, historically specific individuals.

The "history" encompassing the self is not Hegel's history with its teleological framework. Hegel's history (according to some readings) was simply the metaphysically grounded process through which genuine selfhood was achieved. The strong self is undermined by "post-Hegelian" history—still real and deep enough to engulf the self, yet thin, contingent, forever provisional and incomplete. And just as Hegel's history is not the issue, reaction against post-Hegelian history in the quest for selfhood does not simply recapitulate Kierkegaard's reaction against the Hegelian way of embedding the individual in history.

Although Kierkegaard explored the subjectivity that stands in tension with the historical world, his response was against Hegel's theological way of positing history—with God at the other pole. The confrontation between Hegel and Kierkegaard remains instructive,[4] but by the later nineteenth century the most innovative thinkers were trying to see beyond that framework. The challenge was to explore the human experience, the scope for individuality or selfhood in the absence of a transcendent framework for history.

Recent discussion of the self is a chapter in an ongoing exploration that began gathering force around the turn of the century. The discussion so far has led to a premium on the antihistorical self according to which human being becomes possible insofar as the mechanisms of the world as historical are resisted or disrupted. Yet other impulses have suggested a more constructive way of conceiving the tension between self and historical world. From this perspective, the self becomes weak, provisional, historically specific, yet still coherent enough for ongoing self-creation and world-creation through action. And though we can no longer refer to some stable essence as we seek to understand who we are, we can trace the historical events that have created us—deconstruct our present mode of self-understanding and thereby refashion some aspect of ourselves. Such a project would not free us from our history, but it would enable us to make more of it.

Tendencies in both the historical and the anti-historical direction have been at work in recent discussions of the self, but the elements have proven difficult to sort out. My aim is to survey the terrain, looking briefly at the first wave of preoccupations, then at the way several recent thinkers have conceived and responded to the tension between individuality and the world as historical.

The Personal and the Historical: Early Explorations

In early modernist literature, but also in such innovative thinkers as Nietzsche, Croce, and Heidegger, a new axis of possibilities seemed to follow from the overwhelming presence of history. To show, in a post-Hegelian mode, that things are merely historical was to disembed them from any metaphysical framework, any grounding or necessity. I may feel newly limited, determined by a past that has no good reason for having been as it was, and endlessly trapped, because whatever I do will apparently grow from and add to that particular history. But this feeling of suffocation may give way to its opposite, to a sense of uncanny weightlessness, from the capricious quality of the way things happen and history results. Citing the early modernist poetry of Hugo von Hofmannsthal, Georg Lukács worried about the cultural dissolution that seemed to threaten when the individual is left without confidence in the coherence and meaningfulness of the outside historical world:

The individual, retreating into himself in despair at the cruelty of the age, may experience an intoxicated fascination with his forlorn condition. But then a new horror breaks through. If reality cannot be understood (or no effort is made to understand it), then the individual's subjectivity—alone in the universe, reflecting only itself—takes on an equally incomprehensible and horrific character. Hugo von Hofmannsthal was to experience this condition very early in his poetic career:

> It is a thing that no man dares think on,
> And far too terrible for mere complaint,
> That all things slip from us and pass away,
> And that my ego, bound by no outward force—
> Once a small child's before it became mine—
> Should now be strange to me, like a strange dog.

By separating time from the outer world of objective reality, the inner world of the subject is transformed into a sinister, inexplicable flux and acquires—paradoxically, as it may seem—a static character.[5]

Hoffmansthal's self seemed not to hold without a more secure tie to the historical totality. For Lukács, however, his lament stemmed from an overreaction; the historical world remained sufficient, because the Marxist variation on the Hegelian framework specified a certain mode of coherence for the world—*even* the world as history. For Hofmannsthal, however, the possibility of any such framework was part of what had fallen away.

Hofmannsthal's concerns manifest the preoccupation with change, time, and history in relation to individual experience that occasioned a number of the defining themes of early modernist literature—from the overwhelming presence of the past to the fact of temporal finitude and death.[6] As a first response, the new literature often simply invited the individual to turn inward, attending to subjective experience, taken as more real than the public, historical world, which seemed burdensome, incomprehensible, or meaningless. Michel, André Gide's "immoralist," begins as a conventional historian, but he comes to understand history as layer upon layer of mere convention that covers over the authentic self that he feels smoldering within him, beneath the cultural overlay. Only by peeling away those layers can he hope to achieve authenticity. At first that effort encompasses redoing the inherited historical account, which buttresses a certain conventional mode of being, but which stems from merely contingent needs and desires. By forging a different history, connecting with hidden aspects of the past, he could connect with hidden aspects of himself. But Michel ultimately decides that authenticity, creativity, and novelty transcend *any* concern with the past.[7]

As the presence of the past came to weigh as never before, it became possible to envision a kind of uncommitment or disengagement from the actual, the historically-derived conventions that have established what we take as real, rational, normal. Ulrich, Robert Musil's "man without qualities," manages what J.M. Coetzee has called "a certain reserve toward the real world, a living sense of alternative possibilities." Ulrich himself says he is prepared to exist in "a web of haze, imaginings, fantasy and the subjunctive mode," to live a "hovering life" without commitment. Irony seemed the natural mode for such a "man without qualities."[8]

For T.S. Eliot it would not do to disengage and turn inward or to settle for mere self-assertion in the face of a past experienced as either meaningless or suffocating. Rather, the imperative was to confront the world as historical head on, creatively absorbing the whole past, making it one's own.[9] Although it "requires a ridiculous amount of erudition," as Eliot put it, to encompass the entire past as present, he yearned for precisely that wholeness, for "the only real truth is the whole truth."[10] In *The Waste Land* he added reference upon reference, juxtaposing points of view, letting one character melt into another, in order to build the most comprehensive whole he could. For Eliot, however, the satisfaction of such ordering played against the ongoing terror of meaninglessness, from our lurking sense that the world as historical has *only* this merely contingent human ordering. In "The Dry Salvages" he referred to

> The Backward look behind the assurance
> Of recorded history, the backward half-look
> Over the shoulder, towards the primitive terror.[11]

We crave some form of ordering, but we grasp that "recorded history" is only a flimsy human contrivance, a merely historical way of connecting ourselves to the whole. It keeps us only intermittently from the primitive, terrifying experience of the world as fundamentally meaningless. Thus we cannot suppress "the backward half-look."

In light of this painful sense of isolation, it was tempting to try to see through the capricious individualities of history to something deeper, truer—the source of things or the totality of things. A particular artistic approach to the world as historical might open the way to mystical or visionary experience, reconnecting with myth or original revelation. James Longenbach notes that in Eliot's *The Waste Land*, "a primitive revelation of 'the whole truth' (the thunderous 'DA') is disseminated, by the process of tradition, throughout history."[12]

This temptation suggests the ambiguity in these early modernists, who sometimes clung to visions of suprahistorical wholeness, and who never managed to delineate an authentic self in relation to the world as historical. Gide's Michel ends up tormented by his "useless freedom"; Musil's novel remained essentially unfinished and, it has been suggested, unfinishable. Eliot's romantic quest for wholeness, based on the grasp of the visionary artist, jostled with his critical sense, which reflected his grasp of the historicity and finitude of the knower, including himself.[13] But these early modernist explorations indicate the centrality of the new set of preoccupations.

At roughly the same time, Nietzsche, Croce, and Heidegger explored the same set of issues from a different angle, focusing first on the public, historical level. All three took it for granted that what we think of as "individual subjectivity" is always historically specific; my consciousness, subjectivity, or selfhood emerges only in light of the larger historical happening to which I belong.[14] And though their accents differed, each linked this insight to the centrality of language, understood as intersubjective, and as bound up with the ongoing growth of the world in history.[15] At issue for each was individual experience in relationship to the happening of a particular, endlessly provisional world. Public and private, historical consciousness and personal time consciousness, could not be neatly distinguished. The effort to specify the possibilities for inner experience led each of them to fasten upon various quasi-religious categories—responsibility, anxiety, guilt, judgment, grace, redemption, immortality, innocence, the holy. But though Nietzsche and Croce proceeded to-gether for a few more steps, the effort to rethink individuality and selfhood ultimately led the three thinkers in sharply differ-ent directions.

Nietzsche and Croce each posited an affirmative way of experiencing our involvement with the coming to be of our par-ticular world in history. We feel the necessity of all there has been for there to be this moment, which we cannot coherently deny, for to do so would mean denying ourselves and thus the very possibility of such negation. Croce insisted that even our negative judgments presuppose the resultant of history so far—even as they help to change it.[16] Nietzsche deplored the claim "to judge history, to divest it of its fatality, to discover responsibility behind it, guilty men in it."[17] This was the tendency of dissatis-fied individuals who, as the culture came to experience itself as radically historical, could do no better than to blame history it-self for the fact that their historically specific lives had not turned out well.

But Nietzsche and Croce were subject to different preoc-cupations, which ultimately led them in sharply different direc-tions. In his meditation "On the Uses and Disadvantages of History for Life," Nietzsche notes that we moderns are caught up in "the tireless unspinning and historicizing of all there has ever been."[18] History dissolves everything that possesses life, for to understand anything historically is to grasp its real gratuitous-ness, its lack of necessity. Still, our actual world, all there is, has resulted from the particular concatenation of things that has happened so far. Thus the appalling weight of "it was"—the awareness that my whole world, and I myself, have grown out of a particular freakish past.[19] But Nietzsche was also preoccupied with the shadow of the sin, guilt, and judgment he associated with Christianity. The imperative was to restore "the innocence of becoming" in opposition to the notion, traceable to Chris-tianity, that human beings are somehow *responsible* for what becomes.[20]

Through his central categories, *amor fati* and eternal recur-rence, Nietzsche sought to posit a mode of life fully embracing the finitude of the merely historical world, but entailing neither a suffocating experience of confinement nor an anxious feeling of

responsibility. *Amor fati* is the absolute affirmation of this particular world, while eternal recurrence denies novelty and creativity. In this mode we experience reality as a particular circle or
closed system, with nothing but its own excrement to feed on.[21]
There is completeness without telos, history goes limp, and the
individual is freed from history-making to experience each moment as an end in itself. By dissolving the weight of history,
Nietzsche frees the individual to fashion a self—not a centered,
stable, finished thing, but an ongoing living process of playful,
innocent self-creation.[22]

Whereas Nietzsche envisioned experiencing the world as
complete at every moment, the world for Croce was unfinished
at every moment, and we feel that incompleteness as a call to
further action. In Croce's universe, affirmation is simply the
foundation for present action to help shape the next moment as
our history continues. I feel sufficiently at one with the world to
care for it, to feel responsible for it. Thus it is not enough that
what I do be authentic, or self-creating. I want it to last, affecting
what the world becomes. Croce could have said, with Nietzsche,
that "my consolation is that everything that has been is eternal."[23] But the sense for Croce was profoundly different. Though
the world is ever provisional, what I do lives on after me, helping to make reality a particular way at all subsequent moments,
forever. Thus Croce's emphasis on "the immortality of the act,"
the cumulative weight of our actions in the endless coming to be
of the world.[24]

For Croce, then, I experience my connection with the present as "history," as opposed to Nietzschean eternal recurrence,
which concentrates even the future in such a way that any sense
of history-making dissolves. Nietzsche could imagine action as
innocent play because, in the mode of eternal recurrence, action
would not stem from the Crocean experience of the world as
incomplete, and from the consequent sense of responsibility for
what the world becomes next. There is nothing else that needs to
be done because the world at every moment is "perfect"—
complete.

In Croce's world, desire for the immortality that only history can offer helps structure our lives, giving a measure of coherence to selfhood. Because I seek to affect what the world be-

comes, I fear the sense of futility that afflicts us when our actions fail to connect. So I seek a vocation that enables me to focus my efforts and thereby to maximize the effectiveness of my response. Croce's effort to specify how we live in a purely historical world also led him to reformulate certain Christian categories—not only immortality, but also providence, grace, faith, prayer, and even God.[25] We may find ourselves "praying," for example, for the grace necessary to act effectively and thereby mesh with history.

But of course we individuals do not act on our own. Every individual action, if it becomes real at all, interacts with others, so each individual is a collaborator as the world endlessly grows through history.[26] In Croce's world, the sense that we are finite individuals caught up in the history-making process of interaction engenders a broadly liberal humility, tolerance, and pluralism.[27] None of us can foresee the outcome of what we do, which always transcends the intention of any one actor. In our darker moments, our efforts seem futile. But we keep at it thanks to "faith in history," faith that what we do will interact with the contributions of others to respond, in ways none of us can foresee, to the limitations of this moment and produce a richer next moment. In entrusting what we do to history, we hope that those who come after will use our legacies well, just as we feel under obligation to use well what the past has bequeathed to us. For we experience a sense of collaboration and kinship not only with our contemporaries, but with all those who came before us, those whose responses have resulted in the world entrusted to us.[28]

The Crocean individual, then, combines a sense of slippage and risk with a faith that, as we entrust our acts to the future, we have not labored in vain. Concluding his *Philosophy of the Practical* in 1909, Croce noted that because there can be no definitive philosophy in a merely historical world, the philosopher labors knowing that his work will promptly be superseded. But faith in history overcomes the resulting feeling of futility; if he has done his job well, his work will prove an instrument for those who come after, who will respond to it and build upon it. His work will live on, even as he, the individual author, is forgotten.[29] Croce, then, explicitly called his own authority into question, but his thinking, as he understood it, did not thereby self-destruct, or conceive itself as play. He offered his work as an invitation to labor further, a contribution to the ongoing construction. That is all any of us can do—but it makes possible a mode of selfhood congruent with the happening of the particular world in history.

Heidegger, much like Nietzsche and Croce, sought first to explain the sense in which individual experience rests on a relationship to the world as historical, then to specify how we might relate to our own history. In *Being and Time*, he sought to outline the structure of human being, starting for the first time with the fact that individual existence is inherently finite, particular, historically specific. The resulting insights into thrownness and anxiety, and the imperative of authenticity that seemed to follow, helped produce the vogue of existentialism in its later Sartrean formulation. And certain of Heidegger's insights, especially his notion of "care," help us see what a weak, merely historical self might entail.

But Heidegger himself turned from this existentialist direction to focus the fact that being itself is fundamentally historical—and to ask what that means for us, now.[30] This move stemmed partly from his abiding, deeply personal experience of his own time as the debased, inadequate outcome of our particular history. A generally "historicist" and "technological" orientation seemed to be cementing itself in the West, as the nihilistic outcome of the Western metaphysical tradition.[31] Technology was the triumph of subjectivity; human beings make the world, the world is open for human making in history, because there is nothing else. The combination of historicism and technology reflected the loss of any genuinely religious dimension to our experience—and seemed to preclude even the possibility of a new form of religiosity.

Seeking a new way of relating to the history to which we belong, Heidegger set out to explore the history of being—*our* history, the "giving" or "sending" of being that has resulted in our particular world and mode of experience. To say that being is historical means that it is "epochal," that it holds back precisely as it gives itself historically, as some particular history. There is ongoing concealment, forgetting, and loss as any particular world comes to be in history. Worlds come to be in language, but language is itself particular and precluding. We ourselves, with our particular preoccupations and possibilities, are part of a particular sending of being, which has entailed forgetting and loss as its other side.

It might seem, then, that we could deconstruct some mistaken turn and recover something lost at some point in our tradition, with the early Greeks. Heidegger concluded, however, that there is no escaping our particular destiny, the way of being that our particular history has allotted to us. So he sought a different, more passive way of relating to the world as historical. Yet even this response could not be *merely* passive, a matter of withdrawal. Rather, it required a restless, ongoing encounter with the world, first by attending to "the unthought," what did not become actual. Through passive yet restless "thinking," we work back through the course of the actual not to prepare new action upon it, but to *unthink* what actually came to be, to restore openness, not so that we might undo anything in particular, but so that we might simply listen, attuning ourselves to the actualizing itself—to the giving of being as some finite, particular history.[32]

In positing this way of relating to the whole, Heidegger stood in opposition to *both* Nietzsche and Croce, with their contrasting ways of affirming the merely historical world. From a Heideggerian perspective, Nietzsche and Croce offered two modes of complicity. Each was merely settling for the present world, with its tendency to collapse all of being into the actual historical course of things. What Heidegger sought, then, was a post-subjectivist mode of selfhood, wound around neither action as self-creating nor action as history-making, but rather utter and permanent tension with the actual world coming to be in history. In a world that had been reduced to a particular history, the Heideggerian mode of restless disengagement might make possible a new, post-historicist religiosity, or experience of the holy, involving no return to transcendence. Starting from a fundamental alienation from *this* world, to which we have been confined by our particular history, Heidegger posited a new way of relating to the finitude of a merely historical world, a way that was as extreme as Nietzsche's, but at the opposite extreme, since Nietzsche envisioned the full affirmation of this world precisely in its particularity.

Continuing Preoccupation and Response

Recent thinking about the self has operated within the universe of preoccupations that first opened up in the pivotal decades from Nietzsche to Heidegger. Such prominent recent thinkers as Gadamer, Foucault, Derrida, and Rorty have confronted some of the same issues, though they have responded in their own ways, thereby thickening the web of possibilities. Still, the interplay among the responses so far has given the discussion an anti-historical tilt. Selfhood must apparently be conceived in opposition to the world as historical, which seems suffocating, even bound up with authority and domination.

In developing his philosophical hermeneutics, Hans-Georg Gadamer accented the scope for novelty within a particular tradition to counter the sense of confinement that Nietzsche expressed in *On the Uses and Disadvantages of History for Life*.[33] For Gadamer, as for Croce, it is crucial that though we are delimited or channeled by what we have been, we are not fixed. Our horizons move with us; ongoing questioning of our tradition produces an ongoing expansion of horizons, even including the growth of our language.[34] For Gadamer, then, belonging to a particular tradition need not entail an experience of limitation for the individual; rather, the fact that we are fundamentally historical creatures is an invitation to the ongoing growth that starts from a creative encounter with that tradition.

Yet Gadamer, like Croce, accented the sense in which we can only accept the truth of the tradition, inasmuch as we can only start with what has resulted so far, including our ways of understanding what has resulted so far. Even our determination to question and perhaps change our present grows from within the tradition. At the same time, Gadamer emphasized that, as horizons move, we are involved in a process of coming to agreement, of reaching a consensus. Indeed, language is itself the process of coming to agreement, of building up a common world.[35] Ragged though the tradition always is, provisional though every agreement is, the ongoing fusing of horizons brings human responses—criticisms, disagreements, conversations—back to the tradition as that tradition itself grows.

In this double sense, Gadamer's overall accent was conservative, but that accent can easily be balanced by a radical or critical one from within his own framework. However, he himself was so concerned with "the rehabilitation of authority and tradition," partly to head off playful, irrationalist overreaction, that he seemed to preclude the critical moment necessary for openness.[36] This conservatism has reinforced the sense of historical finitude as suffocating that has informed recent considerations of the scope for a post-metaphysical sort of selfhood.

John Caputo, for example, offered a "radical hermeneutics" in response to what seemed an ongoing authoritarian tendency to freeze the present outcome and to "stop the play," the ongoing conversation or dialogue. And as far as Caputo was concerned, Gadamerian hermeneutics, with its emphasis on resolution and agreement, was part of the problem, not the solution.[37] The antidote was in Jacques Derrida's version of deconstruction, with its suspiciousness, its playful, endlessly disruptive capacity, its sense of "the fragility of our thought constructions and the contingency of our institutions." Following Derrida, Caputo warns against taking ourselves seriously, thereby putting an end to the play, the discussion, so that disagreement means "drawing blood." Indeed, he invites us to play "out of bounds" in order to resist the authoritarian tendency to draw blood that lurks even in an endlessly historical world.[38] So Caputo's premium was ultimately on disruption, at the expense of the moment of agreement, of coming back together, or any sense of history-making collaboration.

The generally deconstructive current, centering on Derrida and Michel Foucault, has been attractive to those, like Caputo, who find something suffocating in the experience of the world as historical—and in the Gadamerian way of confining us to it. Although Foucault and Derrida differed considerably, each was explicitly concerned with self and history, and their responses were comparably anti-historical.

In both its Foucault and Derrida variants, deconstruction seems first to specify a form of radical historical questioning that reveals some aspect of "what is" to be merely historical, constructed. Especially by attention to construction *in language*, this approach might serve an endless dialectic of self-creation and world-reconstruction. Selfhood requires the ongoing historical questioning that alone can afford the illumination necessary for us to wriggle free of the contingent coils enmeshing us. Thus Foucault's radical historical inquiries show up the contingency in our ways of understanding sanity and sexuality, for example. His mode of historical questioning, he tells us, does not start with some "given" way we talk about ourselves, because that self-understanding is precisely the problem—and the fundamental object of historical inquiry.[39] And the point of that inquiry can be reconstructive; thus, for example, "We have to promote new forms of subjectivity through the refusal of this kind of individuality which has been imposed on us for several centuries."[40]

Some of Derrida's advocates—Christopher Norris, for example—find in Derridean deconstruction the basis for a still more radical form of reconstructive historical questioning.[41] Yet in the thinking of both Foucault and Derrida, other preoccupations intruded, leading to a premium on ritualistic disruption or play and compromising this potentially re-constructive thrust.

Foucault featured the scope for disruption, which is to be ongoing and global, not a particular moment serving a constructive process of self-formation.[42] The continuity, identity, and coherence necessary for any selfhood whatsoever are somehow illegitimate; Foucault's deconstructive mode of historical inquiry was the antidote, disrupting "reality," "identity," and "truth." Its purpose, said Foucault, "is not to discover the roots of our identity but to commit itself to its dissipation." By displaying "all of those discontinuities that cross us," such inquiry punctures the masks and disguises, undermines the expected identity, and leaves us with intersecting and competing systems that cannot be brought together coherently.[43] More generally, Foucault aimed to disrupt our tendency to invent concepts and categories that shape the world by suppressing "the anarchy of differences." His premium was on liberating difference, in opposition to our tendency to impose some order, even, apparently, if only through the weak, provisional concepts and categories of a merely historical world.[44]

Accenting Foucault's premium on endless subversion, Paul Bové suggests that in Foucault's universe only "failure" can be counted as success, even when modes of opposition are at is-

sue.[45] Even success in building some dominant opposition current partakes of the domination-exclusion that is essential to any
world-making whatsoever.

All of Derrida's work reflected an acute sense of being
caught up in our particular history, which continues to happen,
encompassing whatever we do, no matter what we say, no matter how radically we deconstruct it. We may "seek to contest"
the actual, but we are "trapped," in the sense that whatever we
say or do grows from, belongs to, and returns to the unique,
particular, idiosyncratic history that surrounds us: "We have no
language—no syntax and no lexicon—which is foreign to this
history; we can pronounce not a single destructive proposition
which has not already had to slip into the form, the logic, and the
implicit postulations of precisely what it seeks to contest."[46] As
Derrida saw it, even Heidegger, for all his critique of the tradition, had ended up assuming a place in that tradition, offering
but another particular metaphysics. Derrida wanted to avoid doing the same thing, becoming merely the next phase of the continuous tradition.

Still, Derrida understood that whatever he did in response,
his actions would be beholden to the future. Indeed, he became
increasingly preoccupied by the bizarre, contingent character of
the process whereby whatever anyone writes is taken up by
those who follow—and thereby enters history. In "Otobiographies" (1984) he explored how any project, including his
own, can be exploited for different purposes in different contexts.[47] But Derrida was simply following an insight central to
his thinking from the start. The world as historical is always already in slippage, a notion that he initially dramatized by accenting the primacy of writing, which entails laying oneself open to
unauthorized readings in the future.[48]

How might we respond to a world that enmeshes us in
past and future in this way? Even in his early period, which has
seemed relatively systematic and "serious," Derrida was pleased
to find, opposing the sense of loss and even guilt that might
seem to befall us in this endlessly decentered world, Nietzsche's
"joyous affirmation of the play of the world and of the innocence
of becoming, the affirmation of a world of signs without fault,
without truth, and without origin which is offered to an active

interpretation."[49] But especially by the time he offered *The Post Card* (1980), any concern to offer a "position" of his own had given way. Here Derrida opposed the efficient but authoritarian "postal system," or manner of receiving messages from the tradition, with what Christopher Norris has called "a fabulous realm of messages and meanings that circulate beyond any assurance of authorized control."[50]

Derrida's work increasingly entailed playful "erasure" and evasiveness, rendering any exposition of his own texts problematic. In casting our offerings in playful ways, we undercut the subsequent redescription; we one-up history by doing what it will do—erase, though leaving traces—before it gets the chance. Looked at from another angle, we simply give in to the inevitability of history, which will do with us as it will, as we playfully, but perhaps poisonously, set ourselves up for subsequent deconstruction.[51]

To increasingly aggressive critics, deconstruction has seemed willfully extreme, irresponsible, nihilistic. At the least, it has seemed subject to curious preoccupations, though these, too, apparently respond to the world as historical. As Richard Rorty has put it, spreading his net to include Jean-François Lyotard: "It is as if thinkers like Foucault and Lyotard were so afraid of being caught up in one more metanarrative about the fortunes of 'the subject' that they cannot bring themselves to say 'we' long enough to identify with the culture of the generation to which they belong."[52]

Although it may entail an element of overreaction, deconstruction has not been simply perverse, yet even critics who have convincingly pinpointed certain excesses have had difficulty grasping its basis. John Ellis, for example, offers a good sense of what a constructive form of deconstruction would involve, bound up with an ongoing imperative to question received opinion, and he understands that something *other* than that imperative—something ultimately antithetical to it—is at work in the Derrida current. Ellis notes that whereas feminist questioning, for example, works within history, seeking to overcome a confining, historically specific situation, Derridean deconstruction seeks instead to put *the whole thing* into question, and continually to do so.[53] But Ellis cannot grasp the rationale for this global subversion impulse, for endlessly "putting in question" rather than seeking to overcome, to replace with a better idea, to progress to a "higher level of thought." He does not see why we might prefer to leave superseded ideas in "eternal purgatory," rather than laying them to rest for good, or why we might seek to return from the finite system of language to the "infinite" that was there before the language coalesced, or why we might want to subvert the central/marginal dichotomy and wander aimlessly without judging degrees of importance.[54] In each case, the sort of history-making reconstruction Ellis has in mind is precisely *not* the point, and the question is what deconstruction is doing instead—and why.

Richard Rorty is on the right track in suggesting that something ritualistic, even "religious" was at work, especially in the vogue of Derridean deconstruction among American literary intellectuals within the orbit of Paul de Man. And he notes a crippling ambiguity in Foucault's conception of "power," which functions both as a neutral descriptive term and as a pejorative term, conflated with "domination."[55] But why the overall premium on difference and endless subversion, on anti-historical disruption and play? What experience of the world would lead to the sense that only "failure" can be counted as success?

To the extent that a determination to oppose still-metaphysical pretense is at work, this spin is easy to understand. And both Foucault and Derrida tended to overrate the metaphysical threat because they loaded unnecessary Hegelian baggage onto history, making subversion or play seem the only alternative to metaphysically-grounded authority.[56] But in the final analysis even weak, post-metaphysical history, with no specifically Hegelian admixture, was sufficient to call forth their anti-historical emphases on ritualistic disruption and play. The anti-historical elements that perplex critics like Ellis and Rorty must be understood in terms of the preoccupations stemming from the new experience of the world as historical that we found in Nietzsche and Heidegger.

Foucault's implicit premium on failure responds to a fundamental alienation from the mechanisms—the power, the winning, precluding, dominating, the marginalizing of difference— through which the world endlessly comes to be some particular way. Even the dominant modes of opposition, the dominant ways of conceiving alternatives, partake of the same mechanisms as they succeed, become actual. Foucault's endless disruption affords a kind of ritualistic disengagement from those mechanisms. And because even the self is constructed historically, and thus bound up with particularizing, with domination–exclusion, *any* myself is suspect, so the self, too, must constantly be disrupted, shown up as only mask, theater. The process through which any identity is formed is contaminated precisely because it is historical—because of the mechanisms that the world as historical necessarily entails.

Although he owed a major debt to Nietzsche, Foucault's radicalism was ultimately not Nietzschean, because Nietzschean self-creation was bound up with affirmation of the particular world and even the mechanisms making reality finite and historical. For Nietzsche power was the neutral glue of world-resulting and not "domination," pejoratively connoting an inherent illegitimacy. Insofar as, for Nietzsche, the exercise of power *does* involve "domination," it can be exercised with a good conscience. Somebody wins—some particular world comes to be as some particular configuration of power. The winning, the coming to be in history, is the only measure of power. For Nietzsche, to be sure, critical discrimination remained possible, and a particular power configuration *may* be subject to condemnation as life-debasing; it will not be so, however, simply because, as an instance of power, it entails the concealment and exclusion essential to the coming to be of any world at all.

In a sense Foucault's response was more Heideggerian than Nietzschean because it reflects a quasi-religious orientation to history—to the mechanisms through which some world comes to be. But Foucault's alienation and resentment were deeper than Heidegger's, and thus he saw no point in standing back to seek an opening for religious experience by attuning to the giving itself. Although the religious dimension Heidegger afforded was spare and limited, his orientation was more hopeful because to resist closing up in the actual and to attune to the giving was, first, to experience in a positive way the fact that there is anything at all and, second, to hold open for a different dispensation. Foucault's version of restless, ongoing disruption might seem at first a neo-existentialist, self-justifying, even "human-istic" gesture of resistance to the mechanisms enmeshing us. But his resentment was so extreme that he could envision no scope for a new sense of selfhood in mere Camusian scorn, in lucidly living my life in a certain way.

Although Derrida's anti-historical response was not the same as Foucault's, it stemmed from a comparable resentment, and it was comparably non-Nietzschean. What "there is"—including what we offer now—is only a play of traces that will promptly be displaced, erased, leaving further traces, all in an utterly contingent way. In the absence of settled meaning, Der-rida experienced history as perpetually undercutting us, making of what we say and do whatever it will, beyond our control. Sub-sequent treatment of his own thinking would inevitably delimit, desiccate, and impoverish it by treating it in some particular, contingent way, precisely as we are doing now. This is true whatever we make of him, because making anything of him par-ticipates in the process of actualizing and occasions the suffocat-ing sense of finitude. Yet a giddy sense of lightness promptly follows, affording what seems the only antidote. In a world of these mechanisms, nothing really matters; settled meaning is dead, so everything is permitted. Play becomes the proper way of living the tension between the self and the world as historical.

Although he liberates the text for indeterminate interpre-tive play, Derrida's playful virtuosity is distinctly non-Niet-zschean because the innocent affirmation Nietzsche envisioned was to be an antidote to precisely the preoccupations afflicting Derrida. Nietzsche's mature thinking was an effort to see beyond the experience of suffocation by the particularizing of history. The mode of eternal recurrence, enabling me to experience real-ity as a closed, finite system concentrated at each present mo-ment, dissolves the anxious preoccupation that what I do will be swallowed up by a history imposing its own meaning on what I have done. In affirming the whole as particular, the Nietzschean affirms not only the past and present but also the "future"—what history will make of what I do, the fact that particularizing will encompass this as well. There is nothing I can do about it—but I feel *no need* to do anything about it. Nietzsche, in other words, envisioned affirmation of precisely the thread of what is endlessly coming to be—growing on itself, feeding on its own excrement, producing its future out of its past. Ultimately, the Derridean preoccupation with one-upping history is very nearly the opposite of the kind of oneness with the particular history that Nietzsche valued as the highest form of affirmation.

Some of those troubled by the apparent excess in deconstruction have found an antidote in the down-to-earth neopragmatism of Richard Rorty, who criticized deconstruction effectively, and who seemed to offer a more constructive alternative. Although Rorty became prominent first in the assault on foundationalist philosophy, he has increasingly joined in the wider assault on the strong self and the premium on "self-expression" that followed from the assumption of a prior subjectivity or consciousness. Drawing on Nietzsche, Freud, and Harold Bloom, he insisted that even selfhood is a contingent historical outcome.[57] In some of his moods, he seemed to find, as a result, considerable scope for a weak, merely historical kind of selfhood, bound up with an experience of what we do as history-making that recalls Croce's historicist accents. We hope, Rorty tells us, that our modicum of creativity and novelty will be carried into the future, that our "metaphors" will become part of the future's stock of "truths." And we understand that there is nothing but a process of interaction and persuasion to determine which particular metaphor will most shape the future.[58] So we seek to influence. But for Rorty, as for Croce, the sense that each of us is but one finite component in a merely historical world led to a neo-liberal emphasis on pluralism, collaboration, and humility.

From this perspective, ongoing self-creation is bound up with a positive but critical relationship to the world as historical. Rorty suggested that because "what we are" is but the contingent outcome of past interaction, we can only refer to our particular history in our quest for self-understanding.[59] Again and again, he himself resorted to historical inquiry to dissolve what had seemed fixed, "given," into history.[60] Such deconstructive historical questioning seemed to serve ever-provisional self-making, taking the place of "modern" self-expression. Rorty, then, seemed to open the way for a weak self, embedded, purposive, cognizant of its own historicity and contingency, yet experiencing its involvement with its own time as an opportunity, not as a limitation. But he proved subject to some of the same preoccupations as Foucault and Derrida, so the post-modern self he posited was in important respects an anti-historical self.

In Rorty's universe, once-molten metaphors and ironies continually "objectify" or congeal, and human beings, in their metaphysical necrophilia, tend to worship the corpses.[61] We take the metaphors coming down to us from the past as truths; we take the contingent reality that has come to be in our particular language as metaphysically grounded and thus suprahistorical. If we never overcome the metaphysical temptation altogether, we need to keep undermining that still-metaphysical tendency— and this seems part of the task Rorty has in mind. But even if we were to experience our particular metaphors as nothing but provisional historical resultants, the wider public world seems troublingly confining in one sense, troublingly weightless in another.

Rorty shared something of Nietzsche's suffocating experience of being always already caught up in a particular history, confined to a present that is nothing but the haphazard resultant of an unchosen past. And wherever we go from here can only be some outcome of that particular present. The anxiety led Rorty to a preoccupation with autonomy and a resulting premium on generating new metaphors. In Rorty's universe, the anxiety of influence that Harold Bloom explored with respect to poetry becomes general, because *everything* is wound around past metaphors that threaten our autonomy. And Bloom's corresponding emphasis on "strong misreadings" influenced Rorty's sense of our current priorities.[62] The premium was on actively strong *mis*readings because the alternative, merely to "read," was to be confined to the particular line of the actual, with the present encompassing the embryo of any future. More specifically, to seek "truth" as opposed to a disrupting irony was to remain subservient to metaphors now congealed and dead. Autonomy thus requires irony, discontinuity, even quirkiness, to wriggle free from the historically-resulting world, as opposed to reconnecting with it, seeking to know it, and understanding oneself in terms of that creative, reconstructive encounter with it. Historical inquiry is not the key to self-understanding after all;

indeed, Rorty conflates "the continuity-seeking historian" with the discredited philosopher.[63]

For Rorty, as for Derrida, the effort of wriggling free is endless because the future as well as the past is implicated in the experience of suffocation. Again Rorty invokes Bloom, who "reminds us that just as even the strongest poet is parasitic on her precursors, just as even she can give birth only to a small part of herself, so she is dependent on the kindness of all those strangers out there in the future."[64] Even insofar as I manage to redescribe the whole past into "thus I willed it," I will continually be redescribed in contingent ways by those who come after. This recognition leads not only to anxiety over what will become of what I do, but also to resentment of the mechanisms of the merely historical world, which will arbitrarily make of what I do, even what I am, something I cannot choose or foresee. The particularizing coils of history continue to ensnare us, so the effort of wriggling free is endless. And thus the act of strong misreading is not experienced as history-making, but as defiance of the ongoing happening of history. Creativity must seek private autonomy at the expense of reconstructive reconnection.

In the final analysis, Rorty's way of positing individual experience in relationship with reality-as-history is symptomatically ambiguous. Selfhood entails a premium on autonomy, on edifying novelties, strong misreadings, and brilliant metaphors—as opposed to any sense of myself as participating in a continuing history. Selfhood, autonomy, creation apparently require discontinuity. Yet Rorty's overall emphases undeniably leave us with connection, continuity, history. We are involved in a conversation, as opposed to a sequence of unconnected assertions or descriptions. In the process of social interaction, there is influence, new metaphors connect with earlier ones, influencing the future, so that what is left is "a web which stretches backward and forward through past and future time."[65] A particular history results from the (provisional) triumph of any particular set of contingent metaphors. But though Rorty posited a web of influence, he pulled back from portraying "influence" as a positive opportunity to help shape the future; rather, influence entails anxiety. And thus the overall ambiguity in his thinking, which renews our understanding of liberal interaction, yet places a premium on quirky edification, and which suggests that historical inquiry replaces foundational philosophy, yet submerges history within a larger aestheticism.

Conclusion

For all their differences, Foucault, Derrida, and Rorty manifest new preoccupations stemming from a new experience of the self in a world reducing to mere history. The result was a premium on ritualistic disruption, on playing out of bounds, on autonomy, on quirkiness—all defined in opposition to congruence with history, to any experience of action as history-making. These extreme responses are plausible, in light of the mechanisms that seem essential to the world as merely historical. But as they have entered the discussion so far, those responses have tended to preclude the "moderate" alternative—a weak, merely historical self, caught up in an ongoing two-sided process of self-creation and collaborative world-creation. As the effort to reconceive selfhood continues, we need to deepen our understanding of both the historical and anti-historical impulses, which can best serve the culture in tension, with each as a check to the other.[66]

To posit a historical self entails a renewed understanding of what identity, rationality, morality, and human interaction can mean. While there is endless differing, there is also endless "gathering," endless coming back together as the world keeps becoming some particular way. We unify and create identities, but we recognize the ragged, ad hoc, merely practical nature of the concepts through which we do so. In a merely historical world, we find ourselves confined within our particular tradition, but that tradition invites us to respond to it as we will—or can. Although suprahistorical "principles" or "values" fall away, evaluating goes on, because human being entails care for the happening of the world and individual human beings respond to the world on that basis, though each in an individuated way.

Care and the resulting moral response are not "rational" in the sense of affording an a priori grasp, so that we *know* what to do, but neither are they irrational, warranting license, play, or weightless innocence. To care is to discipline moral response with a rational element, not by invoking "Reason" or claiming enlightened status, but simply by asking historical questions in an effort to understand some particular situation.[67] What is rational is historical inquiry that genuinely seeks to learn, thereby preparing the way for criticism and action. In this sense, seeking to learn from historical inquiry and keeping oneself open to persuasion are moral as well.

Historical selfhood entails precisely the willingness to say "we," to identify with our generation, that Rorty found strangely lacking in Foucault. As Jürgen Habermas has insisted, we have a common interest in undistorted communication, but the basis of our interaction is not the ideal of agreement, but a desire to learn about this particular world from our need to act within it. Knowing ourselves to be partial and incomplete, we seek to learn from others, from the totality of those sharing this particular world with us. And in acting we feel ourselves collaborators in a larger response to our historically specific moment, with its particular challenges and possibilities.

NOTES

1. Ian Hacking, "The Archaeology of Foucault," in David Couzens Hoy, ed., *Foucault: A Critical Reader* (Oxford, 1986), 36.

2. See Bernard P. Dauenhauer, *Elements of Responsible Politics* (Dordrecht, 1991), 111–13, on the inevitable tension between the individual and "the world on its path."

3. There is some ambiguity on this score in, for example, Robert C. Solomon's *Continental Philosophy since 1750: The Rise and Fall of the Self* (Oxford, 1988).

4. See especially Mark C. Taylor, *Journeys to Selfhood: Hegel and Kierkegaard* (Berkeley and Los Angeles, 1980).

5. Georg Lukács, *The Meaning of Contemporary Realism* (London, 1963), 38–39. The Hofmannsthal passage is from "Terzinen, 1: Über Vergänglichkeit" (1894).

6. For example, a "striking new obsession with death," linked to a newly heightened consciousness of irreversible time, became prominent in literature after about 1890. See Theodore Ziolkowski, *Dimensions of the Modern Novel: German Texts and European Contexts* (Princeton, 1969), 221–22.

7. André Gide, *The Immoralist* (New York, 1970), 50–53, 145–46.

8. J.M. Coetzee, "On the Edge of Revelation," *The New York Review of Books*, Dec. 18, 1986, 10.

9. See especially Eliot's famous essay of 1919, "Tradition and the Individual Talent," in *Selected Prose of T.S. Eliot*, edited by Frank Kermode (New York, 1975), 37–44.

10. James Longenbach, *Modernist Poetics of History: Pound, Eliot, and the Sense of the Past* (Princeton, 1987), 174, 200. See also 202, 205–7, on Eliot's yearning for the whole truth.

11. T.S. Eliot, "The Dry Salvages," in *Four Quartets* (1943) lines 101–103.

12. Longenbach, *Modernist Poetics*, 227.

13. Ibid., 209, 220–21, 237.

14. See, for example, Nietzsche's explicit assault on the subject, or Cartesian subjectivism, in Friedrich Nietzsche, *The Will to Power*, edited by Walter Kaufmann (New York, 1968), 267–71 (#s 481–90), and 298 (#552).

15. As Hans-Georg Gadamer frames the relationship at issue, it is through coming to expression in language that being is temporalized (*sich zeitigt*). See his *Philosophical Hermeneutics* (Berkeley, 1977), 50, 77–79. Nietzsche, in contrast to Croce and Heidegger, accented the sense in which the world is forever outgrowing what we can say about it. See especially Friedrich Nietzsche, *Twilight of the Idols*, in Walter Kaufmann, ed., *The Portable Nietzsche* (New York, 1954), 530–31.

16. Benedetto Croce, *Il carattere della filosofia moderna* (Bari, 1963), 100–101, 208–209.

17. Nietzsche, *The Will to Power*, 400–401 (#765).

18. Friedrich Nietzsche, "On the Uses and Disadvantages of History for Life," in *Untimely Meditations* (Cambridge, England, 1983), 108; see also the pivotal section 7, 95–100.

19. On the weight of the past and the possibility of redemption from time, see the famous section, "On Redemption," in Friedrich Nietzsche, *Thus Spoke Zarathustra*, in Kaufmann, ed., *The Portable Nietzsche*, 249–54.

20. Nietzsche, *Twilight of the Idols*, 500–501.

21. Nietzsche, *The Will to Power*, 546–47 (#1062), 547–550 (#1065 – #1067). See 548 (#1066) for the reference to excrement.

22. As Alexander Nehamas has shown in his *Nietzsche: Life as Literature* (Cambridge, Mass., 1985), such self-creation is akin to literary creation. It is crucial, however, that it entails encounter not just with a personal past, but with the totality, the whole world as the resultant of a particular history.

23. Nietzsche, *The Will to Power*, 548 (#1065).

24. Croce's emphasis on the immortality of the act and its corollary, the premium on individual vocation, is most striking in his "Frammenti di etica," now in *Etica e politica* (Bari, 1967); see especially 22–23, 25, 99–101, 123. See also David D. Roberts, *Benedetto Croce and the Uses of Historicism* (Berkeley, 1987), 174–82.

25. Croce, "Frammenti di etica," 93–94. See also Benedetto Croce, *History of the Kingdom of Naples* (1925) (Chicago, 1970), 248; Benedetto Croce, *Conversazioni critiche*, ser. 4 (Bari, 1951), 201–2 (1923); Benedetto Croce, *Terze pagine sparse* (Bari, 1955), 1:97–98.

26. Thus Croce sometimes found it necessary to insist that the maker of the world is ultimately the whole spirit—that the spirit is the only agent. See especially Benedetto Croce, *Filosofia e storiografia* (Bari, 1969), 144 (1946). But this does not mean we individual actors are but shadowy manifestations of spirit, as critics have continually charged. It is simply to say that the individual is a piece of the growing whole—and is inconceivable in isolation. For a recent example of such criticism, see Pietro Rossi, "Max Weber and Benedetto Croce," in Wolfgang J. Mommsen and Jürgen Osterhammel (eds.), *Max Weber and His Contemporaries* (London, 1987), 459–64.

27. For Croce's repeated insistence on world-historical modesty, see "Frammenti di etica," 151–53; *Carattere*, 209–10; and *Discorsi di varia filosofia* 1: 297 (1942). This line of thinking was the basis of Croce's recasting of liberalism during the 1920s. See Roberts, *Benedetto Croce*, chap. 5, especially 216–20.

28. Benedetto Croce, *Ultimi saggi* (Bari, 1963), 263–64 (1930).

29. Benedetto Croce, *Filosofia della pratica* (Bari, 1963), 406. Croce noted explicitly that his fondest wish was that his ideas might pass into common currency in this way. See his *Cultura e vita morale* (Bari, 1955), 206–9 (1916), 210–11 (1917).

30. See Jeffrey Andrew Barash, *Martin Heidegger and the Problem of Historical Meaning* (Dordrecht, 1988), 231, on why the famous "turn" (*Kehre*) in Heidegger's thinking should be understood in this sense.

31. Martin Heidegger, *Early Greek Thinking* (San Francisco, 1984), 17–18. See also Karl Löwith, "Nature, History, and Existentialism" (1952), in *Nature, History, and Existentialism, and Other Essays in the Philosophy of History*, edited by Arnold Levison (Evanston, Ill., 1966), 17–29, for the generally Heideggerian tendency to conflate historicism with a manipulative, subjectivist, and hubristic humanism.

32. Martin Heidegger, *What Is Called Thinking?* (New York, 1968), 76–78; Martin Heidegger, *On Time and Being* (New York, 1972), 8–10, 14–24.

33. Hans-Georg Gadamer, *Truth and Method* (New York, 1975), 271–74.

34. Gadamer consistently denied he was suggesting "that cultural tradition should be absolutized and fixed." See, for example, Gadamer, *Philosophical Hermeneutics*, 31, 56–58. See also Georgia Warnke, *Gadamer: Hermeneutics, Tradition and Reason* (Stanford, 1987), 81–82, 90–92, 96–97.

35. Hans-Georg Gadamer, *Reason in the Age of Science* (Cambridge, Mass., 1981), 166; Gadamer, *Truth and Method*, 158.

36. The conservative accents were not compatible with Gadamer's dominant emphasis on the change, novelty, and growth that follow from ongoing response and dialogue. See Gadamer, *Truth and Method*, 245–53, especially 249, for a key statement of that dominant emphasis. Georgia Warnke emphasizes that Gadamer's conservatism is a kind of overlay that need not follow from his recasting of hermeneutics. Fusion of horizons can include disagreement and "distantiation." See Warnke, *Gadamer*, 136–38.

37. John D. Caputo, *Radical Hermeneutics: Repetition, Deconstruction, and the Hermeneutic Project* (Bloomington, Ind., 1987), 81–82, 96–97, 111–14. See also John D. Caputo, "Gadamer's Closet Essentialism: A Derridean Critique," in Diane P. Michelfelder and Richard E. Palmer, eds., *Dialogue and Deconstruction: The Gadamer-Derrida Encounter* (Albany, N.Y., 1989), 258–64. Although his response differs, Christopher Norris similarly finds something suffocating about Gadamer's way of confining us to history. See, for example, *The Contest of Faculties* (London, 1985), 24–27.

38. Caputo, *Radical Hermeneutics*, especially 97–98, 113, 250–51, 258.

39. As Foucault put it in a 1977 interview:

> One has to dispense with the constituent subject, to
> get rid of the subject itself, that's to say, to arrive at an
> analysis which can account for the constitution of the
> subject within a historical framework. And this is
> what I would call genealogy, that is, a form of history
> which can account for the constitution of knowledges,
> discourses, domains of objects etc., without having
> to make reference to a subject which is either tran-
> scendental in relation to the field of events or runs in
> its empty sameness throughout the course of history.

Michel Foucault, *Power/Knowledge: Selected Interviews and Other Writings,
1972–1977*, edited by Colin Gordon (New York, 1980), 117.

40. Michel Foucault, "The Subject and Power," afterword to Hubert L. Dreyfus and Paul Rabinow, *Michel Foucault: Beyond Structuralism
and Hermeneutics*, second ed. (Chicago, 1983), 216.

41. Accent on the radical and reconstructive implications of Derridean deconstruction has been fundamental to Christopher Norris's
writings. See especially his *Derrida* (Cambridge, Mass., 1987). See also
Michael Ryan, *Marxism and Deconstruction: A Critical Articulation*
(Baltimore, 1982).

42. See, for example, Foucault, "The Subject and Power," 223, 225.

43. Michel Foucault, *Language, Counter-Memory, Practice: Selected
Essays and Interviews*, edited by Donald F. Bouchard (Ithaca, N.Y., 1977),
160–64, 171, 192, 196.

44. Ibid., 186.

45. Paul Bové, "The Foucault Phenomenon: The Problematics of
Style," foreword to Gilles Deleuze, *Foucault* (Minneapolis, 1988), xxix–
xxxvi, especially xxxvi. Criticizing Deleuze's claim to find a "utopian"
element in Foucault, Bové finds instead endless subversion, even of any
such utopian aspiration—*especially* of any such utopian aspiration.

46. Jacques Derrida, *Writing and Difference* (Chicago, 1978), 280–81.

47. Jacques Derrida, "Otobiographies" (1984), in *The Ear of the
Other: Otobiography, Transference, Translation* (New York, 1985). See also
Norris, *Derrida*, especially 194–95, 199–200, on Derrida's preoccupation
with the subsequent uses of the written text.

48. Jacques Derrida, *Of Grammatology* (Baltimore, 1976), 27–44. See
also Norris, *Derrida*, 21, 65–71, 83–86, 121, 187.

49. Derrida, *Writing and Difference*, 292.

50. Jacques Derrida, *The Post Card: From Socrates to Freud and
Beyond* (Chicago, 1987). For Norris's characterization, see his *Derrida*,

116. Richard Rorty similarly finds *The Post Card* pivotal as Derrida abandoned what, for Rorty, was still an effort to do philosophy in a transcendental mode, specifying ahistorical conditions of possibility. See Richard Rorty, *Essays on Heidegger and Others* (Cambridge, Eng., 1991), 128.

51. John Searle notes this tendency in "An Exchange on Deconstruction," *The New York Review of Books*, Feb. 2, 1984, 48, but characterizes it in an especially dismissive way, which does not do justice to the preoccupation at work.

52. Richard Rorty, "Habermas and Lyotard on Postmodernity," in Richard J. Bernstein, ed., *Habermas and Modernity* (Cambridge, Mass., 1985), 172.

53. John M. Ellis, *Against Deconstruction* (Princeton, 1989), 73, 75, 78, 96.

54. Ibid., 41–42, 53–54, 69–71, 81–82, 87, 93–94.

55. Rorty, *Essays on Heidegger*, 113–18, 195.

56. See Derrida, *Of Grammatology*, 10, for an example of the implicit conflation with Hegel. In the same way, Foucault tended to assign unnecessary baggage to "continuity," "identity," and "unity," and to assume that categories of any sort claim to be stable, fixed, and supra-historical. See, for example, *Language, Counter-Memory, Practice*, 181–87.

57. Richard Rorty, *Contingency, Irony, and Solidarity* (Cambridge, Eng., 1989), chapter 2.

58. Ibid., 42, 61.

59. Richard Rorty, *Philosophy and the Mirror of Nature* (Princeton, 1979), 389–92. Indeed, as Rorty notes on 10, this influential work is fundamentally a historical account, explicitly "intended to put the notions of 'mind,' of 'knowledge,' and of 'philosophy' . . . in historical perspective" for such reconstructive purposes. In addition, see 33–34, 123–26, 136, 229, 264; and Richard Rorty, *Consequences of Pragmatism (Essays: 1972–1980)* (Minneapolis, 1982), 60–71.

60. Considering, for example, the enduring desire for some theoretical, suprahistorical grasp of the conditions of free and open discussion, Rorty says he would like "to replace both religious and philosophical accounts of a suprahistorical ground or an end-of-history convergence with a historical narrative about the rise of liberal institutions and customs." And this would be history with immense practical import—as the only way to get our bearings in post-metaphysical world: "Such a narrative would clarify the conditions in which the idea of truth as correspondence to reality might gradually be

replaced by the idea of truth as what comes to be believed in the course of free and open encounters." Rorty, *Contingency*, 68.

61. Ibid., 21. See also Rorty, *Essay on Heidegger*, 103.

62. See especially Rorty, *Consequences of Pragmatism*, 151–54, 157–58; and Rorty, *Contingency*, 24, 24n.–25n., 29–30, 41, 41n.–42n., 53, 61, for his debt to Bloom. For Bloom's elaboration of these two categories, see *The Anxiety of Influence: A Theory of Poetry* (New York, 1973), and *A Map of Misreading* (New York, 1975).

63. Rorty, *Contingency*, 28. Note also Rorty's way of understanding continuity on 25 (n. 2): "Metaphysicians look for continuities—overarching conditions of possibility—which provide the space within which discontinuity occurs."

64. Ibid., 41.

65. Ibid., 29, 41–42, 61. The quote is from 41.

66. Elements for such a new understanding of selfhood as historical can be found in a number of thinkers involved in the loosely historicist and neo-liberal strand in contemporary thinking. See, for example, David Kolb, *The Critique of Pure Modernity* (Chicago, 1986), especially the concluding chapter, 256–70. This direction is evident even in Václav Havel's writing; see, for example, his *Disturbing the Peace: A Conversation With Karel Hvizdala* (New York, 1991), 180–81, 189–90.

67. Compare, for example, Christopher Norris, who seeks to bring Habermas together with Derrida in *The Contest of Faculties*, *Derrida*, and other works. Norris insists on the scope for enlightened critique, even reason with a capital R, because he finds them essential to head off overreaction in non-rational play.

(Re)Educating the Self

Education and the Self in a Postmetaphysical World

Lawrence J. Biskowski

This volume is evidence of the increasing attention being given by theorists and philosophers in a wide variety of disciplines to the self, the nature of human subjectivity, and the politics of identity. The liberal tradition, the general heritage of the Enlightenment, and important elements of Western philosophy and religion have all tended to assume the individual self to be a more or less fixed, unitary, monolithic, homogeneous, and discrete unit, and proceed to make this self the basic building block of both theories and societies. Non-liberal (e.g., Marxian and classical conservative) traditions generally have objected to this conception in various ways, seeing the self as colonized by class interests and understandings or as subsidiary to ongoing, multigenerational, social projects of civilization. More recently, theorists working with feminist, psychoanalytic, and Nietzschean orientations, among others, have pushed the critique of the traditional liberal self still farther, arriving usually at "de-centered" conceptions of a self which is neither fixed, unitary, monolithic, homogeneous, nor discrete. These decentered selves typically are situated in environments full of generally sinister socializing forces and manifestations of power which persistently threaten the ever-diminishing modicum of integrity and autonomy it may or may not retain.[1]

The great insights and enormous liberating potential of these theoretical developments have come at the cost of the need to rethink many crucially important moral issues as well as related questions of public policy. Indeed, the self and the politics of identity are at the center of a number of significant theoretical and practical quandaries. I will focus here on only one example: Reformulations of standard or accepted notions of the self have special relevance to discussions of education and its goals. Educational theory and practice, from Plato's *Republic* to the present day have tended to rely, implicitly or explicitly, on ideal conceptions of a fully and properly developed self, the *telos* of the educational process and target at which educators should aim. But it is becoming increasingly clear not only that such conceptions may be built on faulty assumptions about the nature of identity and the self but also that such conceptions, to the extent that they contain any substance at all, are ultimately arbitrary, contingent, and bound up with various considerations of class, gender, race, culture, and so forth. If our notions of the ideal self, as well as even our most deeply held values and beliefs, are conditioned by the various sites and contexts (linguistic, social, historical, cultural, sexual, etc.) in which we grow, develop, and live our lives, then the aims and purposes of education and the choice of what knowledge, values, skills, and understandings should be taught in our schools all become radically problematic.

This problem is already evident in contemporary controversies over educational policy. Without a relatively clear and widely shared understanding of the desirable self, we have the basis for endless inherently unresolvable arguments about education. Awareness of the contingency of our notions of the self produces decided theoretical advantages, but it also imposes a very important burden: In the absence of any legitimate objective understanding of the flourishing self, how do we orient and structure education? One may push the point even further and ask why education—which seems, inevitably, to condition or socialize people to particular patterns, discourses, and power structures which are ultimately contingent or arbitrary, and thus interferes with individual autonomy—is even *desirable*.[2]

The modern or postmodern world seems to pose problems which make past approaches to these issues obsolete. Contemporary theorists concerned with the self and identity are now inclined to doubt that any single ideal of the self is superior by nature or even appropriate for everyone, and if we cannot establish broad agreement on basic questions of the best possible regime and the most desirable life, all such ideal selves and corresponding theories of education will have no grounding. Even the strategy of basing education on a community's ethos also becomes problematic in large, diverse, multi-cultural, class-divided societies like the United States. As previously silenced and disempowered groups find their political voices, and as people become increasingly aware that the heretofore dominant tradition of Western culture is but one of many, it becomes increasingly clear that one's view of social and political reality, and thus also of the characteristics of the ideal self, is conditioned in large part by the social and cultural role one occupies. The contemporary ethos (if it even makes sense to use such a term) is fragmented and divided—our understanding of social and political reality, of what constitutes the good life, and of what counts as good judgment or a good education are all fragmented and divided to an extent that makes such judgments extremely difficult.

Consequently, while it is relatively easy to criticize the barely hidden cultural biases in such popular objectivist and ostensibly conservative positions on education as are developed by William Bennett, Charles Kimball, Charles Sykes, John Silber, Allan Bloom, and others, rejecting their foundationalism in itself is hardly a panacea. We are left foundering without any clear ideals for orienting our understanding of education. Typically, even the explicit rejection of purportedly objective, socially dominant conceptions of the ideal self has tended to provoke strategies which deny contingency in much the same way. Class perspectives are simply transposed. The viewpoint of the disadvantaged and disempowered, rather than that of the dominant elite, is universalized to society as a whole; in effect, the hegemonic relationship of dominant and subordinate viewpoints is merely inverted. This general strategy, advanced by Paulo Freire and R.W. Connell, among others, has its clear intellectual antecedents in the arguments for the universalization of the proletarian standpoint formulated by Lukacs and Marx. Contingency provokes the very reasonable fear that the lack of any firm standpoint on the substantive characteristics of the selves education is supposed to help develop leads inevitably to conservatism, or even, according to Lawrence Grossberg, to new forms of quietism, elitism, and pessimism (102ff).[3]

But it is difficult to see how the progressive standpoint, formulated in this way, can defend itself from the charge that it too is based on nothing more than another arbitrary cultural norm—and often this leads those of its adherents who are sensitive to the issue into all sorts of complex intellectual gyrations and contradictions. A second and perhaps more promising strategy is to assert, as Benjamin Barber does, that full acceptance of the contingency principle itself points to certain substantive personality traits associated with radical democracy. Barber tells us that democracy is

> how women and men emancipated from the consoling certainties of authority (religious, political, and metaphysical) try to govern themselves in a world without definitive values . . . The prudent democrat . . . teaches how we might survive the passing of values in a world that provides neither escape routes back into the authoritarian past nor ladders leading up into the aeries of the philosopher's republic. The democrat may even promise more: to transform survival into a virtue, by forging an art of politics capable of holding together and giving meaning to beings emancipated from the roots that once imprisoned their spirits even as it grounded their values (169).

The product of education is a democratized version of the Nietzschean *Übermensch*—a literally autonomous self which can face its own contingency with equanimity, throw away its metaphysical crutches, and determine its own identity both individually and collectively (the latter through democratic politics).[4]

But Barber's positing of this sort of self-determining self as a societal ideal begs certain important questions and may amount to a deft dodging of the critical issues. Why should autonomy, to the extent that it reflects the substantive content of the proposed ideal self, be a privileged value? And if we decry all such standards, the effect is a kind of paralysis: On what basis do we make determinations of our own identity? Are all or even most human beings actually capable of creating their own values and identities? If the individual self needs for its own realization the education that society provides, and if society inevitably does at least some violence to the individual by imposing at least some standards on him or her which are ultimately unsupportable in the metaphysical sense—both of which seem to be indisputable propositions—then we seem to be on the horns of an authentic dilemma.

My suggestion here is that this dilemma is in fact yet another product of the long Western infatuation with metaphysics, a sort of metaphysical hangover, and that one possible remedy for the hangover may be found in the political theory of Hannah Arendt. As Arendt points out repeatedly, the metaphysicians who have dominated our thinking for so long have created a philosophical language anchored on the idea of a transcendent reality which existed above or beyond the realm of everyday appearances. In effect, there were alleged to be two worlds, with the transcendent, suprasensory, metaphysical world providing orientation for the mundane world of everyday life. But when our ability to know the upper, transcendent world was denied by Kant and the whole concept ridiculed by Nietzsche, long-standing means of navigating in the world of appearances were cast out as well. Human beings were thrown back upon their own resources; morality lost its former foundation and long accepted ideals lost their plausibility. As Arendt puts it, once the "precarious balance between the two worlds is lost, no matter whether the 'true world' abolishes the 'apparent one' or vice versa, the whole framework of references, in which our thinking was used to orienting itself, breaks down. In these terms, nothing seems to make much sense anymore" ("Thinking and Moral Considerations" 421).[5]

Accustomed as we are to thinking and speaking metaphysically, the demolition of metaphysics leaves us disoriented and unsure of our footing in a newly strange world. Previous strategies for solving practical problems like education become paradoxical and permeated with contradictions.

Arendt is concerned with rethinking these issues in such a way as to avoid the lingering distortions of the metaphysical tradition. At the center of her thesis is her highly complex and somewhat idiosyncratic concept of world. For Arendt, world designates, first of all, the complex web of relationships in which human beings find themselves enmeshed. In the absence of shared metaphysical assumptions and especially in an era when traditions have lost much of their authority, the world can provide the common framework that relates individuals to one another. The apparently atomistic and discrete selves we find in the wake of metaphysics are not necessarily quite so isolated as they sometimes seem. The phenomenological commonality of the world we all share is stressed over and over by Arendt—because the world is something that is held in common by distinct plural subjects, it provides a common point of orientation. Indeed, communication between diverse subjects with diverse perspectives is possible precisely because a world exists between human beings and serves as an enduring point of reference. The world simultaneously separates and relates human beings much in the way that a table separates and relates the individuals who gather around it (*Human Condition* 52ff). The world provides orientation to the diverse selves who hold it in common by giving them at least some common concerns and thereby a common language. We enter into this pragmatic web of relationships or world when we are born and leave it when we die; its existence precedes our own and outlasts our brief sojourn in it (*Human Condition* 58).

Arendt considered the pre-Socratic Greeks to have been the single people to have grasped best the significance of perspectival consciousness and of the sheer human plurality of selves, as well as of the role that a common world plays as both arena and reference point. It is this essentially political epistemology as much as anything else that draws her to them:

> [T]he Greeks discovered that the world we have in common is usually regarded from an infinite number of different standpoints, to which correspond the most diverse points of view. In a sheer inexhaustible flow of arguments . . . the Greek learned to exchange his own viewpoint, his own "opinion" . . . with those of his fellow citizens. Greeks learned to *understand*—not to understand one another as individual persons, but to look upon the same world from one another's standpoint, to see the same in very different and frequently opposing aspects (*Past and Future* 51).

As this common point of reference, world is both a formal condition for political action and, in a very specific manner of speaking, its appropriate object.[6]

But for the world to perform this function, some very important conditions must obtain. The world "depends for its reality and its continued existence, first, upon the presence of others who have seen and heard and will remember, and second, on the transformation of the intangible into the tangibility of things. Without remembrance, and without the reification which remembrance needs for its own fulfillment and which makes it, indeed, as the Greeks held, the mother of all arts, the living activities of action, speech, and thought would lose their reality . . . and disappear as though they had never been" (*Human Condition* 95).[7]

At least in part, the world consists of relatively enduring objects, ideas, and stories. Michelangelo's David, the Eiffel Tower, Hobbes' elaboration of the notion of a social contract, and Homer's *Odyssey* are all features of the common world from which we take our bearings. This is possible—and these objects have meaning for us—because they represent the reification of otherwise fleeting thoughts and actions. This reification itself is the province of art, literature, architecture, and all the other activities which aim at the creation of durable objects that will outlast their mortal creators.

Nevertheless, there is a close and special relationship between authentically political action, which may not leave behind any such tangible object, and the world. For Arendt, action is a special and uniquely human capability very closely tied to issues of self and identity. It is precisely our capacity for action that saves human beings from the futility and pointlessness of simply being the predicates of causally determined natural and economic processes. As Sheldon Wolin puts it, without this capacity there is only "the natural rhythm of coming-to-be and passing away" (97). Through action, at least as Arendt conceives it, human beings can interrupt natural processes and begin something new. We are capable of taking the initiative and doing something that is wholly novel and therefore impossible to predict on the basis of antecedent causes. As such, action has about it a certain "miraculous" quality (*Human Condition* 246) which derives ultimately from the sheer fact that human beings are by their very nature "beginners" ("Labor, Work, Action" 42). Through action we escape the relentless dialectic of cause and effect, and insert our selves into the world (*Human Condition* 176–7).

This is a crucial point for Arendt and for anyone concerned with contemporary understandings of identity and the self. Animals live their lives entirely under the sway of causality; all their activity reflects *what* they are. Their behavior reflects only natural necessity, the instinctual activities necessary to keep them and their species alive. This is also part of the nature of human beings. But a human being is not only a *what* but also a *who*; we are selves. We each have an individual identity entirely different from that of every other human being who ever lived or will live. The relationship between individual identity and the world is essentially dialectical, although Arendt was too wary of the ambiguities and misuses of this term to characterize the relationship as such. The self that I am, and am always becoming, is a product of my interaction with other unique individuals and with the world. But the ontological uniqueness of human beings is that we are also more than mere products.[8] This unique identity makes itself manifest in the world through action, which is the virtual opposite of behavior (conceived of as mere habit, adherence to routine, or instinctual activity, ways of being which we share with every other living creature, and which indeed ultimately *are* causally determined).

In this manner, Arendt's conception of action has a certain self-revelatory or even dramaturgical character. We reveal our selves—our unique identities—to other people. By acting in the world, we reveal our principles, our passions, our virtuosity, and our character. Each action discloses *who* one is ("Labor, Work, Action" 39–40). We act because we want to appear in the world and make our mark on it, either by changing it somehow or preserving it or otherwise imposing ourselves on what would have been, without our action, at least a somewhat different course of events. In so doing, we realize our freedom and reveal our unique identities.

But action is also more than sheer self-revelation and expressivism. By its nature, action is inherently connected to care for the world, not only for what the world thinks (the "glory" for which the Greeks strove) but also for what the world will be like in the wake of one's acting. One's actions originate in the self and exemplify or manifest or embody one's principles; they are not subservient to any practical end in the world. The fact that they may be, and likely will be, frustrated does not impugn the principle involved nor deny the freedom of the agent. Action is an ontological category, a way of being in the world irrespective of the unpredictable practical consequences of any particular action. In this respect, Arendt's concept of action resembles the existentialist concept of the "project."[9] On different levels, the project of the agent is pursued for its own sake, for the sake of the self, and for the sake of the world. Action has no object, strictly speaking, because its contingent nature is such that its consequences are unpredictable; yet we engage in it anyway, and for reasons that may make no sense in terms of instrumental rationality but which are eminently sensible when seen from the perspective of individual identity. Distinctively political actions reflect our hopes for the world regardless of their success, even as they reveal our principles and identities.

The world provides action with context, meaning, a space to appear, and the possibility of remembrance, as well as a common point of reference and orientation. When we lose contact with the world, for any reason, we lose our sense of reality and our orientation in it. Indeed, the various forms of "world-alienation" which have arisen in the West since the fall of the *polis* are the topics of most of Arendt's writing.

This concern is certainly at the center of Arendt's critique of much of the Western philosophical tradition. For Arendt, as for Heidegger, post-Socratic philosophy is itself a form of world-alienation, a turning away from appearance, perspective, and opinion and towards contemplation, *theoria*, and a much more secure (enduring and wholly unperspectival) Truth.[10] In much the same way, Western science seeks to penetrate behind opinion and the mere appearance of phenomena to the reality of the causal mechanisms that produce those phenomena. The test of truth becomes precisely its lack of contextuality and dependence on perspectival appearance. We search, instead, for ever more general causal principles expressed in a form which will enable us to predict and control, at least hypothetically, our environment. In Arendt's terms, we seek an Archimedean point, a perspective on the world that is no longer in it, nor in history or a particular context, nor embodied in a particular person in a particular place and time (*Human Condition* 257ff). We attempt through science and metaphysics to transcend entirely the world and its relativism, our own situatedness and selfhood.[11] But this is a hopeless and ultimately destructive task for creatures whose existence and knowledge is always located somewhere in time and space and for whom being is always being-in-the-world. And the more we seek to transcend the world, the more estranged we are from our common point of orientation and the source of much of our identity, and the more we must seek alternative sources.

In this way, world-alienation has been a distinctive feature of Western society for most of our history. The resulting crises of identity have played an enormous role in shaping that history, sometimes in bizarre and horrible ways. One very important case of world-alienation with which Arendt was especially preoccupied was totalitarian ideology and practice. The totalitarian seeks to impose on people one particular "truth" or one particular perspective on the world without the reality-test provided by discussion and the exchange of viewpoints. This has the effect of depriving everyone of their common point of reference. With the "in-between" that separates, connects, and relates individual selves gone, they are left in a sort of "organized loneliness" in which all that is left to orient thought and action are the premises of the ideology (*Origins* 478). The world itself is betrayed or destroyed, and human existence takes on an unreal quality, almost as if it were lived "on another planet" ("Social Science Techniques" 63). In totalitarianism, irrespective of the particular substantive ideology, the principle of the plurality of selves is abolished in the sense that individual perspectives on the world no longer matter and are replaced by the mechanical logic of one idea or ideal. The perspective of the leader (or of the ideology) is substituted for the perspectives of everyone. Thus, while the world ought to serve to secure the unique perspective of individual subjects and yet relate them one to another externally, totalitarianism, by abolishing the world or unweaving the previously existing web of relationships, seeks to press diverse selves together into a single, unified perspective.

As the world "disappears" before the very eyes of these subjects, their sense of reality, the community's common sense, and everyone's capacity for good judgment also disappear. Their former means of orienting themselves is replaced by the inherent distortions of a single perspective without the reality check provided by the dialogical presence of other selves with other perspectives. Under totalitarianism, and as exemplified by Adolf Eichmann,

> [a]ll the moral norms of behavior in the Western tradition collapsed overnight and it seemed as if the original nature of morals (*mores*—custom, manners) and ethics (*ethos*—custom, habit) had suddenly revealed themselves for what they were—that is, customs or behavior patterns which could be changed as easily as table manners. This arouses our suspicion that morality was never more than that—as if morality was a dream from which we had suddenly awakened.[12]

Without the enduring point of reference the world gives us, one belief system indeed becomes just as good as any other. We become ensnared in utter relativism and can find escape only through single-minded faith in suprahuman principles and processes that serve as the initial premises of totalitarian ideologies. When these initial premises are accepted, what matters thereafter is only consistency, and sometimes not even that. Without the world, individual identity becomes problematic and *anomie* provokes desperate searches for alter-native orientation, including grotesquely exaggerated forms of nationalism such as Nazism but also sublimation of the drive for identity into various projects of world mastery or into the workings of historical laws and processes.[13]

Concern for the world also animates Arendt's notorious but usually misunderstood separation of social and economic questions from politics and her refusal to accept pity as a legitimate basis for political action. Authentic politics, as far as Arendt is concerned, always respects the natural plurality of individual selves separated but related to one another by a common world. The French Revolution, in Arendt's view, illustrates the dangers both of allowing economic or social questions to intrude on or overwhelm politics, and of allowing sentiment or emotion rather than principle to guide political action. Thus, Robespierre and his associates began to glorify suffering, "hailing the exposed misery as the best and even only guarantee of virtue . . . [and] set out to emancipate the people not *qua* prospective citizens but *qua malheureux*" (*On Revolution* 111). When it was brought out in public, the depth of Robespierre's pity for the poor turned into the boundlessness of an emotion that seemed to respond only too well to the boundless suffering of the multitude in their sheer overwhelming numbers. By the same token, he lost the capacity to establish and hold fast to rapports with persons in their singularity; the ocean of suffering around him and the turbulent sea of emotion within him . . . drowned all specific considerations, the considerations of friendship no less than the considerations of statecraft and principle (*On Revolution* 90). The plurality of particular selves became the singular abstract mass, *le peuple*. Pity turned into delirious rage, and thence into the Terror.

Arendt insists that concern with social questions should be inspired by principle rather than sentiment. It is justice and not pity or even compassion that makes the welfare of the poor a political question. When our actions are inspired by pity or some other emotion, we begin to lose our bearings, precisely because such emotions take no account of, and are harmful to, the "in-between," the "world," that separates and relates human beings. Eventually, "the social" may entirely replace "the political," and the public realm may become preoccupied with nothing more than the maintenance and smooth operation of the life-process itself. The web of relationships that constitute the world is collapsed into and increasingly dominated by the economic demands of the life process, and human beings become more and more closely identified with their economic roles. One concern or process—production—comes to dominate politics, and people increasingly can find their identities only in the roles they play in this process, e.g., as particular types of producers and consumers.

The common theme running through all of these arguments is the unique nature of action and the nature and fragility of the common world. The world provides a public realm in which there are many voices and where the announcement of what each "deems truth" both links and separates men, establishing in fact those distances between men which together comprise the world. Every truth outside this area, no matter whether it brings men good or ill, is inhuman in the literal sense of the word . . . because it might have the result that all men might suddenly unite in a single opinion, so that out of many opinions one would emerge, as though not men in their infinite plurality but man in the singular, one species and its exemplars, were to inhabit the earth. Should that happen, the world, which can form only in the interspaces between men in all their variety, would vanish altogether (*Dark Times* 30–31). An absolute or transcendental Truth, even if it were possible, would mean a fundamental change in the human condition, an end to politics and discourse, the disappearance or occlusion of the world, and thus a change in the way human identities are formed and stabilized.

Arendt makes clear that the world, at least as she conceives of it, is perishable. It can be undermined or dissolved or obscured in any number of ways. Like Aristotle's *ethos* and Kant's *sensus communis*, the world provides intersubjective criteria for making judgments, for guiding and evaluating actions and potential actions, and for the formation of the individual selves who in turn shape the world. Such criteria are by no means absolute, and cannot be, but they do save us from pure subjectivism. Moreover, in view of our growing post-Nietzschean awareness of the contingency of even our most deeply held values and assumptions, they provide us with perhaps the only orientation we have. Equally important, this conception of world offers the hope of a reconciliation between the ideals and demands of both autonomous selfhood and community, a safe passage between the Scylla of domination by socialization and the Charybdis of a noncommunity of disoriented, atomistic, isolated, unrealized selves. But if the world is to endure, it depends on our care for it.

Our understanding of education must reflect the various existential dimensions and political implications of this complicated relationship between the individual self and the world. According to Arendt, "the essence of education is natality, the fact that human beings are *born* into the world" (*Past and Future*

174). Children are new arrivals, newcomers to this joint project of ours, and must be introduced to it. "But the child is new only in relation to a world that was there before him, that will continue after his death, and in which he is to spend his life. If the child were not a newcomer in this human world but simply a not yet finished living creature, education would be just a function of life and would need to consist in nothing save the concern for the sustenance of life and that training and practice in living that all animals assume in respect to their young" (*Past and Future* 185).[14] But human children are selves in the process of becoming. They form their selves and become who they are in relationship to the world.

The authority of the educator thus lies in the function of introducing and representing the world to the child:

> The teacher's qualification consists in knowing the world and being able to instruct others about it, but his authority rests on his assumption of responsibility for that world. Vis-à-vis the child it is as though he were a representative of all adult inhabitants, pointing out the details and saying to the child: This is our world (*Past and Future* 189).

This authority, however, does not extend to the determination of whom the child becomes, but rather only to the provision of choices and opportunities by which the child may become a self in our world.[15] Human beings are essentially incomplete without an identity that relates us to one another and the world; education plays a large role in helping us to develop that identity.

The crucial problem is that every identity that education enables also is a form of limitation: Every social form contains within it certain subjugations and cruelties. No identity is sufficient to contain and express the being behind it. An educational theory attentive to the politics of identity must therefore respect *différance*, that curious quality of existence which always exceeds and makes inadequate our various concepts, catgories, and constructions of identity and difference (Derrida 3–27). Lessons, skills, basic information thus should be provided less to make the child develop according to a certain, pre-established pattern than to minimize the repression of *différance*, to allow the child to become who she is, but also to introduce her to the world. This means that the skills, values, and information passed on through education can not be selected on the basis of metaphysical or transcendent principles which, as we have seen, deny the fundamental relativity of the world and would tend to generate a narrow range of identities, narrow standards of normality and worth, and so forth.

An alternative to metaphysics would be the formulation of education policy through political discussion by concerned adults in general, and educators in particular, who must take responsibility for introducing children to the world in all its relativity. The authority of adults and educators to decide what needs to be taught comes from their experience as well as from their having taken upon themselves responsibility for the world (including the role of introducing the newcomers to it). The lessons should reflect this process in such a way that the child may become conscious of the contingent nature of the lessons, as if each were accompanied by a message from the adults saying in effect that "this is what we think you should know to live in our world." And the selection of lessons is a continuing process, because the world too is always in a state of becoming.

Children depend upon adults for their educations precisely because they are newcomers to the world and have not yet developed even their own identities. They are not yet selves in the ways that adults are, and they cannot even decide what they need to know to navigate in the world and find their place in it. They need to be protected from the world, from the fact that they are strangers who do not yet know their way around. But when they become adults, this paternal responsibility must end, because the world itself is threatened by efforts to collapse the infinitely plural and diverse perspectives it exists between and from which it is known. Our common point of reference and even our capacity to become distinct selves are threatened when, owing to the demands of economics and other life processes or to the existential anxiety and resentment that lead many of us to seek the security of transcendental groundings, our ways of being are regularized, disciplined, and reduced to a limited number of approved patterns. At this point, education becomes no more than political control and domination.

But even as children *qua* newcomers must be temporarily protected from the world, Arendt makes clear that the world must also be protected from them:

> Because the world is made by mortals it wears out; and because it continuously changes its inhabitants it runs the risk of becoming as mortal as they. To preserve the world against the mortality of its creators and inhabitants it must constantly be set right anew. The problem is simply to educate in such a way that a setting-right remains actually possible, even though it can, of course, never be assured . . . Exactly for the sake of what is new and revolutionary in every child, education must be conservative; it must preserve this newness and introduce it as a new thing into an old world, which, however revolutionary its actions may be, is always, from the standpoint of the next generation, superannuated and close to destruction (*Past and Future* 192–3).

Without this essentially conservative or conservationist[16] education, we become little more than Burke's famous "flies of a summer." We lose our conscious connection to our own past as well as to the world; we are no longer partners in the joint intergenerational project of making a common home for ourselves and our children. And to the extent that we define our selves against and in relation to our common world, we lose sight of who we are and whom we may become.

Thus the point of education is to introduce newcomers to the world in all its richness and diversity, not to foist upon them one particular perspective on or experience of the world as universal. This means, for example, not only providing children with the traditional works of the dominant culture but also encouraging them to listen to voices from previously suppressed or ignored perspectives, without which our understanding of the world and of our own possibilities is distorted and undermined. But tolerance and respect for diversity is only one side of the issue; the point of education must also be to inculcate a sense of responsibility for the world. As Arendt puts it:

> Education is the point at which we decide whether we love the world enough to assume responsibility for it and by the same token save it from that ruin which, except for

> renewal, except for the coming of the new and the young,
> would be inevitable. And education, too, is where we de-
> cide whether we love our children enough not to expel
> them from our world and leave them to their own devices,
> nor to strike from their hands their chance of undertaking
> something new, something unforeseen by us, but to pre-
> pare them in advance for the task of renewing a common
> world (*Past and Future* 196).

And if Arendt's teaching about selves and the world constitutes
in effect only another arbitrary norm, then at least this much can
be said for it: Arendt's conservative orientation for education is
consistent with democracy, liberal concern for the individual,
and postmodern anxiety about the autonomy of the self in the
face of ubiquitous power and domination. It poses no direct
threat to the purely private manifestations of other belief systems, modes of self-expression, or ways of being in the world.
And it does so without recourse to metaphysical pretension,
aesthetic expressivism, or transcendental ideals of selfhood.

NOTES

1. Examples of recent works preoccupied with issues of self and
identity include Connolly, Taylor, Norton, Kateb, Lash and Friedman,
and Young.

2. The easy response here, that education's aim is the *enabling*
rather than the repressing of autonomy, only skirts the deeper issues
surrounding the penetration or colonization of the self. Education, and
socialization processes generally, tend inevitably to encourage some
substantive personality traits and not others, to encourage the development of some value systems and not others, and to enable some self-un-
derstandings and not others.

3. As Jürgen Habermas makes clear, moreover, education has
important functions to perform in the broader socioeconomic system,
and system level imperatives are powerful enough that education is
perpetually in danger of disappearing into the economic, technological,
and administrative functions of society. Without an independent ideal

to orient education, the school may be reduced to an appendage of the economy, helping to create selves which merely reflect the characteristics presently needed by the economic system (*Toward a Rational Society* 3–4; c.f. *The New Conservatism*).

4. Barber's conception is in some ways a more radical version of Amy Gutmann's ideal of "conscious social reproduction" as the guiding principle of democratic education.

5. Also of relevance here are Arendt's discussions of Nietzsche and Heidegger in "What is *Existenz* Philosophy?" and especially in *The Life of the Mind*.

6. The world is the arena in which we judge and act, and also the object of our judgments and political deliberations. Action may be distinct from work in having no object outside of itself, but the world is the medium in which actions are performed and hence, in a slightly different sense, its object.

7. Hence we speak of a "work" of art and not a "labor" of art or "act(ion)" of art. Much of *The Human Condition* is devoted to the distinctions between, and existential implications of, these important concepts.

8. Developing a position initially formulated by Augustine, Arendt argues that the existential or ontological uniqueness of human beings is that we are by nature "beginners." We are not simply the products or predicates of processes we do not and cannot control, but rather are beings who also begin processes of their own, creators as well as creatures (*The Human Condition* 175–81). In this way, I can be who I am by virtue of my interaction with our common world (e.g., through having a particular language and culture, and thus certain concepts for understanding and defining myself and not others; through having the opportunities for certain experiences and not others; and so forth) and yet still be able to make choices. The historical and contextual nature of our existence "goes all the way down"; and yet we are more than the determinate products of historical, economic, and other processes.

9. One acts politically for the sake of the world, but the meaning and motivation of one's actions are not exhausted by instrumental calculation. Even when the cause is hopeless people may act because the principles embodied in their identities demand that they take a stand and show themselves for who they are. See Kateb for a discussion of similarities between action and project:

> The project is a task without boundaries; one can never say that it is done, yet the whole meaning of it is found in every action done for its sake . . . It is never realized. The fact that I adopt a principle prevents no

one else from adopting it too; it is inexhaustible. To
act from a principle is not only to be inspired by it but
to manifest it. A political actor does not *pursue* honor,
for example; he does all that he does honorably, or he
does honorable deeds (153).

I differ from Kateb in asserting that two particular principles—love of
freedom and care for the world—are inherent in the political tradition as
described (and exemplified) by Arendt.

10.   This is a constant theme in many of Arendt's writings, but the
most detailed statement of her position is found in *The Life of the Mind*,
Vol. 1.

11.   Perversely, it is the philosopher's insistence on leaving the
world of appearances ("the beastliness of the multitude") that makes
him begin to doubt its reality and eventually gives rise to Cartesian
skepticism and solipsism (*Life of the Mind I* 47–53). This is also the root of
the false choice between transcendent foundations and solipsism.

12.   These remarks derive originally from Arendt's lecture course
"Reconsiderations of Basic Moral Propositions" held at the University of
Chicago in 1966. They are quoted in Hill (254).

13.   The general theme of world-alienation is also at the heart of
Arendt's critique of Christianity and her complicated interpretation and
critique of Kant. Purportedly transcendent principles, such as those offered by Christianity and by Kant, become substitute sources of identity
and orientation. Ultimately, they devalue and threaten the world and all
that is distinctively human in human affairs. For example, with the Cat-
egorical Imperative, Kant attempts to introduce into human affairs

something that runs counter to its fundamental relativity. The inhumanity which is bound up with the
concept of one single truth emerges with particular
clarity in Kant's work precisely because he attempted
to found truth on practical reason; it is as though he
who had so inexorably pointed out man's cognitive
limits could not bear to think that in action, too, man
cannot behave like a god (*Dark Times* 27).

Kant proclaims a transcendent principle, a monological moral Truth
which overwhelms human plurality and transcends perspectival consciousness. In much the same way, other-worldly religions attempt to
provide world-substitutes as sources of identity and orientation. These
too run counter to the fundamental relativity of the world, human affairs, and human identity.

14. Arendt, *Between Past and Future*, 185.

15. Clearly the constellation of choices and opportunities change over time and culture. Not every identity is available to me in the particular circumstances in which I find myself. To a considerable extent, we are *thrown* into the world, and we find ourselves and become ourselves in particular contexts which inevitably make some possibilities available to us while precluding others. But within these parameters, education is an introduction to the world and the possibilities for identity that it makes available.

16. It should be stressed, however, that an authentically conservative education (in contrast to much of what often passes for conservatism in current debates about education) is not oriented by or to metaphysical principles. Indeed, metaphysically-oriented education is far more radical than it is conservative, and constitutes in effect a destructive and ultimately doomed attempt to dissolve the world and make it over again from a single privileged perspective.

The Self En Route

The Human Way of Being and Its Political Implications[1]

Bernard P. Dauenhauer

One would be hard-pressed to maintain that one's view of politics, with its possibilities and requirements, is conceptually independent of one's interpretation of what it is to be human. At the very least, "ought" implies "can."

Most Western political thought since the seventeenth century has rested on some version of an interpretation of human beings, the political agents and patients, as more or less well defined, self-possessed entities which are in crucial respects independent both of one another and of their material and cultural contexts. Accordingly, human beings either possessed or could attain stability and totalized self-integration. Indeed, this stability and self-integration were marks of the fully developed, accomplished person. They were characteristics which did or should provide the basis for one's political activity. And that activity either did or should preserve or enhance this stability and totality.

The Cartesian doctrine of the ego is a prime example of this view of human beings. But many of the principal competing views, e.g., those of Hobbes, Locke, Rousseau, Kant, and Mill, also emphasize stability and self-integration of this sort.[2] Even Hume emphasizes at least stability, if not totality.

The stable, totalized person is, for the tradition, the responsible agent of politics, the one who acts in his own name for his own purposes in pursuit of his own objectives. Because he is stable and whole, he can be identified and held responsible for what he does or fails to do. He is likewise the one to whom political appeals can be addressed and who can respond at his own discretion.

Heidegger, however, with his critique of the Cartesian doctrine of the ego, initiated a line of criticism that can be and has been extended to show that all versions of a stable, self-sufficient, self-contained human person are untenable (*Being and Time* 122–134, *Nietzsche* IV: 96–122). Among the most prominent thinkers to have taken up and amplified the Heideggerian critique are those who are today called post-structuralists.

Post-structuralism is at most a movement. It is surely not a doctrine. Each of its leading figures—e.g., Roland Barthes, Gilles Deleuze, Jacques Derrida, Michel Foucault, Julia Kristeva, Jean-François Lyotard, Ernesto Laclau and Chantal Mouffe—has articulated a distinctive position differing in important respects from the others. Nonetheless, they are linked by a common foe. They are all unremittingly hostile to the claims of stability and totality (Jay 515). And their critiques of traditional interpretations of human existence, as they explicitly recognize, likewise vigorously challenge traditional Western political thought.

Given the force of the post-structuralist attacks, is there nonetheless a defensible interpretation of what it is to be human that provides grounds for attributing political responsibility? What must a human being be if he is to bear responsibility of this sort?

In this paper, I will first briefly explore a few post-structuralist proposals for understanding human beings and their transactions, linguistic and otherwise. Proposals of this sort, I will argue, are insufficient to support an appropriately strong attribution of political responsibility. I will therefore propose and defend an alternative. This alternative does not seek to restore the now discredited emphasis on stability and totality. But it does provide grounds for an appropriate sense of political responsibility. I do not claim that I can definitively establish the proposal I advance. But the evidence in its favor is strong and, for want of a sufficiently comprehensive and articulated competitor, compelling.[3]

I

In general, post-structuralist accounts of the ego, the subject, or the self have treated it as a construct or an effect, as something derivative, something constituted by more elementary processes or forces. In place of the modern view, according to which the ego, subject, or self is a fundamental, independent given which grounds or constitutes cultural processes and artifacts, the post-structuralist or post-modernist treatment stresses its dependence upon factors logically or conceptually, if not temporally, prior to and independent of it.

Nietzsche's critique of the notions of the ego or the subject foreshadows that of the post-structuralists. In *The Will to Power* he says:

> The "subject" is not something given, it is something added and invented, and projected behind what there is. . . . Is it necessary to posit an interpreter behind the interpretation? Even this is invention, hypothesis. . . . Our belief in the concept of substance . . . is simply a formulation of our grammatical custom that adds a doer to every deed. . . . The concept of substance is a consequence of the concept of the subject: not the reverse! If we relinquish the soul, the "subject," the precondition for "substance" in general disappears. . . . "The subject" is the fiction that many similar states in us are the effect of one substratum. . . . Everything that enters consciousness as "unity" is already tremendously complex: we always have only a semblance of unity. . . . The assumption of one single subject is perhaps unnecessary; perhaps it is just as permissible to assume a multiplicity of subjects whose interaction and struggle is the basis of our thought and our consciousness in general? A kind of aristocracy of "cells" in which dominion resides? To be sure, an aristocracy of equals, used to ruling jointly and understanding how to command? *My hypothesis*: The subject as multiplicity (267–270).

Echoes of Nietzsche's critique have reverberated and continue to reverberate in many recent theoretical discussions in literary criticism, historiography, and philosophy. For a sample, let me draw upon remarks of Barthes, Foucault, Deleuze and Guattari, and Stanley Fish.[4]

In "The Death of the Author," Barthes speaks of the author as a product of modern society with its emphasis on the individual "human person." For modern society, the author is one who gives expression to a thought, point of view, etc., which has its source within the depths of his consciousness. But in truth, Barthes claims, "to write is . . . to reach that point where only language acts, 'performs,' and not 'me'" (143). The same holds for the *I* which in speaking says *I*. This subject, this *I*, is not a 'person.' Apart from the enunciation which defines it, it is empty. Thus "the modern scriptor is born simultaneously with the text, is in no way equipped with a being preceding or exceeding the writing, is not the subject with the book as predicate" (145).

Instead of an author, a text, which is made of multiple elements drawn from multiple sources, has a reader. But this reader is not an independent, self-sufficient ego or subjectivity either. Rather, Barthes says:

> The reader is the space on which all the quotations that make up a writing are inscribed without any of them being lost; a text's unity lies not in its origin but in its destination. Yet this destination cannot any longer be personal: the reader is without history, biography, psychology; he is simply that *someone* who holds together in a single field all the traces by which the written text is constituted (148).

The ego, subjectivity, or self, then, is simply a function or product of language and its deployment.

Deleuze and Guattari, in their turn, consider the subject to be at most an ephemeral, ultimately insignificant, thing. The subject has no fixed identity and is always peripheral to the organic body, the desiring-machine. It is never more than a function, a transient function, of the transient sensuous states of the body (*Anti-Oedipus* 16). The subject is produced as a residuum alongside the machine, as an appendix, or as a spare part adjacent to the machine. . . . This subject itself is not at the center, which is occupied by the machine, but on the periphery, with no fixed identity, forever decentered, *defined* by the states through which it passes (*Anti-Oedipus* 20).

At the beginning of *A Thousand Plateaus*, they playfully reiterate this view of the subject, the I. They say:

> The two of us wrote *Anti-Oedipus* together. Since each of us was several, there was already quite a crowd. . . . We have assigned clever pseudonyms to prevent recognition. Why have we kept our own names? Out of habit, purely out of habit. To make ourselves unrecognizable in turn. . . . To reach, not the point where one no longer says I, but the point where it is no longer of any importance whether one says I. We are no longer ourselves. Each will know his own. We have been aided, inspired, multiplied (3).

For Stanley Fish, all objects with which we deal, linguistic or otherwise, are made and not found. But they are not made by individual subjects drawing upon their own inner resources. Rather, they are the products of social or communal conventions. In fact, Fish says, we ourselves as individuals are products of social and cultural patterns of thought. The notion of an independent, unconstrained self is incomprehensible, for the self is a social construct whose performances and activities are delimited by the systems of intelligibility informing it. Hence "the self does not exist apart from the communal or conventional categories of thought that enable its operations. . . ." (325). It is a function of one or more interpretative communities.

Foucault, at least during his middle period (1966–1975), similarly rejected any notion of a subject or self which in any sense constituted the discourse or practices in which it was implicated.[5] In *The Order of Things* Foucault entertains the possibility that man is no more than the contingent product of a particular historical configuration of language. Man, he says, is a recent invention, an invention perhaps nearing its end. If the conditions which brought man into being disappear, as it is easy to imagine, "then one can certainly wager that man would be erased, like a face drawn in sand at the edge of the sea" (387).

More clearly, in *The Archeology of Knowledge*, Foucault holds that discursive formations and practices are historical, determinate bodies of rules which define for some spatio-temporal period and some social, geographical, linguistic, or economic zone the conditions for enunciation (116–117). This domain of enunciation refers neither to an individual subject, nor to some kind of collective consciousness, nor to a transcendental subjectivity; but . . . it is described as an anonymous field whose configuration defines the possible position of speaking subjects. Statements should no longer be situated in relation to a sovereign subjectivity, but recognized in the different forms of speaking subjectivity effects proper to the enunciative field (122). Discourse, then "is not a language (*langue*), plus a subject to speak it. It is a practice that has its own forms of sequence and succession" (169). Inasmuch as what we do is a function of what we know and inasmuch as what we know is indistinguishable from what we can say, our practice, like our enunciation, and hence our very selves are effects of the discourse or discourses which define us.

These examples illustrate the roots of the widespread contemporary critique of any interpretation of what it is to be human that is couched in terms of a stable, totalizable, independent subject or self. They stress the importance of either language or desire, both of which display discontinuity and inconstancy. There is good reason to agree that this critique has served to call attention to features of human existence which have all too often been overlooked. And in doing so, it has shown the indefensibility of any view of the self like that of the Cartesian ego. Whatever it is to be human, it is surely not to be sovereignly in control of either language or desire.

But not infrequently those who espouse this critique make the further claim that the human subject or self is *wholly* constituted, *wholly* an effect or product of intersecting forces and circumstances all of which are in some respect prior to it, either logically or temporally. It is this further claim which I believe to be ultimately indefensible. And the error it embodies is not innocuous. For it undercuts the sensefulness of either making or trying to accede to calls for rationally warranted political conduct. That is, if the human self or subject is wholly constituted, is wholly a product or effect, how could it be held responsible for engaging in or acting on the basis of a critique of the conditions in which it itself lives? Even if Lyotard is right in claiming that there is no politics of reason but only a politics of opinion, the self must, as Lyotard himself sees, have the ability to decide among opinions, to adopt some and to reject others (73–88). An "opinion" which one cannot help but hold or reject is an obsession, not a genuine opinion.

Writing specifically of Foucault, Charles Taylor asks whether not only can there be, but even must there be something between maintaining on the one hand so total a constituting subjectivity that every pattern discernible in history is necessarily attributed to conscious designers and holding, on the other hand, that no patterns or structures owe what they are to purposeful human action. Taylor grants the importance of emphasizing that every human act "requires a background language of practices and institutions to make sense; and that while there will be a particular goal sought in the act, those features of it which pertain to the structural background will not be objects of individual purpose" (89). But still one must explain diachronic changes in these structures. One cannot do so by giving unqualified priority to structure or language over action or speech. Rather:

> Structures of action or languages are only maintained by being renewed constantly in action/speech. And it is in action/speech that they also fail to be maintained, that they are altered. . . . To give an absolute priority to the structure makes *exactly as little sense* as the equal and opposite error of subjectivism, which gave absolute priority to the action as a kind of total beginning (90).

Taylor's critique of Foucault fits well with the critique Ian Saunders has made of the widespread tendency shared by poststructuralists and others totally to reduce the subject, self, or ego to a function or effect wholly determined by some impersonal system. And Saunders explicitly ties his critique to the matter of politics.

This widespread tendency, Saunders claims, rests upon some version of two, or sometimes three, assumptions which, taken together, are inconsistent. He gives two versions for the first two assumptions. The first version is:

> 1. Our thoughts and perceptions are fundamentally *determined* by the semeiotic system in which we operate. 2. It is possible to specify the mechanics of that system.[6]

The second version is:

> 1. The subject, and the sense it makes of the world, is fundamentally *determined* by the universe of discourse in which it is embedded. 2. It is possible to specify the mechanics of that discourse and the procedures by which sense is produced, and the way in which the subject is imbedded in it.[7]

If one takes the term 'determined' in a strong sense and not merely as the equivalent of the weaker 'influenced,' then, Saunders persuasively argues, assumptions 1 and 2, in either version, are inconsistent. If the former is true, then the latter is false and vice versa. If the subject is wholly determined by its linguistic context, then it cannot explicate the mechanics of the way the context works. Any so-called explication could only be something just as fully in need of explication as the initial explicandum. Conversely, if the subject can give an explication which is genuinely distinct from the initial explicandum, then it is not wholly determined in its performances by its linguistic context, the initial explicandum.

More pertinent to my present concerns is Saunders' further claim that the widespread third assumption, namely that "political change is possible only where that mechanism is itself identified and changed" (230), is possible only if either assumption 1 or assumption 2 is false. If both assumptions 1 and 2 were true, there could be no intentional change, political or otherwise. That is, if assumption 2 were true, assumption 3 could also be true only if the outcomes of the mechanics of discourse and its procedures were *not* wholly determined by the universe of discourse whose mechanics are in question. If they were wholly determined, then the system would be absolutely closed and hence impervious to intentional change. For intentional change, if it is anything at all, is at least partially extrasystematic.

Saunders, however, is mistaken when he says that if we substituted 'influenced' for 'determined' in both of the first two assumptions we would reduce them to triviality. Much contemporary study of both individual and social human existence, whether by post-structuralists or others, has helpfully specified these influences and constraints. Just to know that human beings are not Cartesian egos is, of course, important. But it is no small matter to be able to go further, as these recent studies have made possible, to see the multiple ways in which we are subjected to constraints we cannot remove.

Saunders' mistake notwithstanding, his work and Taylor's each in its own way prods one to look for an interpretation of what it is to be human which is compatible with the possibility of deliberately initiated or fostered political change. The requisite interpretation, however, must not surreptitiously reintroduce a Cartesianesque self. I turn now to propose a candidate for this interpretation.

II

Though it is necessary to interpret the human condition as one which is not wholly determined by "extrinsic" forces if deliberately sought political change is to be possible, an interpretation that did no more than allow for change would be insufficient to provide the basis for distinguishing responsible from irresponsible political thought and action. A sufficiently comprehensive interpretation is one which also accounts for the persistent, apparently intractable tension between the individual and the social and/or communal dimensions of human existence. This tension subtends the more specific tensions among such matters as freedom, authority, and justice, however they are defined. Thus an acceptable interpretation of what it is to be human must construe this fundamental tension in such a way that it can make sense both of oppositions and conflicts on the one hand, and of convergences and cooperation on the other. And it must account for the irreducibility of this tension's polyvalency.

The interpretation that I propose of what it is to be human has its roots in the works of Heidegger and Merleau-Ponty. I concede that not everything that either of them says supports my account. This is particularly true of Heidegger, especially the post 1930 Heidegger.[8] Nonetheless, if there is merit in my account, it is owed largely to them.

To be human is always to be implicated in a world of things and other people. But it is to be implicated in this world in a specific way. To be human is to be in the world interrogatively.

To interrogate is to struggle, though not necessarily with hostility. This interrogatory struggle constitutes the human being as one who is always and essentially *en route*.[9]

In *Being and Time*, Heidegger repeatedly insists upon Dasein's implication in a world with others. Dasein's way of being is such that it can both be and understand itself as being assigned to a world of things with which it is unavoidably concerned (114–122). Among the worldly entities with which Dasein finds itself involved are other Daseins. This involvement with others is not something that Dasein, once already constituted, achieves or recognizes. For Being-with is an existential characteristic of Dasein even when no Other is present-at-hand or perceived. Even Dasein's Being-alone is Being-with in the world. The Other can *be missing* only *in* and *for* a Being-with. Being-alone is a deficient mode of Being-with (156–157). Thus, Being-with Others, in solicitude, is constitutive of Dasein's very way of being.

These involvements, which constitute Dasein, induce anxiety in it. This anxiety is anxiety precisely about Being-in-the-world itself. In anxiety Dasein finds itself as free, free for authenticity. Anxiety thus individualizes Dasein. But, in so doing, it does not isolate it. Rather, "what it does is precisely to bring Dasein face to face with its world as world, and thus bring it face to face with itself as Being-in-the-world" (233).

Heidegger's treatment of these themes in *The Basic Problems of Phenomenology* is, if anything, even more clear. Though there can be Nature even if there is no Dasein, world as that wherein things and people can appear and be understood can only be so long as Dasein exists. But because Being-in-the-world is constitutive of Dasein's way of being, Dasein can discover and understand itself only by way of its encounters with the world and its entities. Thus:

> Because as existents we already understand world beforehand we are able to understand and encounter ourselves constantly in a specific way by way of the beings which we encounter as intraworldly. . . . In understanding itself by way of *things*, the Dasein understands itself as being-in-the-world by way of its world (171).

As being-in-the-world Dasein is likewise being-with other Daseins. Dasein does not just discover among the things of its world some other Daseins. Instead, as the being which is occupied with itself, the Dasein is with equal originality being-with others *and* being-among intraworldly beings. The world, within which these latter beings are encountered, is . . . always already world which the one shares with the others (278, 297). Thus, equiprimordially existent Dasein is always and essentially being-with others as being-among intraworldly entities (278–279). Hence human freedom can in no wise consist in either establishing or maintaining independence either from things or from other people.

What deserves emphasis for present purposes is the irreducibility of the human way of being to that of intraworldly entities. They do not come to be what they are in the same way as things do. In whatever way they are effects or products, they are not such in the same way as intraworldly beings might be.

The political pertinence of Heidegger's Dasein analysis is enhanced by his "The Origin of the Work of Art." Politics, like art, requires both creators and preservers who are in turn made possible and constituted, as creators and preservers, by politics as they are by art (*Poetry, Language and Thought* esp. 62, 66–68, and 77–78). The creation and preservation of the political community, like that of the work of art, takes place in an enduring struggle in which the work, here the body politic, is continually wrestled from the earth upon which it must nonetheless always rest and back into which it always is in danger of collapsing (*Poetry, Language and Thought* esp. 46–50, 63–64, and 68–70). The political domain, like that of art, is always possible but also always historical and precarious. It is possible only because there are people and equiprimordially people are what and as they are because politics, like art, is possible.

Heidegger's Dasein analyses can be fruitfully linked to Merleau-Ponty's interpretation of the human way of being as fundamentally interrogative. This interrogation is not directed toward a world to which the interrogator is irrelevant. Rather interrogating, and hence the human way of being itself, responds to a world which does not merely confront us but which elicits our questioning.

Interrogation, Merleau-Ponty says, presupposes nothing more than an indubitable encounter between "us" and "what is." Without this encounter we could not ask questions. This inaugural encounter requires interpretation both of the "us" and of the "what is." At the start we must interpret this encounter neither as an inclusion of what is in us nor as an inclusion of us in what is.

From the outset we address ourselves to our experience because every question is addressed to someone or something and we can choose no interlocutor less compromising than *the whole of what is for us*. But the choice of this instance does not close the field of possible responses; we are not implicating in *"our experience"* any reference to an *ego* or to a certain type of intellectual relations with being, such as the Spinozist "experiri." We are interrogating our experience precisely in order to know how it opens us to what is not ourselves. *This does not even exclude the possibility that we find in our experience a movement toward what could not in any event be present to us in the original and whose irremediable absence would thus count among our originating experiences.* . . . We situate ourselves in ourselves *and* in the things, in ourselves *and* in the other, at the point where, by a sort of *chiasm*, we become the others and we become world (104, 159–160).

This inaugural encounter between "us" and "what is" is not the encounter between "probers" and "the inert." What we encounter is no naked thing, but rather the thing *ready* to be encountered. We interrogate it, Merleau-Ponty says, "according to its own wishes" (120, 124, 133).

The chiasm, the intertwining, of which Merleau-Ponty speaks, does not merge either me with the rest of humanity or humanity with things. But it holds us together in such a way that neither we nor things can either be nor be thought except as intertwined. It is as intertwined that both people and things both have their distinctiveness and affect one another.

If the human way of being is fundamentally interrogative, and if human interrogation is essentially responsive to a world which in effect asks to be interrogated in certain ways (perceptually, imaginatively, memorially, cognitively, in productive enterprises, etc.), then both we and the world interplay in a domain of openness. But this openness is not without bounds, even if the bounds cannot be named.

If my interrogation is indeed a response, it cannot be wholly determined in advance by that to which it answers. But neither can it ignore what calls it forth. What calls forth my response today includes not merely things ready for interrogation but also previous responses both of my own and of other people.

Thus when I think or act I am responding to a world already bearing the mark of prior human questioning. There is neither a distinguishable first call issued by something showing no trace of the human nor a first response wholly innocent of antecedents.

Pressing these leads provided by Heidegger and Merleau-Ponty, I propose that we interpret the human way of being as that of being *en route*. This interpretation gives perhaps more emphasis to the distinctiveness of each person as initiating doer than either Heidegger or the later Merleau-Ponty explicitly does. But given the difference between their rhetorical situation, namely a situation in which Cartesianism is not yet overthrown, and ours, instructed as it is both by them and by post-structuralist work, I believe that my proposal is consonant with their positions.

In *The Human Condition*, Hannah Arendt makes two points concerning human action which, taken together, epitomize the interpretation that I offer. She says, first:

> Because the actor always moves among and in relation to other acting beings, he is never merely 'doer' but always and at the same time a sufferer. To do and to suffer are like opposite sides of the same coin, and the story that an act starts is composed of its consequent deeds and sufferings. . . . Since action acts upon beings who are capable of their own actions, reaction, apart from being a response, is always a new action that strikes out on its own and affects others (169).

Second, she links action and the unpredictability of its outcome with the doer's self-disclosure. She says:

> This unpredictability of outcome is closely related to the revelatory character of action and speech, in which one discloses one's self without ever either knowing himself

or being able to calculate beforehand whom he reveals. . . . This unchangeable identity of the person, though
disclosing itself intangibly in act and speech, becomes
tangible only in the story of the actor's and speaker's life
(171–172).

But whereas Arendt distinguishes both thought or contemplation and labor from this account of action, my proposal takes
what she says about action to hold good for all aspects of the
human way of being.[10]

All the performances of those who are *en route*—percep-
tual, imaginative, cognitive, volitional, etc.—are nondefinitive.
They are essentially finite. But to say that they are finite is not to
say that they are either immature or flawed. Nor is it to say that
they are finally futile. Rather, it is simply to acknowledge that
each of us is always involved with other people in a material
world not of our own devising. The context we inhabit always
presents itself as already articulated into other people and entities which are not human. All of these, and each of us in our own
ways, have their own specific weights or differentiated
"gravitational pulls." Each of these weights is reciprocally, but
not uniformly, correlated with the others.

To be *en route* is not, however, to have a clear cut destina-
tion which is fundamentally distinct either from oneself or from
one's context. There is no fixed anterior goal which one either
misses or hits or approximates. There is no *terminus ad quem*
whose achievement would eliminate one's routedness. On my
interpretation, the specific *telos* of the human way of being is to
persevere *willingly*, in both thought and deed, in one's essential
routedness.

Thus, to be *en route* is to find oneself always already linked
to a route which is there to be trod and tended. Without route,
there is no human way of being. Without people, there is no
route. A person fails to achieve his *telos* if he insists upon trying
to bring his routedness to an end. Even should there be some ul-
timate *terminus ad quem*, some heaven that comes after this life,
one who would insist that only such a well defined culmination
can give point to our path treading, would effectively deprecate
human existence. Deprecation of this sort is tantamount to

nihilism. It denies that human life as presently constituted is of *intrinsic* worth.[11]

To be *en route* is to walk a path, to be a path dweller (Dauenhauer, "Heidegger" 189–199). To walk a path is, of course, to follow it. But it is also to break it. Path walking both brings about something new and preserves something old. It is also to be sustained by the path. To be *en route* then is to struggle with and for the path.

This struggle with and for the path is, of course, a struggle in which each person is inextricably involved with other people. It manifests itself in the three-fold sorts of mediational performances people engage in, namely discursive, actional, and productive-destructive performances. And among these three types of performances, the discursive holds a certain pride of place because without discursive performances, actional and productive-destructive performances, if they would be possible at all, would be fundamentally opaque. And when actional or productive-destructive performances are discursively articulated, they acquire a durability they could not otherwise achieve.

To be a path dweller is not to be a Sisyphus, condemned to futile exertions. The world elicits our interventions. Thus, both they and time matter. It is through our interventions that both what the path is and what each of us is can come to be and to appear. Our interventions, however, whether they are innovative or preservative, are not necessarily "progressive." The metaphor of linear progression is inappropriate to the interpretation of the human way of being as being *en route*.

What Paul Ricoeur says of political experience is a special case of our fundamental experience of being *en route*. Political experience, he says,

> is never an acquired experience; both progression and regression are possible. The same pretensions, the same illusions, the same faults can be repeated at different moments of history. . . . History—as history of power—is uncertain. It is the collection of chances and perils, the possibility of gaining everything or losing everything (Ricoeur, "Tasks" 145).

But at the same time, each of us is the beneficiary of a specific heritage which, though we can corrupt it, we can also enhance to bequeath to our successors.

In plying our path(s) each of us is constantly confronted by the confluence of the settled and the open, the old and the new. This confluence constitutes the unique present which in effect interrogates us. In turn, it elicits from us an interrogating response. This double interrogation thus constitutes our basic encounter with the world and others. That encounter gives rise to our path treading, our play-struggle, in a world which both invites our interrogation and yet remains finally ungoverned by any of our particular interrogations and the control they tend to aim for.

We path dwellers are thus not coequal to the world. We reply to a path that the world itself plies. Willy-nilly, all human replying both springs from and interrogatively responds to the world and its path. This replying is in the service of the world plying its path. Whether we recognize it or not, tending the world on its path is the intelligible point of human performances of any sort.

To be human, then, is to be for the world. This does not mean that the world so dominates people that what they do is really its doing and not theirs. We can be for the world and serve it only if we remain its other. The world allows, at least for a time, its other to be genuinely other. In maintaining our otherness, we remain for the world. Our otherness from the world is finally for the world.[12]

This interpretation of the human way of being as being *en route* fully respects the achievements of recent critiques of the Cartesian subject. It acknowledges the ineluctable finitude, historicality, and intersubjectivity of human existence.[13] But it does so in such a way that it shows how it is that we can be and are responsible both to the world and to others. We are in some measure always responsible both for the way they are and the way we are. Our interrogatory response to our ongoing encounter with the world and others is never so tightly constrained that it is effectively their response which we merely enact. It is our response, one in which we pose a new question to them. But at the same time our question is responsive to a world which allows us to be and which furnishes both the stimulus and the resources with which we respond.

The interpretation of the human way of being as being *en route* has widespread consequences for thinking and practicing politics responsibly. Let me simply mention, in conclusion and without argumentation, just a few topics, central for politics, for which this interpretation has important implications. I do not, of course, mean that this interpretation solves specific political problems or mandates specific policies. Rather, it provides a crucial orientation for addressing political issues of all sorts, both conceptual and practical.

My proposal to interpret the human way of being as being *en route* provides a sound basis for considering ecological issues, for if we are to serve the world, we must preserve it. And we must preserve it as habitable for other preservers. My interpretation also shows how and why considerations of economics are always relevant to politics. Economics always depends in part upon available material resources. These resources are constitutive of the path available for treading. But inasmuch as economics is not merely a matter of available material resources but also always involves human endeavors, it is always in some important respects at the disposal of politics (Ricoeur, "Ethique" 1–11).

Further, my proposal accounts for why whatever we do has consequences which never perfectly match our intentions. All of our sayings and doings are interventions in a game which is already under way before we arrive on the scene and which will continue after we die. The path we have for treading both goes its own way and is fashioned in part by other treaders. And the effects of our own treading are never fully isolable from those of other treadings.

And finally, understanding the human way of being as being *en route* shows why it is impermissible and ultimately impossible either to seek at all times and in all respects to be independent and autonomous or, on the other hand, to surrender ourselves wholly and without reserve to that which is other than us. To be *en route* is to maintain oneself, in struggle, both as a unique individual and as one who belongs with and to the world and other people.

Responsibly lived, this struggle respects the historicality and finitude characteristic of everything human. As a path treader, when I struggle responsibly I struggle for myself against the stasis of self-satisfaction. I struggle against myself for the sake of being available to and for my fellows (Marcel 38–57). I struggle for others against their oppressors, always however struggling for all-encompassing reconciliation. I struggle against those who would coopt me lest I fail either to maintain my own distinctive treading or to do what I can to support others in their struggles. The struggle constitutive of the human way of being, then, is the struggle to abide as path dweller with other dwellers.

This interpretation provides underpinnings, and in some aspects, correctives for studies showing the ineliminability of certain tensions and struggles in social life. The struggle for autonomy or radical democracy against hegemony, for example, which Ernesto Laclau and Chantal Mouffe speak of unifying is not the struggle of the good, the diversifying, against the bad, the unifying. It is the always ambivalent and ambiguous struggle to preserve and elaborate a tension whose reduction, in either direction, would be destructive.

To be sure, I have not proven, in any strong sense, that we should interpret the human way of being as being *en route*. But the argumentation I have presented on its behalf and the light it sheds upon the perplexities of political thought and practice give one good reasons for adopting it. No competitor, so far as I can see, has comparably strong credentials.

NOTES

1. Calvin Schrag's comments on an earlier version of this essay were most helpful.

2. A case can be made for also mentioning Hegel and Marx in this context. But this is not the place to make it.

3. The interpretation I propose, though developed independently, fits well with the interpretations of the 'I' in evidence in Robert

Sokolowski's *Moral Action* (Bloomington: Indiana University Press, 1985), esp. 156–174. See in this connection my "The Ego Revisited," *Journal of the British Society for Phenomenology* 21 January (1990): 48–52.

4. I do not suggest that these writers all share a common position. Nor do I suggest that I have done justice to the complex thought of any one of them. I make no claim to contribute here to the scholarly discussion of any of their works taken as a whole. Rather, I want to assess a widespread contemporary view in support of which these writers have regularly been invoked.

5. There is some evidence that Foucault was not wholly hostile to a constituting subjectivity in his last works. But exactly what he pointed to, as Hubert L. Dreyfus and Paul Rabinow show, is by no means clear. See their "Conclusion" and Foucault's "Afterword" in their *Michel Foucault* (Chicago: University of Chicago Press, 1982) 205–226.

6. Ian Saunders, "The Concept Discourse," *Textual Practice*, 2, 1988, 230. My emphasis. Hereafter cited as FCR.

7. *CD*, 231. My emphasis.

8. An excellent source for the contemporary status of criticism concerning Heidegger's views on what it is to be human is the set of papers of the 1989 Spindel Conference published in *The Southern Journal of Philosophy* 28, Supplement.

9. Conversations with Fred Dallmayr have helped me to clarify my account of the human. Whatever flaws remain are, of course, wholly mine.

10. Calvin Schrag's reply to my critique of his *Communicative Praxis* at the October 1989 meeting of the Society for Phenomenology and Existential Philosophy shows that there is substantial agreement between us about what it is to be human. See *Communicative Praxis* (Bloomington: Indiana University Press, 1986), esp. Parts 1 and 2.

11. I acknowledge a tension here between my position and that of some versions of religious thought which speak of our destiny to an afterlife. Though I do not think my position is incompatible with one which looks to an afterlife, it does conflict with any view which permits slighting this life for the sake of an afterlife.

12. I have developed in more detail the interpretation of the human way of being as being *en route* and the political consequences thereof in my *The Politics of Hope* (New York and London: Routledge & Kegan Paul, 1986).

13. For more detailed discussion of these characteristics of human existence see my "Relational Freedom" in this volume.

The Potential Self

Self-Questioning: An Afterword

Bernard P. Dauenhauer

What is it to be a self? To be a human being? Will we ever finish with these questions? As numerous recent studies, including those in this volume, indicate, the answer is probably no. And from what these studies bring to light, that is probably a good thing. Perhaps really good questions, like these, have no definitive answers. Nonetheless the answers they provoke give one good reason to think that taking them up again and again will reward those patient enough to do so.[1]

This Afterword, then, is not a closing word. It is only another word awaiting its own sequel. In it I want to make just a few remarks that amount to a call for more detailed reflection. These remarks touch upon two topics that are epistemically tied to one another. They are: (a) temporality and (b) bodiliness, especially human bodiliness. What we know of temporality we know in large measure, if not wholly, only by way of attending to bodies. And we make sense of bodiliness only by way of attending to the temporality of bodies.

If one were to believe Descartes, there would be no complexity about either time or bodiliness. Time would consist exclusively of discrete instants, each self contained and fundamentally unrelated to any other instants.[2] Bodies would be not only distinct from but also separable from minds (egos). Each would have its own temporality composed of discrete nows. And in principle, what transpired in one sequence would be both in fact as well as in thought independent of what transpired in the other.

Our experience, though, of what it is to be bodily and to be temporal through and through gives us scant encouragement to endorse these features of Cartesianism. We do, it is true, find strong reason to acknowledge two distinct orders of causality. There is the order of physical causality. Thus, she turned 180° from me, took ten steps, and placed her lips against John's, as a consequence of which my heart rate increased 10%. And there is the order of social or human causality. She abandoned me for John, and, kissing him, filled me with anger (Atom, 209).

But if we are attentive to our experience of being implicated in these two orders of causality, we find that the Cartesian conceptions of both time and bodiliness are wanting. They both badly oversimplify matters.

Consider first the matter of time. Reflecting on the two orders of causality that we inhabit, we find that each of us is inextricably geared into three irreducibly distinct, though inseparable, modes of temporality. Indeed, I would say that a sufficient condition for x to be a self, a person, is that it inhabit all three of these modes. Whether this is also a necessary condition for being a self is an issue that I will return to shortly but will not pretend to settle.

These three modes of temporality are (a) one's "own-time," (b) social time, and (c) cosmic time. My own-time is the time in which I deliberate and choose, I evaluate what I have done or suffered, and make plans for what I will try to do in the future. It is the time, as Heidegger has stressed, that is always under the mark of my death that is to bring it to a close. It is the time in which I experience my own unattenuated individuality.[3] (Heidegger 231–235 and 299–304). Each of us normal adults experiences his or her own-time as unique. Social time is the time in which I find the sayings and doings of human beings, including my own, prompting rejoinders that interrogate their propriety. This is the time in which we receive our cultural heritage as a heritage and pass it along to others, modified now by the peculiar ways we have made it our own. Social time is thus the time of gaining and losing, of loving and hating, of building and destroying. Cosmic time is the time of sun and moon phases, of locomotion, of blossoming and fading, of all living things' coming to be and passing away. It is the time for which the distinction between what is alive and what is not is irrelevant.

These three modes of time, our experience tells us, all bear in some fashion upon every facet of our waking lives, including our wakeful sense of what it is to sleep and dream. One reason that this is so is that each of these modes has its own sort of past and future as well as present. And I am implicated in all of them. My own-time is a time in which I always figure. Its span is my span. Social and cosmic times, though, are times that I know both antedate me and will outlast me. Even their presents are presents that could do without me. They are times from which I am in principle always expendable. Cosmic time is a time that outstrips not only me but all selves. It outstrips social time as well as my own-time. Indeed, it outstrips the time of any life at all.

Each of these modes of time has its own pace. And both my own-time and social time have their own rhythms. My own-time passes sometimes slowly and sometimes rapidly. And it is rhythmically marked at least as much by starts and stops as it is by stretches of ongoingness. The pace and rhythm of social time are rarely if ever all of a piece. For social time is a time, on the one hand, of surprises and disappointments that come in a frequency and order that is never settled. And yet, on the other hand, it is the time of a relatively stable cultural milieu upon whose regularity people count in living their lives together. In fact, this stable cultural milieu is the precondition for the recognition and assessment of the surprising and the disappointing. Cosmic time, like Ol' Man River, just keeps rolling along inexorably, to all appearances headed nowhere.

The trimodal temporality that we inhabit gives an anxious urgency to each of our lives. If my life is to matter, it must do so before impending death brings it to an end. If I am to find recognition, I must struggle for it, and now before it is too late. But my struggle to matter and to gain recognition is waged in the face of a cosmic time that shows no interest in human existence of any sort, much less in my own individual existence.

It is not too much to suggest that a fundamental task for human beings is to determine how to deal appropriately, in concept and deed, with their trimodal temporality. How one deals with these three modes amounts to making an interpretation of what it is to be a self. It amounts to an interpretation of the meaning and significance of many of the attributes we regularly ascribe to one another, such as rights-and-duties-bearer, freedom, and autonomy. Whichever mode of time one gives priority to will modify the significance of all of these attributes and others like them. For example, do I have to try to keep the world habitable for future generations? If so, why? If not, why not?

There is probably no single unequivocally proper interpretation of how one should deal with this trimodality of time that we inhabit. But it is likely that wholly to ignore the claims of any one of them is either folly or knavery. To think well and to act well is to respect in some way the claims made and the opportunities afforded by all three of these modes.

Perhaps every appropriate way of living out the trimodality of our time is akin to a successful jazz improvisation. None of them calls for repetition but each of them respects the complexity of the musical soil that made it possible.[4]

But if experiencing time in its full trimodality is sure evidence that the one experiencing it is a full-fledged self or person, what is to be said of those human entities who do not so experience it? Are such human entities not selves?

Consider the following groups of human entities: normal human embryos, normal newborn babies, lifelong severely mentally disabled adults, and the terminally comatose or brain-dead.[5] By hypothesis, no member of any of these groups can give us an account of the temporality he or she experiences. All we can know of their involvement in time's trimodality we know by observing their bodies and comparing these observations with our experience of our own bodiliness.

For those of us who are normal adults, the experience of our bodiliness is not like that described by Descartes. Rather, we experience our bodily being in an irreducibly double way. On the one hand, I experience my bodiliness as ingredient in the agency of which I am capable. Thus, I can walk, I can talk, I can embrace you. I do not do these things with my body as a mere instrument. I do them by virtue of being bodily. On the other hand, my body is that from which a mole can be removed or into which a kidney can be transplanted without my suffering a change in my selfhood. My bodiliness then is such that it is irreducibly both agent and patient, in both orders of causality, physical and social.[6]

But what about those human entities that are not or are not yet normal adults? How do they experience their bodiliness? So far as we can tell from the contact we have with them, whatever experience they have of time and bodiliness is quite different from our own. Nonetheless, we make sense of them at least partially in terms of the closeness or distance we find between what we can experience and what we find reason to believe that they can.

The terminally comatose show no sign of either physical or social agency. Though they once were agents they are not and will never be agents again. Their bodiliness is the bodiliness of patiency alone. Similarly, though we normal ones locate them in cosmic time, and by our concern or attention, give them a place in social time, they themselves apparently take no notice of either of these modes of time. And we can only acknowledge that, whatever experience they may have had of their own-time, they will never have it again.

The severely mentally impaired are not merely patients of physical or social causality. They can also be agents of both sorts. Their social agency has a narrower range than that of normal adults. But their range is not negligible. Similarly, there is no good reason to deny that they inhabit all three temporal modes. But here again, the evidence we have indicates that their sense of these modes is vague or distorted in comparison with our own. And we do not set much store by whatever interpretations they give about how to integrate these three modes. Further, and of considerable importance, we have no reason to think that the severely mentally impaired's experience of either time or bodiliness will ever become more like our own adult experience of them.

Normal newborn babies exercise some minimal physical agency. But it is much harder to ascribe any social agency to them, especially when they are genuinely newborn. To talk about the wants or aims of the newborn seems exaggerated. Of course, like all human entities they can be patients of social as well as physical causality. And though it is not unlikely that newborns have some sense of time, we would be hard pressed to justify the claim that they inhabit time trimodally. We place them in social and cosmic time. And perhaps they have some recognition of their mothers as other than they. But we have scant basis for attributing an own-time to them. Crucially, though, we know enough about the world to recognize that these normal newborns are on their way to having just as nuanced an experience of time and bodiliness as we do. They now already have what is necessary to come to fully adult experience.

Normal human embryos, so far as we know, show no awareness of time at all. Their physical agency, to the extent that it exists at all, has less scope than that of newborns. And they show no recognition of their mothers as other than they. But again, a crucial feature of normal embryos is that they are on the way to become normal newborns. Thus, in an already predelineated future of cosmic time, they are likely to become normal adults with experiences of time and bodiliness just like ours.

These far from fully developed remarks are surely insufficient to support very strong conclusions. Nonetheless, they permit a few observations of some interest. These remarks in effect raise the following question: If simple membership in the class of genetically complete human entities is insufficient to establish that the member is a self or person, then what further criteria are appropriate for making that determination?

If the experience of time and/or bodiliness is relevant to this determination, then the differences among the four groups of human entities that are not normal adults become significant. On these grounds, normal human embryos appear to be at least as good candidates for selfhood than either the severely mentally impaired or the terminally comatose are. But if the experience of time or bodiliness is either irrelevant or insufficient to determine the matter of selfhood, then what other considerations should one bring into play?

I need not, I am sure, belabor the bearing of these observations on such thorny issues as abortion, euthanasia, and the distribution of medical care as well as upon the central question: What is it to be a self? Even if there are no knockdown arguments to answer this question, entertaining it does not go unrewarded.[7]

NOTES

1. See in this connection, Charles Taylor, "Atomism," in his *Philosophy and the Human Sciences* (Cambridge: Cambridge University Press, 1985), 204. Hereafter, Atom.

2. On the punctiliar character of Cartesian time, see Jean Wahl's brief but masterly *Du Role de l'Idée de l'Instant dans la Philosophie de Descartes* (Paris: Librairie Felix Alcan, 1920) esp. 5 and 25–30.

3. See Martin Heidegger, *Being and Time,* tr. John Macquarrie & Edward Robinson (New York: Harper & Row, 1962), esp. 231–235, 299–304.

4. See Atom, 204–208. See also Paul Ricoeur's fine treatment of the connection between human time and cosmic time in his *Time and Narrative,* tr. Kathleen Blamey and David Pellauer (Chicago University Press, 1984–1988), esp. I, 5–30; II, 104–126.

5. Here I want to single out as lifelong severely mentally disabled adults those who can engage in only rudimentary communication and who, though they are mobile, capable of feeding themselves, etc., cannot provide for their own physical needs. For present purposes, there is no need to give rigorous specification to this group.

6. See in this connection Paul Ricoeur, *Soi-même comme un autre* (Paris: Éditions du Seuil, 1990) 68–72. [Editor's note: *Oneself as Another,* tr. Kathleen Blamey (Chicago: University of Chicago Press, 1992)]. I leave aside speculation about what would happen to selfhood in the event of brain transplants. I simply have no clue about what would be the outcome.

7. My colleague, Frank R. Harrison, raised the questions to which these remarks are a partial response. His questions deserve a much fuller response than I can give.

PART FOUR

Self and/as Other

The Caring Self

Autonomy, Integrity, and Care

Victoria Davion

I. Introduction

In *In a Different Voice*, moral psychologist Carol Gilligan claims to
have discovered a distinctive approach to moral deliberation
which she refers to as the care perspective. The care perspective
in ethics involves seeing oneself as connected to others within a
web of various relationships. Rather than seeing moral problems
as conflicts of rights to be solved by ranking values, moral problems are seen as embedded in a contextual framework of others.
Moral deliberation from within the care perspective aims to
maintain these relations. "From within the care perspective, the
relationship becomes the figure, defining self and others. Within
the context of the relationship, the self as a moral agent perceives
and responds to the perception of need. The shift in moral perspective is manifested by a shift in the moral question, from
'What is just?' to 'How do I respond?'"[1]

The care perspective in ethics can be contrasted with a
more traditional rights-based approach. Adherents of rights-
based ethics include John Locke, Immanual Kant, and John
Rawls. One central feature of this tradition is the importance of
personal liberty. Each individual is seen as having certain basic
rights, such as the right to life, liberty, and property. The self is
seen as an autonomous individual, free to make choices that do
not infringe upon the basic right of others. "From a justice perspective, the self as a moral agent stands as the figure against a

ground of social relationships, judging the conflicting claims of others against a standard of equality or equal respect" (Gilligan, "Moral Orientation" 23).

I will not address questions concerning the accuracy of Gilligan's research. Rather, my discussion will focus on philosopher Nel Noddings' attempt to develop the care perspective into a fully developed ethical theory to serve as an alternative to ethics that treat justice as a basic concept and as an alternative to an ethic of principle (*Caring*). On Noddings' analysis, caring requires actual encounters with actual individuals. One's ethical responsibility is to meet others as one-caring. For Noddings, caring is more than simply being concerned about others. It has three elements: (1) motivational engrossment and displacement in another, (2) feeling with the other, and (3) actual care-taking. Noddings tells us to "always meet the other as one caring" and to "maintain caring relations."

In this paper I will focus on Noddings' first component of caring, motivational displacement and engrossment in another. According to Noddings, when one becomes engrossed in another, one suspends evaluation of the other and is transformed by the other. In motivational displacement, one allows the other's goals to become one's own. I will show that both of these involve a significant moral risk. If someone is evil, and one allows oneself to be transformed by that person, one risks becoming evil oneself. If the other's goals are immoral, and one makes those goals one's own, one becomes responsible for supporting immoral goals. This raises the issue of whether one can be in a caring relationship with someone who has immoral goals, while avoiding moral responsibility for promoting those goals. I will argue that in caring, one must nurture the other, and in doing this, one supports the other's goals in various ways. I will argue that because caring, as described by Noddings, involves supporting another's goals, the choice of with whom to enter a caring relationship, and choices about whether to continue a caring relationship, become significant moral issues. Therefore, we should not always meet the other as one-caring, and we can not always maintain caring relations. We must *evaluate* potential and ongoing relationships.

I will show that the evaluation of caring relationships requires knowledge of values more basic than care, because for any caring relationship to be morally good, it must not require parties to violate deeply held convictions in order to be in it. Each must be able to maintain moral integrity. Caring itself can not be the most basic value in such an ethic. Therefore, I will argue that other values must be more basic than care, otherwise there is no basis for the evaluation of caring relationships.

In arguing that one must be able to maintain deeply held convictions in order for a caring relationship to be morally good, I do not mean to preclude the possibility that one could change one's deeply held convictions, but this raises interesting issues concerning self-deception. It is one thing to change deeply held convictions because one is honestly convinced they were misguided, and another to change merely to enter or maintain a caring relationship with someone.

Two related difficulties will be discussed in this paper: (1) We cannot expect to agree with all of a person's projects. To what extent is agreement necessary? (2) To what extent does the suggestion that at least some agreement regarding moral convictions is necessary fuel for prejudice by implying that we should avoid caring relationships with people different from ourselves? This is especially significant given the importance of respecting cultural differences in fighting against prejudices such as racism, xenophobia, homophobia, and so forth. I will argue that my suggestion neither implies that we should avoid people different from ourselves, nor encourages the making of unreflective judgments without considering such things as cultural differences. However, if after spending the time necessary to understand another person's values and projects, one finds such values and projects reprehensible, if one cannot see oneself supporting those values even indirectly, other things being equal, one should avoid a caring relationship with that person. Not to do this would be to sacrifice one's moral integrity, given that entering into a caring relationship involves engrossment and motivational displacement. This does not mean that one should not help that person in various ways, but one should avoid becoming engrossed and/or motivationally displaced in that person. Finally, I will argue that the process of evaluating ongoing and potential caring relationships can be seen as an exercise in moral autonomy. Diana T. Meyers presents an account of moral autonomy as a competency that can be exercised by responsibility reasoning. She suggests that in responsibility reasoning, "the individual's moral sense gains expression through an exercise in imaginative introjection by asking what choices are compatible with or reinforce desirable aspects of one's personal identity".[2] I will show that the evaluation of caring relationships can be seen as an exercise of moral autonomy using Meyers' account. Thus, I will show that the evaluation of caring relationships involves the concepts of moral integrity and moral autonomy. Their place within a care ethic has been an important question in the literature on this topic.

II. Caring

Although my focus will be on two particular components of caring, motivational displacement and engrossment, I shall begin with a general sketch of Noddings' ethic as a whole. This will allow us to see the risks involved in motivational displacement and engrossment more clearly. In developing the care perspective into a full-blown ethical theory, Noddings attempts to offer an alternative to rule-based action-guiding ethical theories. The project of such theories is to generate universal moral rules, applicable to all moral agents in similar situations. These theories typically contend that there are objective facts in moral situations. Any moral agent can in principle "see" these facts. Once the facts are obtained, the theory provides a universal moral principle which tells the agent which actions are either permissible or obligatory in that particular situation. Because the facts are objective and available to all moral agents, and because the moral principles are universal, to be used by all moral agents, these theories prescribe the same actions for all moral agents in similar situations.

Noddings rejects these kinds of theories for important and interesting reasons. She claims that the idea of universality depends on an erroneous concept of sameness.

> In order to act on principle we must establish that human predicaments exhibit sufficient sameness, and this we cannot do without abstracting away from concrete situations those qualities that seem to reveal sameness. In doing this we often lose the very qualities or factors that give rise to the moral question in the situation.[3]

Thus, while these theories may tell us that agents should behave the same way in similar situations, all things being equal, other things rarely, if ever, are equal.

The alternative offered by Noddings is an attempt to ground morality in the understanding of individual others with whom one interacts. Rather than seeking similarities between moral agents, this theory attends to differences. Before one can act morally in relation to another, one must attempt to understand the other's reality. This understanding is more than gaining an objective understanding of the facts. It involves attempting to see the other's reality as one's own. Only then can one act as one-caring towards another. Hence, for Noddings, morality is grounded in the experience of caring, to act as one-caring is the ethical ideal. She states "One must meet the other as one-caring. From this requirement there is no escape for one who would be moral" (*Caring* 201).

Noddings grounds her ethic in a relational ontology. Because human beings are constructed out of our relations with others, we must, in order to survive, remain in relation. She states: ". . . 'we' are the products of relation, not mere constituent parts."[4] The fact that the self is a product of relation is a central aspect of this ethic, and one which leads to many of the problems I shall discuss.

III. Some Problems with Caring

In this section I shall review some important criticisms of Noddings' ethic. My purpose in reviewing these is twofold: (1) I want to place my concerns and recommendations in the context of other discussions concerning Noddings, and (2) I hope to show that my suggestions for improvement speak not to my own difficulties, but address these other concerns as well.

Noddings has been widely criticized for her position regarding the termination of caring relationships. For Noddings, the ethical ideal is to act as one-caring by meeting others as one caring and maintaining caring relationships. Whenever one can not do this, one acts under a diminished ethical ideal. One may terminate a caring relationship when it threatens to prevent one's ability to act as one-caring towards others with whom one is also in caring relationships, but this seems to be the only justification for doing so. She states that although there are situations when there are no alternatives other than to cease caring, when one does this, one acts under a diminished ethical ideal. Thus:

> The perceived lack of alternative induces minimal ethical functioning under the diminished ideal. The ethical agent accepts responsibility; it is she who is, personally, committed to caring ... When the one-caring is driven to the point where she perceives only one solution, and that in opposition to the enhanced ideal, she is badly shaken and, in extreme cases, broken. For while she must still say, "it is I performing this act," it is clearly not the "I" she would have chosen. There can be no greater evil, then, than this: that the moral autonomy of the one-caring be so shattered that she acts against her own commitment to care (*Caring* 115).

And:

> When one intentionally rejects the impulse to care and deliberately turns her back on the ethical she is evil, and this evil can not be redeemed (*Caring* 114).

Thus, although someone may be justified in terminating a caring relationship, she still participates in evil and acts under a diminished ethical ideal. Several critics have argued this is a major flaw in Noddings' account. If one is justified in terminating the relationship, if one needs to do this in order to maintain oneself as one-caring, then surely one is not acting under a diminished ethical ideal. By doing the right thing one acts in accord with the ethical ideal; one does not somehow diminish it. In addition, some have argued that Noddings fails to value the one-caring sufficiently. Her discussion of when it is morally permissible to leave a caring relationship focuses on one's ability to continue caring for others. In discussing the case of a wife who kills her husband after many years of abuse she cites the diminishment of the children's ethical ideals and their increasing fear and pain, as reasons for the woman to act. "Assuming that her receptivity was adequate and that her motivational displacement was directed towards the needs of her children, she acted as one-caring but under a diminished ethical ideal" (*Caring* 114). Critics have argued that someone is also justified in ending a caring relationship for the sake of his or her own well-being and not only out of concern for others. This possibility is not even mentioned by Noddings.

IV. Caring and Moral Risk

I now turn to the two aspects of caring as described by Noddings that I wish to focus upon, motivational displacement and engrossment. Using the mother-child relationship as a paradigm she states:

> My motive energy flows toward the other and perhaps, although not necessarily, toward his ends. I do not relinquish myself; I cannot excuse myself for what I do. But I allow my motive energy to be shared; I put it into the service of the other. . . . When this displacement occurs in the extreme form, we sometimes hear parents speak of "living for" their children.
>
> In such a mode we receive what is there as nearly as possible without evaluation or assessment. We are in a world of relation, having stepped out of the instrumental world; we have either not yet established goals or we have suspended those we have established. We are not attempting to transform the world but we are allowing ourselves to be transformed (*Caring* 34).

Noddings claims that there is reciprocity in a caring relationship. However, although she speaks of reciprocity, she states:

> It is important to re-emphasize that this capacity is not contractual; that is, it is not characterized by mutuality. The cared-for contributes to the caring relation, as we have seen, by receiving the efforts of one-caring, and this receiving may be accomplished by a disclosure of his own sub-

jective experience in direct response to the one caring or
by a happy and vigorous pursuit of his own projects
(*Caring* 151).

Sarah Hoagland has objected that this model is unidirectional so
that one person in a relationship can always be the one-caring
and the other the cared-for.[5] In the case of mothering a small
child, this seems fine. A small child cannot understand the projects of the mother and is not really in a position to help her try
to pursue them. However, in adult relationships, or relationships
between equals, something is wrong where one person does all
the care-taking and the other receives all the care.

Reciprocity doesn't mean we play the same roles at the
same time, or even that we are cared-for and one-caring exactly
one half of the time. It means we are equally prepared to be
ones-caring when it is necessary; that neither of us expects to be
cared for all of the time. In what follows I will assume that Noddings is right in claiming that caring involves engrossment and
motivational displacement, although I want to insist that between adults, other things being equal, for an ongoing caring relationship to be morally good, it must involve equal commitments on behalf of all parties to be the one-caring when this is at
all possible.

The fact that the role of care-giver involves engrossment
and motivational displacement, and the fact that reciprocity demands that one be willing to provide care for those who care for
one, means that one's choice of caring relationships is an ethical
matter. To see this, one need only look again at what is involved
in engrossment and motivational displacement. When one is engrossed in another one receives what is there as fully as one can
without judging what one sees. One is not trying to transform
what is there but to let what is there transform oneself. In doing
this, if one becomes engrossed in someone who is morally corrupt, one risks being transformed into someone morally corrupt
oneself. One risks character damage. To avoid this one must be
critical *before* becoming engrossed. Becoming engrossed appears
to involve a certain loss of control, and before one abdicates this
control to another one has an obligation to be sure that the
changes in oneself will be changes one can support.

Engrossment leads to motivational displacement in which the other's goals become one's own. One's motive energy flows towards their ends. Again, a moral risk is involved, depending on what the cared-for's ends are. Here the issue is highly complex. In caring for others one sustains them, providing them with energy to pursue their own projects. Even when one does not pursue their projects directly, one may contribute to the cared-for's ability to do so. A closer look at Noddings' model reveals this.

According to Noddings, caring involves putting one's motive energy into the service of another. This may involve directly working to promote the cared-for's goals. However, even in situations where one does not directly pursue the cared-for's projects, one may indirectly support them by nurturing the cared-for. In caring for someone, one may provide a generally nurturing atmosphere from which the cared-for gains energy to pursue his or her goals. If the cared-for gets strength from the care-giver and uses it to support the Ku Klux Klan, and if the care-giver knows this is what is happening and continues to provide support, the care-giver is supporting the Ku Klux Klan, even if the care-giver regrets this. Thus, if one has dinner on the table every Thursday night at six o'clock sharp so that the other can get to the Klan meeting on time, one is indirectly supporting the activities of the Klan. In entering caring relationships one promotes the goals of the cared-for in various ways, even if this is not directly intended.

Obviously one is causally responsible for promoting the goals of the other in the situation described above. However, this does not yet settle the issue of moral responsibility. Noddings explicitly states that the care-giver can not excuse himself or herself for what he or she does in the service of the ends of the cared-for. In cases where nurturing involves directly promoting the goals of the other by attending political meetings for example, the question of moral responsibility is clear. One is morally responsible for one's choices. However, in cases where the promotion is indirect, questions of moral responsibility are more complex.

A look at Aristotle's analysis of moral responsibility is instructive here. According to Aristotle, one is morally responsible for actions which are (1) not done under compulsion, (2) done with knowledge of the circumstances, and (3) chosen. One is not morally responsible for actions done out of ignorance, or where the moving force is wholly outside the agent.[6]

Using Aristotle's framework, we can examine individual cases. Within the context of a caring relationship, it is possible that the care-giver does not know what the cared-for is doing with all the positive energy gotten out of the relationship, or does not know that the cared-for needs dinner at six-thirty sharp in order to make it to a Klan meeting. In these cases, ignorance is involved, and so perhaps the care-giver is not morally responsible for promoting Klan activities. It is unclear whether these examples reflect true caring relationships as described by Noddings. In order for a caring relationship to be intimate, knowledge of the other's personal commitments is needed. However, relationships vary in degrees of intimacy. It is possible that one could make sure to have dinner on the table for a casual acquaintance at exactly six-thirty without knowing why she needs to leave by seven-thirty. In such a case, the care-giver would not be responsible for promoting the goals of the cared-for.

The interesting and more complex cases involve situations where the care-giver knows that her activities are helping the cared-for promote certain goals, but the care-giver does not believe in those goals. In such cases, the question of the care-giver's moral responsibility for promoting something wrong arises. We can not simply assume moral responsibility here. The care-giver may be coerced into the service of the cared-for by the threat of physical violence. Domestic abuse cases are good examples. If the care-giver is acting out of the fear of battery, for example, she may not be morally responsible for her assistance. In such cases, I question whether these are genuine caring relationships rather than simple acts of self-preservation.

There are, however, cases where the care-giver is clearly morally responsible for supporting the goals of the cared-for, even when this support is only indirect. Suppose the care-giver is aware that the gun she is purchasing is to be used in Klan activities, and assume her choice to buy the gun is not made under coercive conditions. Her purpose in buying the gun is not to support the Klan, but to support a loved-one who has asked her to run this errand. In this case, she is morally responsible for providing the gun, and morally responsible for what the gun is used for, though perhaps to a lesser degree than the person who actually fires it. The care-giver voluntarily purchases the gun, is not ignorant of what it will be used for, and is not coerced into this choice. Even though her purpose in buying the gun was to support a loved one, she is partly responsible for what the gun is used for because she knew what it was to be used for when she bought it.

I have not attempted to offer a full account of moral responsibility in cases of caring relationships. There are a wide range of possible cases I have not discussed. However, I hope to have shown that there are at least some cases where caring is problematic from the standpoint of the care-giver, and therefore, a discussion of moral responsibility in such situations must be central to any ethic of care. It is dangerous to "always meet the other as one-caring" and to "maintain caring relations." Critical evaluation *prior* to motivational displacement and engrossment is necessary for responsible action.

Noddings misses these aspects of moral responsibility because she denies the absolute value of anything other than caring. This is shown in the passages discussed earlier where she insists that there is unredeemable evil in ending a caring relationship, even when doing so is necessary for the health and well being of the one-caring. It is also shown in the following example. She describes the situation of a person whose relatives are racist and involved in a violent battle against people of color. This person genuinely believes that her relatives are wrong. Yet she loves them for their past kindnesses to her personally. She is also aquainted with Jim, described as a black man fighting on the other side, against racists, for his basic human rights. Noddings says of Ms. A:

> She saw clearly what she would do, would really do. I could not, she said, ever-not ever-oppose my bigoted old father or my hysterical Aunt Phoebe with physical violence. I do not agree with either. Aunt Phoebe! Imagine a person in this day and age who would actually say (and demonstrate her statement by fainting at the thought) "Ah would just die if a niggah touched me!" Oh, she is wrong

and my father is wrong. But there are years of personal kindness. They must count for something must they not? I know I could not fight on the other side. And what of the black man, Jim, who is after all "right"? If my sights picked him out, says Ms. A, I would note that it was Jim and move on to some other target (*Caring* 110).

I find this example disturbing for several reasons. Jim is after all "right." But why is Jim "right" instead of RIGHT? The quotation marks around the word "right" indicate that in the mind of the thinker perhaps others think it is right, but the word "right" has lost its original meaning for her. Thus, she can put her relationships with her father and aunt before the rights of people to be treated with minimal human dignity. What about the other target at whom she aims instead of Jim? This person is also "right," yet she is killing him or her in order to fight on the same side as racists.

Perhaps the most telling aspect in this example is that she feels she cannot fight on the other side. Why not? Why can't she fight on the other side and aim at another target if her sights happen to fall on either her father or her aunt? If she did this she would be fighting on the right side while still refusing to use violence against her father and aunt. I think it is significant that not only can she not bear to use violence against her father and her aunt, neither can she join the other side. Her inability to join the other side somehow stems from her caring for her father and aunt. The metaphor of standing with her father and aunt is important. When someone stands with someone else, or stands by someone else, they support those people. If she joins the other side this amounts to severing connections between herself and loved ones which she cannot bear to do. Therefore, she will stand with them in order to maintain certain ties, and will fight against what she really believes is right in order to do this. I think what she does is wrong. In "Caring and Evil," Claudia Card argues that because we cannot have caring relationships with most people in the world, we need other grounds for moral obligations towards them. In arguing that justice is necessary as well she states, "life can be worth living in the absence of caring from most people in the world, but in a densely populated world life is not apt to be worth living without justice from a great

many people, including many whom we will never know."[7]
Card is absolutely right about this. In fact, this point can be extended. Considerations of justice are necessary so that all decisions aren't made on the basis of whom one happens to care
most about at a given time. Ms. A has chosen with whom to fight
on the basis of loyalty to those she cares about. She has ignored
considerations of justice completely. This includes ignoring justice in the case of someone she knows, namely Jim, and those she
doesn't know, all the others fighting with Jim. The fact that she
will not shoot at Jim does not mean she treats him justly, as she
fails to fight for his basic human rights. With regard to the others
whom she has chosen to kill, she becomes a murderer fighting
for racism.

Noddings implies that Ms. A makes a morally acceptable
choice in the example discussed above. She argues that the idea
of someone willing to sacrifice loved ones for principles is frightening. I think she is right. However, it is also frightening to think
about someone who will stand by their loved ones no matter
what those people do. I find this kind of unconditional love
problematic as well. Some middle ground is needed. I believe
that in this case, the middle ground is to fight with the side one
believes in, but not to aim directly at one's father or aunt. This
doesn't involve sacrificing them, although it may involve sacrificing the relationship.

Although I believe Ms. A reached the wrong decision in
the dilemma stated above, I can also understand the emotional
trauma involved in risking personal relationships for a cause.
When loved ones take opposing sides in important moral struggles, relationships can be endangered. Thus, many will sacrifice
their beliefs and values to remain in caring relationships.

In the above example it is important that the people involved are family members. In some sense they didn't choose
each other. Families are a kind of given. Under normal circumstances a child will grow to love caring (and even uncaring)
adults well before she can judge their projects and commitments
for herself. She may then find herself in a situation where she
must choose between principles and loved ones. However, this
case is instructive as we think about forming new relationships.
Although we may find ourselves having to choose between prin-

ciples and loved ones, we can work to minimize this by finding people whose basic principles we can support. This is like an insurance policy against being in the kinds of situations described above. In doing this we can take responsibility for who we are becoming by taking responsibility for who we allow into our transformative process. In becoming involved with someone whose projects one can not support, one sets oneself up to become like Ms. A, betraying one's own beliefs. If one chooses this path one is responsible for having put oneself into a position where one can not bear to do the right thing. This is not simply a matter of fate; one has, in an important sense, chosen it. Thus, it is not totally a matter of what Thomas Nagel and Bernard Williams refer to as "moral luck".[8] We can maintain at least some control in decisions about with whom we become involved. This is another reason why I believe literature on caring should avoid focusing on mother-child relationships as paradigm instances of caring. These relationships involve moral luck in ways that many other relationships may not.

V. Autonomy and Integrity in Caring Relationships

How can a care ethic provide guidance in evaluating caring relationships? In order to answer this question I shall first examine what is missing in Noddings' account, and then attempt to enrich the account to take care of the problems I shall discuss. As I have already stated, I believe the central problem is a failure to recognize absolute value in anything other than caring. Noddings privileges the caring relation because of her relational ontology: According to Noddings, we must maintain connections in order to survive. We do not *have* connections, we *are* connections. We naturally desire to care for others as a survival mechanism. Hence, Noddings, like Aristotle and many others, attempts to ground her ethic in an account of the type of beings humans are.

There are many problems in attempting such a project. I will focus on two. The first concerns the jump from the idea that maintaining caring relationships is necessary for human survival to the idea that all caring relationships are good. Even if Noddings' relational ontology is correct, it does not follow that all caring relations are good. One can consistently hold that caring is necessary for human survival, and distinguish between morally desirable and morally undesirable instances of caring.

The second problem concerns the valuing of relationship more than the individuals who are relating. Sarah Hoagland points out that one can not have a relation without having at least two beings to relate. Even if one is the product of one's relations, in making decisions about continuing caring relationships and about forming new ones, one acts out of a sense of oneself as a being separate from others. According to Hoagland:

> Relation is central to ethics. However, there must be two beings, at least, to relate. Moving away from oneself is one aspect of the dynamic of caring, but it cannot be the only defining element. Otherwise, relationship is not ontologically basic, and the self ceases to exist in its own ethical right (Hoagland, 111).

Thus:

> One who cares must perceive herself not just as both separate and related, but as ethically both separate and related. Otherwise, she can not acknowledge difference (Hoagland, 111).

Hoagland is correct. Furthermore, if one can not acknowledge difference, one can not evaluate the projects of others *as* the projects of others, in order to make a responsible decision as to whether to promote those projects oneself.

I believe what is missing from Noddings' account is an account of the individuals within caring relations as important in themselves. This is reflected by the fact that the ethical ideal is to be one-caring and to maintain caring relations. What is needed is an enrichment of the ethical ideal to reflect not only the positive aspects of the self as one-caring, but also the self as a being with other important ethical commitments that make up its moral identity. One major problem in the example discussing Ms. A and Jim is that Ms. A must suffer a loss of moral integrity in order to maintain her relationships with her aunt and father. She must turn against important values which are part of her ethical ideal, her image of her best self. This indicates that there is more to her ethical ideal than merely maintaining certain relationships. Our account of the ethical ideal must be sensitive to this.

In order to enrich an account of the ethical ideal we need an account of moral integrity, a vision of a best self including more than an image of oneself as one-caring. Elsewhere I have argued that in order to have moral integrity, one must have at least one unconditional commitment.[9] This is the commitment to keep track of oneself, not to betray oneself. I argued that this kind of unconditional commitment, while highly abstract, doesn't imply a lack of attention to context. It requires that in each situation one pay careful attention to what one is doing and who one is becoming in doing it. It embraces the idea that we are dynamic beings, constantly growing and changing, but insists that we keep track of these changes rather than letting them happen randomly. Thus, monitoring who one allows into one's transformative process is essential in maintaining moral integrity. Seeing oneself as a being with moral integrity is part of seeing oneself as one's best self. Hence, it must be part of the ethical ideal. Thus, in order for caring to enhance the ethical ideal it must not require a loss of moral integrity. At least one criterion for a caring relationship to be morally desirable is that all parties be able to maintain moral integrity within it. When a person must lose their integrity in order to care, caring does not enhance her ethical ideal, and therefore, caring is undesirable.

Recently, Diana T. Meyers has suggested that an ethic of care can incorporate a sense of autonomy. This autonomy is different from the standard sense of autonomy based on allowing rules and principles to guide behavior. Meyers suggests that autonomy is a kind of competency. She states:

> . . . one asks what choices are compatible with or reinforce desirable aspects of one's personal identity. Questions like "what would it be like to have done that?" and "Could I bear to be the sort of person who can do that?" are foremost. To answer these questions satisfactorily, the individual must be able to envisage a variety of solutions, must be able to examine these solutions open-mindedly, must be able to imagine the likely results of carrying out these options, must be attuned to self-referential responses

like shame and pride, must be able to critically examine
these responses, and must be able to compare various possibilities systematically along sundry dimensions. Each of
these abilities constitutes a complex skill, and, together,
these skills equip the individual to make a choice by con-
sulting her self. Thus, it is possible to say that people who
deliberate in this way are self-governing ("Socialized Self"
151).

I want to suggest here that these are the kinds of questions one
must ask oneself in order to determine whether a particular existing or potential relationship is morally desirable. One must
ask what it would be like to support the other's projects, whether
one could live with oneself, morally, if those projects were one's
own. This is necessary in order to decide who one should allow
into one's transformative process, which as I stated above, is
necessary in order for an agent to maintain moral integrity.

VI. Caring and Difference

The value of differences between people, and the importance of
accepting difference as a way of overcoming such things as
racism, anti-Semitism, and xenophobia as well as enriching our
lives by associating with people different from ourselves, has received much attention recently. It may appear that I am recommending close association only with people who are similar to
ourselves as a way of insuring morally good associations. This
could increase tendencies towards racism, anti-Semitism, homophobia and xenophobia, and limit our associations with those
different from us. I do not mean to encourage parochialism. In
order to make an informed decision about entering into a caring
relationship with another, one must get to know the other. If one
makes snap decisions based on prejudice or superficial differences, or even on deep differences that one fails to try to understand, one acts too quickly. We may have a tendency, for example, to find certain cultural differences distasteful because they
are unfamiliar. However, to refuse a relationship without really
examining oneself and the other person, without trying to understand the difference, would be a mistake, and this is not what

I am suggesting. Yet, there are differences that make morally good caring relationships impossible. If one finds certain deeply held values in the other to be truly wrong, if the person is committed to things that after searching oneself, being aware of aspects such as cultural differences into account, one finds morally reprehensible, one will be unable to maintain integrity within that relationship. Embracing difference is very important. However, not all differences are good simply because they are different. We still have important judgments to make.

One might wonder, at this point, about the possibility of attempting to change a person in order to make caring morally desirable. Once again, we must consider different cases. First, one might be in a caring relationship with another who has changed over the years, so that one can no longer support the other's projects, or one might be considering whether to *enter into* a relationship with someone whose projects one knows one can not support, with the hope of changing that person.

Aristotle speaks to the first situation in his discussions of friendship. In discussing the question of ending friendships when a friend changes for the worse he states:

> Must the friendship, then, be forthwith broken off? If they are capable of being reformed one should rather come to the assistance of their character or their property, inasmuch as this is better and more characteristic of friendship. But a man who breaks off such a friendship would seem to do nothing strange; for it was not to a man of this sort that he was a friend; when his friend has changed, therefore, and he is unable to save him, he gives him up (*Ethics*, Book IX: 3).

The issues involved in attempting to change another person are highly complex. When is someone incurable? Also, what are the ethics of attempting to change another's values? Once one is already in a caring relationship with another, one may incur an additional obligation to help the other that is the product of the relationship.

Because we may incur special obligations to help friends, it is important to learn about the character of a potential friend before becoming too intimately involved in a caring relationship. In attempting to change another, one must be aware that one might be changed in the process. If this occurs one bears some responsibility for whom one has become. Under certain circumstances ending a relationship may be the only ethical choice. I believe the kind of unconditional commitment that allows us to go against our important values is not a good thing. When we go against our most deeply held values for the sake of unconditional commitment to another person we do wrong. One can never be sure how another will develop, thus unconditional commitment to another cannot be ethically acceptable. It amounts to the willingness to support anything a loved one is involved in, even things one finds morally outrageous. This is what makes the commitment unconditional. I believe that some things are wrong, no matter who does them. This is incompatible with an unconditional commitment to support another's goals, no matter what they are.

My analysis might strike some as chilling. Many of us were raised with the idea that the most important goal in our lives is to find unconditional love and support. It may seem as if I am advocating sacrificing loved ones for abstract ideas. However, this isn't so. I am not advocating sacrificing people, it is relationships I am recommending sacrificing under certain conditions. Many of us have been taught the value of unconditional commitment to other people. It is precisely this value that I am calling into question here.

VII. Conclusion

This analysis demonstrates why a good caring relationship, one which allows both parties to maintain integrity, must incorporate values other than caring itself at a fundamental level. In order to know whether one can support another's projects, one must have some knowledge of one's fundamental values. Answering to oneself that one could not live with oneself if one was involved in *that!* means knowing what one's values about *that* are. Thus, one's thoughts about justice, fairness, human rights and dignity, animal rights, environmental concerns, racism, sexism and many other issues will play a part in guiding with whom one can have a morally desirable caring relationship.

The ability of both parties to remain true to deeply held values within a relationship may not in itself make the relationship morally good. Two evil people can engage in horrendous things together, and their relationship would then be bad, however strong. Hence, while the ability of both parties to maintain integrity is not sufficient for caring to be good, it is necessary. I have not dealt with the problem of jointly held bad values. The aspect of integrity I have focused on involves not betraying oneself. There may indeed be other aspects. However, my analysis as it stands leaves room for the fact that while a certain two people may not be able to engage in a morally good caring relationship, each person might be able to do so with others who can support them. I have not unconditionally ruled out any particular values here (although there are some things I find unconditionally wrong).

I have suggested a strategy one might use to see if integrity can be maintained, one that involves the exercise of personal autonomy. Thus, the notions of integrity and autonomy have a central place within an ethic of care. While many of the recent discussions of the place of other values in an ethic of care have been concerned with obligations to those about whom one does not care, I have argued that values other than care determine whether a particular relationship between two people is itself a good instance of caring.

Although I have focused upon a particular example of an ethic of care in this analysis, I believe I have shown something that is important more generally. Any ethic of care that offers only caring itself as of absolute value can provide only an impoverished ethical ideal. There is more to ethical life than being one-caring, and sometimes it is wrong to be one-caring if this involves motivational displacement and engrossment in someone whose projects are wrong. What I want to say about caring is rather like what Kant says about happiness. He distinguishes between a thing's being good and useful, and a thing's being good without qualification. Thus, he claims that while happiness can be good it can also be bad when not under the direction of a good will.[10] I want to say something similar about caring relationships. Caring can be good when certain conditions are met. However, caring itself is not good without qualification, as some instances of caring are bad. A viable ethical theory must provide an ethical ideal rich enough to distinguish between good and bad instances of caring, and therefore must incorporate moral integrity and autonomy into its ethical ideal.

NOTES

1. Carol Gilligan, "Moral Orientation and Moral Development," in *Women and Moral Theory*, (Maryland: 1987), 19–33; 23. Hereafter, "Moral Orientation."

2. Diana T. Meyers, "The Socialized Self and Individual Autonomy: An Intersection Between Philosophy and Psychology," in *Women and Moral Theory*, 139–53; 150. Hereafter, Meyers, "Socialized Self."

3. Nel Noddings, *Caring: A Feminine Approach to Moral Education* (Berkeley: 1984), 85. Hereafter, *Caring*.

4. Nel Noddings, "A Response," in *Hypatia: A Journal of Feminist Philosophy*, 5.1 (1990): 120–27; 124. Hereafter, "Response."

5. Sarah Lucia Hoagland, "Some Concerns About Noddings," in *Hypatia: A Journal of Feminist Philosophy*, 5.1 (1990): 109–114. Hereafter, Hoagland.

6. Aristotle, *The Nicomachean Ethics*, (London: 1980), Book III: 1–5. Hereafter, *Ethics*.

7. Claudia Card, "Caring and Evil," in *Hypatia: A Journal of Feminist Philosophy*, 5.1 (1990): 101–08; 107.

8. Thomas Nagel and Bernard Williams, "Symposium on Moral Luck," in *Proceedings of the American Aristotelian Society*, 1 (1976): 115–51.

9. Victoria Davion, "Integrity and Radical Change," in *Feminist Ethics*, (Kansas: 1991): 180–92.

10. Immanuel Kant, *Groundwork of the Metaphysic of Morals*, (New York: 1964), 61.

The Maternal Self

The Maternal Gaze: Women Modernists and Poetic Authority

Margaret Dickie

"Stealing the language," "the art of deception," "the poetics of deflection," these are the terms that feminist critics use in discussing women poets and poetic authority (Ostriker, Homans, Diehl). Placing the woman poet in an indirect, if not oppositional, relationship to literary expression, these terms are not a radical departure from those pre-feminist descriptions of women Modernists which called Marianne Moore "mistress of quirks and oddities" or claimed that Gertrude Stein "walked the swampy field between brilliance and looniness" or relegated H. D. to her role as an Imagiste (Nitchie vi, *Yale Gertrude Stein*, xvii). This agreement among critics of widely disparate ideological positions is puzzling, and the terms they use—stealing, deceiving, walking—are peculiar since they are hardly appropriate descriptions of poetic activity, and especially of those experiments in perception which absorbed the women Modernists.

The focus of these experiments is evident in the titles of the women Modernists' early works: Stein's portraits of painters in *Camera Work*, H. D.'s *Notes on Thought and Vision*, and Moore's *Observations*. These women put themselves self-consciously in a new position that may seem "deceptive" or "looney" only because it is so radical and untried. Conventionally women are looked at.[1] But here are women looking and trying to develop language and metaphors that will express not just what they see but how they look. Although H. D. and Moore were friends and all three knew each others' works, these poets were trying very

221

different experiments and writing quite independently (unlike their male contemporaries, T.S. Eliot and Ezra Pound, for example, who worked closely together in the early stages of the Modernist movement). So, it is all the more surprising that each of these women poets turned to the model of maternity and especially to the maternal gaze as they began to develop a radically new lyric "I."

Although it is the first one, the maternal gaze has never figured prominently in discussions of women writers even in psychoanalytic analyses of creativity where the maternal is tracked through the child's development, and so it has been easy to overlook its prevalence in these women poets. But, as feminist theorists like Julia Kristeva and later Madelon Sprengnether begin to explore the whole idea of female subjectivity, the maternal gaze needs to be looked at more carefully.[2]

Stein's concern with bringing the inside out, H. D.'s interest in the vision of the womb as opposed to the vision of brain, and Moore's "watchful maker" are acts of perception that draw their metaphors from childbirth and from the mother's reaction to her child. Such a model has its roots in a conventional conception of the distinct self, but it pushes that conception toward its breakdown as the self and the other interact and interpenetrate.

These poets look at people or things to which they feel both intimately attached and disturbingly detached; they are aware of the other's fragility, protective toward it, identify with it, and yet remain alarmed at its otherness. Such experience approximates that of the mother looking at her creation, the child. Only one of these women was a mother and an indifferent one at that, and, thus, it cannot be argued that they are writing from actual experience.[3] Rather they use the maternal metaphor in all its complexity as a way of expressing how women look, developing an experimental language of perception and a radically new conception of the self. Bold poetic innovators, they rely on an age-old image to express a way of looking that disrupts the conventions of ordering and controlling the object of their gaze. Rather they activate heterogeneous elements in what they see.

These poets may have anticipated the insights of such feminist theorists as Julia Kristeva and later Madelon Sprengnether who have attempted to imagine and interpret female subjectivity. Sprengnether, developing some of Kristeva's insights, writes, "The condition of pregnancy creates a radical paradox in terms of subjectivity. The mother is neither one nor two but two-in-one, her body the ground of an otherness that is nevertheless experienced as an aspect of self" (235). She goes on to argue:

> If the mother's body in its otherness represents estrangement as well as origin, it also provides a paradigm for the construction of the ego, itself a form of memorial, or a presence that enfolds absence (233–34).

Theorizing from the mother's body, Sprengnether develops Kristeva's more radical insights about the mother as a continuous separation, a division of flesh, to identify the mother's body and not the phallus as the source of signification.

Decades before these theorists, Stein, H. D., and Moore were working toward an understanding of subjectivity as an experience of division and attachment. Like their contemporaries among male poets, they were experimenting with new ways of presenting the lyric "I" that would break up the coherent self and the boundaries between that self and the other. The women poets differ from the men in the participatory pleasure they express as a result of this process. For example, whereas Eliot's Prufrock presents himself as alienated from his surroundings, Moore's speakers are interested in participating in the life they observe. Or again, Pound's speaker in "Portrait d'une Femme" seeks to control his subject, while Stein's speaker wants to open up to the subjects of her portraits. And H. D. felt herself flooded with the other.

If the poets took as their model the maternal gaze, it may be because, unlike the much discussed male gaze, it is less restricted by convention, more open to new ways of seeing, looking not on a distinct and distant object, but on an object that has come out of the self. In this scopic economy, because the separation between the subject who looks and the object she sees is never complete, the maternal gaze is cast both inside and outside or, as Stein writes, it mixes the inside and outside. It is not properly a look; rather it is a channel through which energies pulse. Unlike the proprietary male gaze, the maternal gaze is both protective and celebratory, acknowledging at once the vulnerability and the power of the other, the other's familiarity and its difference from the self. Such an attitude suggests possibilities for the lyric "I" that are quite different from the long literary tradition of the male gaze.[4]

The woman's position is not easily explored because there has been, even in women's writing, a general silencing of the maternal, as Margaret Homans has argued.[5] The possibility of maternal discourse, even the conception of motherhood, is difficult because in our civilization motherhood is, as Julia Kristeva has noted, "the *fantasy* that is nurtured by the adult, man or woman, of a lost territory" and involves "the idealization of the *relationship* that binds us to her" ("Stabat Mater" 234). Even when the mother herself provides her own testimony, she too will be heavily invested in the idealization of her position.

Nonetheless, Kristeva has begun to explore the subject. Writing in "Stabat Mater," a clearly bifurcated text in which she offers an analysis of the cult of the Virgin Mary on the right side of the page and the testimony of her own intense personal experience of motherhood on the left side, Kristeva acknowledges the difficulty of her subject. Her critical analysis is as tentative as her personal testimony is exclamatory. In her testimony, she presents the mother's gaze in its full ambivalence:

> For a mother, on the other hand, strangely so, the other as arbitrary (the child) is taken for granted. As far as she is concerned—impossible, that is just the way it is: it is reduced to the implacable. . . .

Kristeva then goes on to argue:

> rooted in that disposition of motherly love, besides, we find the leaden strap it can become, smothering any different individuality (263).

Kristeva's testimony of mothers as "crossroads beings" in a position of "continuous separation" (254) points to the constant movement of that role. Far from the passive instinctual role to which women have been traditionally relegated and in contrast to Homans' identification of the woman with the literal, the woman as mother in Kristeva's view is at the center of the signifying process.[6] It is her body and the child's separation from it that provides the source of signification for the child.

But the mother cannot be seen completely from the child's point of view. The object-relations view of development depends upon a mother-infant symbiosis which, Madelon Sprengnether argues, is "an obvious absurdity, for a mother can only act as a mother if she perceives herself as such, as separate and different from her infant" (233). Like object-relations theorists, Lacan too views the mother from the child's perspective by placing her in the Imaginary, from which the child must separate as he develops and moves into the Symbolic. As Sprengnether argues, Lacan excludes the mother's body as the fleshly origin of human subjectivity (236).

But the mother is, as Kristeva states, "a continuous separation, a division of the very flesh. And consequently a division of language" (254). In this view, Sprengnether writes, the body of the mother offers "a model for the radical paradox of absence-in-presence which propels the process of signification" (245).

The maternal gaze, then, is that look of estrangement as well as familiarization that the mother casts on her child and that the child sees as a recognition of the other and the other in the self. It is this strategy of the maternal gaze that the Modernist women poets used in developing their lyric "I," writing from the new location of the woman as subject.[7] To express it, they have not had to steal a language but rather to create one; if they have developed a poetics of deflection, they have also worked toward a poetics of recognition. If these women poets were inspired by the revolution in the visual arts at the turn of the century no less than by the Modernist revolution of the word, they were also attempting a revolution of their own by trying to articulate their own difference as they separated themselves from their male colleagues.[8]

Stein established herself early as a poet of portraits. She made her first appearance in a periodical in the special issue of *Camera Work* which Alfred Stieglitz put out as an immediate response to the critical rejection of Cubism that had followed its introduction to the American scene in the 1911 issue of the journal. Stieglitz printed Stein's two portraits along with illustrations of paintings and sculptures by her subjects, Matisse and Picasso, and argued that Stein's "articles themselves, and not either the subjects with which they deal or the illustrations that accompany them, are the true *raison d'etre* of this special issue" (Brogan 13). Thus, before the famous Armory Show of 1913 that has often been cited as the beginning of the Modernist revolution, Stein was established as a major innovator whose work paralleled the innovations in the visual arts.

Her "portraits" are not simply views; they are written views, and, as such, they are double experiments in looking and writing that attempt nonetheless to erase the dualities they set up between painter and model, subject and object, imagination and reality, creation and representation. In doing portraits, Stein was participating in an experiment common among the Modernists; but, it is generally agreed, Gertrude Stein's portraits are different and designedly so.

First, they are not the work of a man looking at a woman. They are rather the work of a woman looking and sometimes looking at a man. And it is work. She does not assume the controlling role and easy manipulative style of the speaker in T.S. Eliot's "Portrait of a Lady," for example, who frames and limits the object of his vision. Rather, she claims that she was trying for "what I at that time called the rhythm of anybody's personality" (*Lectures* 174). Imagining personality as a rhythm anticipates Kristeva's idea of the semiotic as a pulsion always threatening to disrupt the symbolic. Moreover, Stein identifies personality as a force rather than a fixity, a *sujet en procès* in Kristeva's terms. Stein places herself in the role of the analyst in identifying the difficulty of expressing "the rhythm of anybody's personality," admitting in *The Autobiography of Alice B. Toklas* that, "Gertrude Stein, in her work, has always been possessed by the intellectual passion for exactitude in the description of inner and outer reality. She has produced a simplification by this concentration, and as a result the destruction of associational emotion in poetry and prose" (174). Here, Stein wants to locate herself both inside and outside the signifying process, boasting of her paradoxical "intellectual passion."

Such exactitude as she claims here allowed her nonetheless not only to destroy "associational emotion" but to destroy the barriers between inner and outer, to participate in the creativity of those whom she observed, rather than to fix them in form. In this process, she had to be very attentive. Like childbirth, her writing was, she writes in *The Autobiography*, "a long tormenting process" in which she seems to labor to create: "she looked, listened, and described" (112).

One metaphor she discovered for the problem of describing the outside and inside was the maternal child-bearing act. Thus, Stein can find in Picasso's genius a kind of generative power that is maternal in its production of something out of himself, as she writes in this portrait:

> This one was one having always something being coming out of him, something having completely a real meaning. This one was one whom some were following. This one was one who was working. . . . This one was one having something come out of him and this thing the thing coming out of him always had real meaning (*Selected Writings* 335).[9]

Having something coming out of him, Picasso is further identified with a libidinous, instinctual voice as opposed to a rational one in a notebook entry: "Leo does his [job] with his brains. . . . Matisse, Pablo, and I do not do ours with either brains or character we have all enough of both to do our job but our initiative comes from within a propulsion which we don't control, create" (quoted in Ruddick 104). Again, Stein's words anticipate Kristeva's ideas about the split in the subject between the pre-Oedipal semiotic pulsions and the Law of the Father evident in the symbolic that such pulsions threaten always to disrupt.

In identifying herself with Matisse and Picasso, Stein also makes them into herself; they may be men and painters whose eyes were seeing new things, but they are also seen anew in Stein's generative act of producing something out of herself. The rhythm of inner and outer reality that Stein seeks to capture in their portraits is the rhythm she creates by repetitive and incantatory words.

She traces this style to the other experiments in the arts, claiming, "Portraits of men and women and children are differently felt in every generation," and, for her generation, the new art of portraiture would be influenced by the cinema (*Lectures* 165). Portraits that are "felt" rather than seen are again rhythmic forces, Kristeva's *sujet en procès*. Stein claimed, "I was doing what the cinema was doing. I was making a continuous succession of

Gertrude Stein Sitting in Front of Picasso's Portrait of Her, 1922. Photo by Man Ray. Courtesy of Artists' Rights Society.

the statement of what that person was until I had not many things but one thing" (*Lectures* 176–77).

Thus describing herself as working in a way that she did not control and, at the same time, in absorbing the techniques of the new art form of her day in the cinema, Stein appears to minimize her own creative role in experimental writing. In simply being where and what she was, she saw and wrote as she did, or so she seems to say. Such modesty would not appear to have generated either the relentless experimentation of her writing or her view of herself as one of the three geniuses of her day along with Pablo Picasso and Alfred Whitehead (*The Autobiography* 5). But what appears to be modesty may be actually a new way of describing the artist's eye. Like childbirth, creative production is a process to which the artist submits. She saw herself, as she saw others, powerfully significant not because she could control and manipulate other people, but because she could release their power by her own listening, observing, and describing.

Creating a portrait in words to be read rather than in a picture to be looked at, Stein also activated the creative imagination of her audience. To do this, she experimented tirelessly, never listening nor looking in the same way. At first listening and talking until she could get the inner rhythm of the personality, then not listening and talking but simply looking, she went through constant changes in writing "portraits." In the process, she discovered that "words which were the words that made whatever I looked at look like itself were not the words that had in them any quality of description" (*Lectures* 191). She was experimenting with words that would not "mean it" but be "equivalent to it," as if she could create rather than name what she saw.

If she was the boldest of the Modernist experimenters in poetic portraiture, she was also the most open to its possibilities and anxious to follow her experiments from looking to listening to pure rhythms. In Stein's portraits the distinctions between the speaking subject and the object she views are obliterated; personality is converted into rhythm which emanates from language itself. In fact, so remote is looking from portraiture in Stein's work that when she came to concentrate on looking, she gave up portraits, claiming, "I for a time did not make portraits because as I was trying to live in looking, and looking was not to mix itself up with remembering I wished to reduce to its minimum listening and talking" (*Lectures* 189). So she began to write about "Objects," "Rooms," and "Food," as the sections of *Tender Buttons* are named.

> Looking appears to have led her away from not only portraits, but even from her sense of herself. In fact, looking was for Stein a way of abstracting herself and others from view, as she admits in "Portraits and Repetition."
>
> All this time I was of course not interested in emotion or that anything happened. I was less interested then in these things than I ever had been. I lived my life with emotion and with things happening but I was creating in my writing by simply looking. I was as I say at that time reducing as far as possible for me to reduce them, talking and listening (*Lectures* 191).

This split between living and creating recalls Eliot's split between the man that suffered and the mind that created. But while Eliot describes poetic creation as a kind of chemical experiment closed off in the mind of the poet, Stein considers that creation is an opening up of herself to others. She describes one stage of her portraits as listening and talking until "I had the existence of that one inside in me until I had completely emptied myself of this that I had as a portrait of that one" (*Lectures* 198). The filling up and emptying out carried her into the experiment with melody until she was, she claims, "getting drunk with melody and I do not like to be drunk I like to be sober and so I began again" (*Lectures* 199). And here, Stein is at the farthest remove from Eliot's controlled artistry; even the metaphors for creativity of filling up and opening out that recall the natural act of childbirth are remote from the scientific experiment of Eliot's metaphor.

For Stein, looking was not a matter of fixing an object, but of participating in an identity. She wanted to ask, "How could a thing if it is a human being if it is anything be entirely contained within itself" (*Lectures* 201). And, of course, she questioned the possibility of such a containment in both others and herself. She claims that she began to feel "something outside me while I was writing, hitherto I had always had nothing but what was inside me while I was writing" (*Lectures* 205). She goes on to experiment and claims that "now I suddenly began, to feel the outside inside and the inside outside and it was perhaps not so exciting but it was very interesting" (*Lectures* 205).

What Stein is describing as the creative process of her portraits is very close to Kristeva's description of motherhood:

> A mother is a continuous separation, a division of the very flesh. And consequently a division of language—and it has always been so.
>
> Then there is this other abyss that opens up between the body and what had been its inside: there is the abyss between the mother and the child. What connection is there between myself, or even more unassumingly between my body and this internal graft and fold, which, once the umbilical cord has been severed is an inaccessible other? . . . .
>
> What connection is there between it and myself? No connection, except for that overflowing laughter where one senses the collapse of some ringing, subtle, fluid identity or other, softly buoyed by the waves (254).

This collapse of identity in Kristeva's experience of motherhood as in Stein's experiments with portraits is an act of affirmation, rather than an act of criticism. Kristeva's "overflowing laughter," like Stein's excitement, is a positive response to the creative act, to the pleasures of authoring, if not authority, and to the connections between the artist and what she has created out of herself and into herself. In her portraits, Stein anticipates Kristeva's maternal gaze. Looking at the child to confirm its separateness, its otherness, Kristeva also confirms its identity with her. The inside and outside interconnect in Kristeva as they had in Stein.

Stein is not alone among her generation of women writers in adopting the maternal metaphor for the creative act. For H. D., the maternal position was an actual and important precipitating moment in her creative life. Like Stein, who viewed creation as a propulsion that could not be controlled, H. D. also identifies creative vision with a state of consciousness that is achieved through the body and especially through pregnancy and childbirth.

Although Ezra Pound presented H. D. to the literary avant-garde in the January 1913 issue of *Poetry* as "H. D. Imag-

Gertrude Stein, 1913. Photo by Alvin Langdon Coburn. Courtesy of International Museum of Photography at George Eastman House.

iste," when she herself came to write her own poetics, H. D. moved beyond the restrictive tenets of Imagism to found her art on a much more elaborate idea of vision than the Imagistic "direct treatment of the thing." *Notes on Thought and Vision* details an experience that H. D. had during a healing visit to the Scilly Isles in 1919, three months after her miraculous survival of the birth of her daughter while she had influenza. It is intimately connected with both her experience of giving birth and the maternal affection and care she received at the time from her friend Bryher. Although she never published this text, it contains the germs of ideas about creativity that would inform her later work.[10]

For H. D., creative vision is not a picture, but an entrance into the "overmind," which she describes as "a cap of consciousness over my head," "like water, transparent, fluid yet with definite body, contained in a definite space. It is like a closed seaplant, jelly-fish or anemone" (*Notes* 18–19). Although H. D. admits that these jelly-fish states of consciousness are of two kinds, "vision of the womb and vision of the brain," and that before the birth of her child such states seemed to come definitely from the brain, she claims that most dreams are visions of the womb (20–21). The womb or body is itself most creative, as H. D. concludes, "The oyster makes the pearl in fact. So the body, with all its emotions and fears and pain in time casts off the spirit, a concentrated essence, not itself, but made, in a sense, created by itself" (51).

Here again, the metaphor of birth serves to explain this woman writer's conception of creativity. By contrast, commenting perhaps on the published list of Imagist Don'ts, H. D. claims, "The new schools of destructive art theorists are on the wrong track" (24). She indicates the right track: "memory is the mother, begetter of all drama, idea, music, science or song" (23). Her maternal memory includes "certain words and lines of Attic choruses, any scrap of da Vinci's drawings, the Delphic charioteer"; they are "straight, clear entrances, to me, to over-world consciousness," she claims (24). Moreover, such a consciousness is revolutionary and life-giving, as she argues, "Two or three people, with healthy bodies and the right sort of receiving brains, could turn the whole tide of human thought, could direct lightning flashes of electric power to slash across and destroy the world of dead, murky thought" and bring the whole force of power back into the world (27).

Notes on Thought & Vision owes an obvious debt to the body consciousness of D. H. Lawrence whom H. D. knew and to another friend, Havelock Ellis, whose work on sexuality interested her; but its emphasis on the womb and on creativity as begetting distinguishes her work from theirs. Although she uses language that echoes Nietzsche's, hers is no will to power, but rather a desire to open up to the power of art, to be one of its "receiving centres." As such, H. D. provides a receptacle in *Notes* for a variety of ideas and voices: Socrates' "doctrine of love," Biblical stories, Eleusinian rites, Greek myths, philosophies of Tao and of the Hebrew and Greek, Christian symbolism.

Unlike Pound and Eliot who wanted to find a place for themselves in the history of art and wrote their critical essays toward that end, H. D. blurs the boundaries between herself and others by creating an experimental text which is organized in the form of a montage, that she, like Stein, took from the cinema and modern art, as she was to explain much later in her pamphlet on Kenneth McPherson's film, *Borderline*, in 1930. Although she has a prophetic message about the importance of a creative and constructive vision for her own age, she writes a text that is composed of random and fragmentary "notes" rather than of a continuous and coherent argument. Claiming that "No man by thought can make the grain sprout or the acorn break its shell," she puts her faith in nurturing a natural growth, emphasizing love over power.

If, in writing criticism, H. D. is unwilling to govern the text from an authoritative point of view, in her poetry she is even more open and receptive or more willing to be infiltrated and perhaps hidden entirely within another identity. In this state, she sees division as the beginning of signification, identifying with the god of crossroads, as she writes in "Hermes of the Ways": "But more than the many-foamed ways / of the sea, / I know him / of the triple path-ways, / Hermes, / who awaits" (37). "Dubious, / facing three ways," Hermes like H. D. is a crossroads figure, split and yet optimistically awaiting. In this, he re-

H.D. Courtesy of Perdita Shaffner and New Directions Publishing Corporation.

sembles as she does Kristeva's image of the mother as well as Stein's portrait writer.

Open, receptive, even dubious, H. D. is nonetheless no passive receiver, writing unreflectively from an "over-world consciousness." She is an active creator, inspired by "lines of Attic choruses," but writing against "dead, murky thought." Speaking in the voice of mythic women, H. D. enters freely into their stories, infiltrating their experience in order to revise their destinies from conventional stories of sacrifice to statements of defiance. "Eurydice" is typical: the speaker starts in regret with the statement, "So you have swept me back," but she goes on to discover the power of her own position and concludes, "At least I have the flowers of myself, / and my thoughts, no god / can take that." Refusing the repression of the woman in myth, H. D. reimagines the female body as fertile, flowering, generative.

The poetics of visionary affirmation developed in *Notes* allows for a layering of vision and revision like Stein's mixture of the inside and outside. It is a looking both ways. For example, "Helen" is a double vision and judgment: the poet looking at Greece looking at Helen. The speaker attacks the traditional image of Helen as the desired object: "All Greece hates / the still eyes in the white face" (154). She sees rather that "Greece sees unmoved, / God's daughter, born of love." Greece "could love indeed the maid, / only if she were laid, / white ash amid funereal cypresses" (155). In this process of indirection, the silenced woman speaks.

This interpenetration of voices in H. D.'s early poetry was a way of disrupting order and tradition by affirming a chaotic, if creative, force. If it can be seen as a poetry of deflection that allowed the poet to hide from full revelation and, at the same time, expose deeply disturbing emotions, it also provided H. D. with the possibility of channeling energies that might otherwise have been unavailable to her. The strategy allowed her to conceal and affirm simultaneously the pleasures of a lesbian relationship that absorbed her emotional energy and provided her with maternal protection. As a new mother herself at this time, H. D. felt nevertheless the need of mothering. If Stein had, as she claims, a life of intense emotions in her new relations with Alice B. Toklas at the moment that she was trying to exclude emotions from her writing, H. D. was no less aroused to creativity by the experience of Bryher's maternal care. She did not directly acknowledge this relationship in the poetry published in her lifetime, although it is encoded in what she calls the vision of the womb.

The paradox of an affirmative vision that is refracted through an other has its source in the vision which H. D. had in the Scilly Isles, which she described much later as "an impulse to 'let go' into a sort of balloon, or diving-bell." It is reminiscent of Stein's affirmation of the outside in herself and the inside of her subjects. Poetic authority in both these poets derives from participation in the other, from a suspension of control, and a relaxation into an intuitive apprehension.

Although Marianne Moore could never be imagined as letting go of her artistic control, she too, like Stein and H. D., writing in what Sandra Gilbert and Susan Gubar have called this most Satanically assertive of genres, the lyric poem, assumed poetic authority by granting it to others whom she had first absorbed by careful observations. Like Stein's tormenting process of looking, Moore's observations were meticulous. Her own view of viewing was established early in a peremptory review of T.S. Eliot's *Prufrock and Other Observations in Poetry* (April 12, 1918) where she fixes that poet's portrait-drawing abilities at somewhat below the mean. Reviewing Eliot's view, Moore attacks "the ungallantry, the youthful cruelty, of the substance of the 'Portrait'" (*Complete Prose* 35). She objects to the ease with which Eliot can differentiate himself from the woman he treats as an object.

In her own poetry at this time, Moore was attentive to skilled observers such as the "Old Tiger," which she addresses with sympathetic attachment:

> you to whom a no is never a no, loving to succeed where
> all others have failed, so constituted that opposition is pas-
> time and struggle is meat, you see more than I see but
> even I see too much;[11]

Unlike Eliot in his portrait, Moore identifies with the old tiger, presented as itself a model for the poet with an "eye which is characteristic / of all accurate observers." Unlike the "cultured, the profusely lettered" (one might even say the literary establishment, mostly male), the tiger, "scorning to / push," knows "that it is not necessary to live in order to be / alive." This watchfulness and patience between the eye and its object (the habits of the poet and the mother, no less than the predator) are what Moore missed in Eliot's "Portrait of a Lady."

Late in her life, when she was asked about the source of her poetry, Moore quoted George Grosz's explanation of art, "Endless curiosity, observation, research, and a great amount of joy in the thing" (*Collected Prose* 592). It is this joy that connects Moore with Stein and H. D. as celebratory seers and with the maternal laughter of Kristeva. And it is this joy that separates all these women writers from the male Modernists. It allows Moore to be what she calls an "imaginary possessor" both of the pictures she looks at and of those she creates. Like Stein and H. D., when she looks, Moore opens herself to the other, not to appropriate it or triumph over it, but to appreciate it, aware, as she writes in "The Labors of Hercules," that "one detects creative power by its capacity to conquer one's detachment" (53). Besides, she writes in "Critics and Connoisseurs," "What is / there in being able / to say that one has dominated the stream in an attitude of self-defense" (39).

Moore's openness is not exactly the same as Stein's mixture of inside and outside nor does it share with H. D. a source in visionary consciousness. It comes rather from an insatiable curiosity and the conviction that "To have misapprehended the matter is to have confessed that one has not looked far enough," as Moore writes in "England" (47). Combined with this willingness to look far enough is a reluctance to be too familiar, to imagine that the other is fully understood, to settle finally on a view. Moore's interest in observation would appear to be entirely intellectual except that, as she admits, "Too stern an intellectual emphasis upon this quality or that detracts from one's enjoyment" (48).

Moreover, for all her interest in formal qualities, Moore engaged in a constant process of blurring boundaries, first in her habit of composing through a collage of quotations so that the division between her work and that of others is never clear, and then in her tireless revisions of poems from one highly stylized form to another where order is always being disrupted. The distinct voice is hard to distinguish, and the distinct form is never fixed permanently.

It is not surprising then that, like Stein and H. D., Moore finds maternity a subject of interest and a metaphor for the creative process. Herself the daughter of a particularly dominant mother, Moore could also see her own creative activity as maternal in its agonized watchfulness, its division of the self, as in "The Paper Nautilus," which, Bonnie Costello claims, compares maternity to poetry. She argues that Moore depicts "the process of nurture as a struggle beneath an apparent gentleness" and sees "the creative process as a highly precarious restraint of energy" (119). Birth is a differentiation that frees both the nautilus and its offspring: "the intensively / watched eggs coming from / the shell free it when they are freed" (121). The shell is language itself which can never fully contain the poet's feelings and yet which must release them, knowing that "love / is the only fortress / strong enough to trust to" (122). The paper nautilus is "the watchful / maker" which buries her eggs "eight-fold in her eight / arms" "hid" "but not crushed" (121). She is "hindered to succeed," not anxious to relinquish her eggs and yet freed by doing it.

A more elaborate maternal image is another eight-armed animal, "An Octopus," where Moore displays her skills as a tireless observer in describing "twenty-eight ice-fields" (71).[12] The maternal image here is all encompassing and unknowable. Although Moore moves through eight pages toward the compliment that "Relentless accuracy is the nature of this octopus / with its capacity for fact" (76), she appears to be more interested in detailing its capaciousness than its accuracy, declaring at the very start that the "octopus" is "Deceptively reserved and flat." Moving around it, "Completing a circle," she claims, "you have been deceived into thinking you have progressed" (71).

The elusiveness of the glacier is Moore's subject, and she shares and mirrors the octopus/glacier's "capacity for fact," again enveloping her own "relentless accuracy" in a capacity for fact that is commodious without being complete. She acknowledges the unknowable in the glacier: it is the "property of the exacting porcupine," unapproachable, and of the bears whose "den is somewhere else, concealed in the confusion" (72). This glacier incorporates absence in presence; its location is the site of "somewhere else" and nothing is itself here. Even the "goat" in those altitudes assumes another identity, a "stag-at-bay position," and water is "immune to force of gravity in the perspective of the peaks" (72). Unfamiliar, strange, and other, the glacier is also familiar, a domestic place: "Big Snow Mountain is the home of a diversity of creatures" (73). But, again, it is a home to otherness: its inhabitants are outlaws or mavericks (the chipmunk, "running with unmammal-like agility," for example), all "happy seeing nothing" (73). Spotted ponies, "hard to discern," fungi "magnified in profile," leaves "upon which moisture works its alchemy," all testify that the landscape and its inhabitants are tricky, changeable, impossible to fix accurately in view.

By contrast to this "original American menagerie of styles," Moore claims, "The Greeks liked smoothness, distrusting what was back / of what could not be clearly seen." She can settle on no such "Neatness of finish!" despite the repetition of this exclamatory phrase. Instead, she pictures the octopus-glacier "'Creeping slowly as with meditated stealth, / its arms seeming to approach from all directions'" (76). The final image is even more ominous as she leaves "the glassy octopus symmetrically pointed, / its claw cut by the avalanche" (76).

Here is no "'deliberate wide-eyed wistfulness'" (Diehl) in the description of nature, but rather a constant reiteration of the impossibility of "relentless accuracy" in seeing this glacier-octopus. Like the unicorn in "Sea Unicorns and Land Unicorns," the glacier has a "miraculous elusiveness" (78). The fabled unicorn, "not seen except in pictures," although "Upon the printed page, / also by word of mouth, / we have a record of it all" (79), and the glacier of "An Octopus" are occasions for Moore to display her scepticism about capturing anything in language at the same time that she is able to acknowledge and refuse to resolve "'complexities which still will be complexities / as long as the world lasts'" (75).

But "An Octopus" is not simply an exercise in looking. It is a view of the inscrutability of nature imagined *by* a woman and *as* a woman. The glacier is "of unimagined delicacy," "it hovers forward 'spider fashion / on its arms' misleadingly like lace" (71). It is "Distinguished by a beauty / of which 'the visitor dare

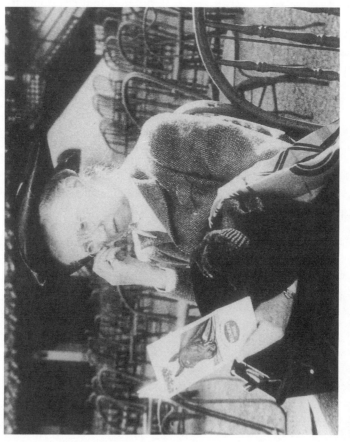

Marianne Moore at the Belmont Park Racetrack. Photo by Esther Bubly. Courtesy of Esther Bubly and The Rosenbach Museum and Library.

Marianne Moore in Her Brooklyn Apartment. Photo by Esther Bubly.
Courtesy of Esther Bubly and The Rosenbach Museum and Library.

never fully speak at home'" (73), and finally veiled "'in a curtain of powdered snow launched like a waterfall'" (76). Hovering forward with arms approaching from all sides, this glacier would appear to be the very image of an engulfing mother, and yet, unlike Whitman's old crone out of the sea, this feminized landscape is imagined as not so much personally threatening as stalwartly resistant. It creeps slowly forward but "receives one under winds that 'tear the snow to bits'" (76). It is a "hard mountain 'planed by ice and polished by the wind,'" (76). Its mysteries are those of "doing hard things," of endurance, of unimaginable resistance to the poet's imaginative grasp. They are mysteries appreciated and confirmed here, traits identified with a woman and admired here by this woman poet who imitates them.

"An Octopus" is a good poem to keep in mind when contemplating the frequent charge of timidity that is made against Moore imagined as a brilliant woman but writing in a world where literary authority was male. Although the natural landscape she describes is formidable and she has behind her the powerful male tradition of Romantic nature poetry, Moore makes her independent way, intent on celebrating rather than dominating the world she creates even when that world is "unimaginable" and overwhelming. She sees herself perhaps ultimately shut out from an accurate view of all the glacier's facts and mysteries, but she celebrates its power.

"An Octopus" is certainly the most menacing maternal image among these three poets. Unlike Stein's "having something come out" of herself and H. D.'s vision of the womb, the hovering many-armed octopus seems as ominous as it might be delicate, beautiful, and durable. In Moore's poetry, the maternal image is embodied in "the unegoistic action of the glaciers" (73) where this remarkably unegoistic poet can locate the interaction that forms the bond between nature and poet, reality and language, as between mother and child.

When Stein, H. D., and Moore began to experiment with looking from the position they occupied as women, they were moved to make a radical break with even those among their male colleagues who were experimenting with multiple perspectives or voices, with mythic structures, and with varied personae. They went to extremes certainly: Stein followed her friends among the painters to the limits of non-referentiality where language became meaningless and subsequently lost her audience; H. D. was so overwhelmed by a visionary experience and a private life of such conflicted emotions that she exhausted her creative impulse, fell silent in mid-career, and did not resume writing until the shock of the Second World War drove her to produce her major long poems; and Marianne Moore made such a great effort to distinguish her characteristic style of presentation from that of others that she seemed to be at times merely idiosyncratic even when she could not settle on a final form for her work. Perhaps these extreme solutions and the poetic silences they occasioned are cause and effect; they may indicate an insistence on independence that was ultimately too exhausting. Or perhaps these women were writing from a wholly different and more revolutionary attitude toward poetic authority than the so-called High Modernists.

Stein, H. D., and Moore all expressed their resistance to their own generation of male poets. Stein claimed "she did not understand why since the writing was so clear and natural they mocked at and were enraged by her work" (*The Autobiography* 32–33). H. D. set herself in opposition to the "new schools of destructive art theorists," among which she must have numbered her friend Pound, and Moore attacked Eliot's cruelty and indifference in her review of *Prufrock*. In contrast to this negation and destruction, these women poets were to establish a poetics based on generativity and the maternal metaphor. In their work, the lyric "I" confirms others and otherness in itself. The "I" engages in an interactive process that allows a participatory celebration even of such a thing as a glacier's obduracy or a "dubious" crossroads god.

Writing as subjects, as the eye of the lyric "I," Stein, H. D., and Moore were beginning to articulate what women saw through the maternal gaze that first affirms identity and then acknowledges the other as different from and part of the self. This gaze recognizes separation and division at the same time that it confirms inseparable bonds. It is interactive, receiving back what it is giving, taking in and giving out. It is the way these women poets looked when they began to look for themselves.

NOTES

1. In her study of the way women have been denied the status of
subjects and producers of culture in the cinema, Teresa de Lauretis calls
for a feminist theory that may be sought "in that political, theoretical,
self-analyzing practice by which the relations of the subject in social reality can be rearticulated from the historical experience of women"
(186). These women poets may, in fact, provide such a practice, which
has yet to be acknowledged and understood.

2. The maternal gaze, prominent in object-relations theory, fades
out of view in psychoanalytic discussions of the child's development.
Even literary critics interested in women's writing express a certain resistance to it. Does it need to be tied to the experience of motherhood,
readers, who never want to know if the Law of the Father derives from
actual fatherhood, ask. What can the mother/child relationship tell us
about it, other readers ask. Who knows? What does the father/child relationship tell us about the Law of the Father?

3. In "Mallarmé as Mother," Barbara Johnson also makes the case
for a writer who was not a mother writing from the mother's position.
She uses Margaret Mahler's scheme of the separation-individuation
process to describe how one can write from a maternal position. Of the
four sub-phases of the process, she chooses the third phase, rapproche-
ment, to explore the undecidability of Mallarmé's poetry. But these sub-
phases are part of the child's development and not the mother's, and I
want to suggest that the mother's experience in this process is the important one. See Johnson's interesting essay (137–43).

4. Luce Irigaray writes, "Women find pleasure more in touch
than in sight and her entrance into a dominant scopic economy signifies,
once again, her relegation to passivity: she will be the beautiful object"
(101). By contrast, I want to explore the kind of pleasure women find in
looking.

5. Margaret Homans has examined the intersections of women's
reproductive and literary roles in nineteenth-century British fiction in
Bearing the Word. She sees women as culturally identified with the literal
that both makes possible and endangers the figurative structures of literature. In Homans' view, the dilemma of the woman writer is to be
caught between her own interest in a literal mother-daughter language
and her desire to placate and enter the symbolic realm of literary language. It cannot be denied that the twentieth-century women poets I
discuss here were interested in the literal; but I find them to be more

disruptive of the symbolic realm than their nineteenth-century prede-cessors in prose, in part because Modernist poetry itself had a more revolutionary potential than nineteenth-century realistic fiction and in part because these women poets put themselves deliberately outside cultural models of behavior.

6. For a brief survey of the issues at stake in recent feminist re-considerations of *the maternal*, see Marianne Hirsch.

7. Carolyn Burke has discussed the women Modernist poets as "an important counterstrain of modernist poetics—centered on the modalities of joining and separation, union and disunion—that was first exemplified in the paratactic and gender-conscious writing of Gertrude Stein" (100). She looks at Moore, Stein, and Mina Loy; but she is inter-ested in the erotic underpinning of "getting spliced," rather than the maternal.

Kristeva writes of the subject-in-process (*sujet en procès*) of po-etic language in *Desire in Language* (136–47). The speaking subject in po-etry for Kristeva is always a questionable subject-in-process which reac-tivates the instinctual maternal element repressed in language as a sym-bolic function. In *Revolution in Language*, Kristeva writes of this subject-in-process in terms that will be relevant to these women poets, "The best metaphor for this transversal rhythmicity would not be the gram-matical categories it redistributes, but rather a piece of music or work of architecture" (126).

8. The story of the relationships Stein, H. D., and Moore enjoyed with Eliot and Pound, for example, is a varied and intricate one; but in every case the women broke free or remained independent from them. The exclusion of these women from the canon of High Modernism is proof enough of their treatment by their male contemporaries.

9. It could be argued that what is "coming out" of Picasso is se-men or excrement. But since Stein is talking about Picasso's creative ge-nius, "something being coming out" would not be excrement, and since it is "something having *completely* a real meaning," it would not be se-men which has a real meaning only when combined with something else.

10. Dianne Chisholm suggests that the presence of Bryher may have enabled the vision. She writes "What might have been merely a disturbance of consciousness becomes with encouragement an experi-ment in autohypnosis, hallucination, and hypnoid states" (21). Chisholm's study is an important reading of the post-Imagist long po-ems and autobiographical prose in which H. D. challenges Freud's the-ory of femininity and provides a "wholly affirmative vision of woman's libidinal resources and her capacity for creative sublimation" (6).

11. This poem is not included in *The Complete Poems*, but it is reprinted with an accompanying discussion in Grace Schulman, *Marianne Moore* (18–25).

12. I am indebted here to the elaborate reading of "An Octopus" as a revisionary Romantic Sublime, a female-centered Family Romance by Feit Diehl (71–85). In her discussion, Feit Diehl draws on biographical information about Moore's relationship with her mother as well as passages from the poem as it was published in the December 1924 *Dial* that were excised from the version in *The Complete Poems*. Feit Diehl notes identifying signs of the glacier as a mother who is threatening and nurturing at once.

The Theatrical Self

Aporias of the Self

James J. Dowd

In his essay on sincerity and authenticity, Lionel Trilling wrote that the hypocrite-villain of literature "has become marginal, even alien, to the modern imagination of the moral life" (17). Dissemblers and parvenus are so commonplace in the present age, that they no longer compel our interest or stimulate our imagination. "The deception we best understand," Trilling explained, "is that which a person works upon himself."

Trilling's observations are fascinating for their suggestions about the self in the modern, or postmodern, age. Does the self still exist in the same sense as it once did? Do the categories of authenticity and sincerity remain relevant to theoretical analyses of human action? In Trilling's assessment, based upon the work of Freud and Marcuse, authenticity resides only in the unconscious. Conscious social activity, in contrast, is contrived and, therefore, only sincere in the sense that the individual may also be taken in by a good performance, his or her own included. Unlike the concern of modernist writers with the problem of alienation, the theme of much postmodern theoretical writing is precisely with this question of authenticity. In Eagleton's view,

> "The depthless, styleless, dehistoricized, decathected surfaces of postmodernist culture are not meant to signify an alienation, for the very concept of alienation must secretly posit a dream of authenticity which postmodernism finds quite unintelligible. Those flattened surfaces and hollowed interiors are not 'alienated' because there is no longer any subject to be alienated and nothing to be alienated from,

'authenticity' having been less rejected than merely forgotten (1985:61).

Postmodern social theory challenges the assumption of a world of differentiated and autonomous social actors whose behavior and motivations stubbornly resist our attempts to account for them. Postmodern theory is also at odds with the traditional role theory approach to the self that acknowledges its socially constructed nature yet which emphasizes the constraints on the self that are embedded in social systems and which induce alignment between individual capacities and social requirements (Riley, 1985). It encourages instead a recognition or reappreciation of the once remarkable notion that the self is an image we construct from the materials at hand. In a sense, a self resembles a wardrobe: we pick up bits and pieces of identity along the way and, as long as these elements fit and are suitably stylish, we will wear them for the time being.

This is not to argue, however, that the self is incapable of substance, depth, or a sense of genuineness. The mistake is to situate such qualities deep within the core of the individual's real self rather than in performance. In the present age, the individual is expected to construct a convincing public self from the means at his or her disposal and to remain true to this public self (more properly, selves) by segregating one's audiences and not having them find oneself "out of character." In the current age, civilization's discontents are not restricted to those with unruly ids but include those who have failed to acquire a self that is estimable in some way and that can withstand public scrutiny.

Approaches to the Self

To differentiate a modern from a postmodern approach to the self, it may be useful to compare the self-monitoring theory, a traditional or modern viewpoint, developed by social psychologists such as Mark Snyder, with the dramaturgical approach of the late Erving Goffman. Goffman's career spanned a 25-year period from approximately 1955 to 1980. Although he was not then known as a "postmodern" writer, his work is distinguished by its focus on social interaction and his use of the metaphor of the theater, and related ideas such as roles and stage, to explain social interaction. Goffman, in retrospect, is probably sociology's first theorist of the postmodern self.

Let me begin with a sketch of self-monitoring theory. A central question of interest to researchers on self-monitoring is why can't we all be ourselves. Snyder (1987: 1), for example, asks why, "do some people [appear] to be living lives of public illusion, when others are content just to 'be themselves,' without constantly assessing the social climate around them?" This question presumes that we do not attempt, as the poet Auden confessed to have done, to create an image "in the minds of others in order that they may love me." Self-monitoring theorists contend instead that there are people who "express what they really think and feel" and others who do not (Snyder, 1987: 5). High self-monitors are vigilant in their observations of the reactions of others to their words and behaviors. They "monitor" these reactions and respond accordingly. Low self-monitors, in contrast, are both less vigilant in their observations and less inclined to adapt their behaviors to fit the prevailing circumstances (Snyder and Swann, 1976).

Snyder (1974; 1979) has tested his ideas on self-monitoring with various populations, including actors. Actors, as one might expect, were found to be disproportionately high on the index of self-monitoring. The recently published autobiographies of the actors Hume Cronyn and Katherine Hepburn seem to attest to Snyder's conclusion. Hume Cronyn, in his memoir, *A Terrible Liar* (1991), writes about attending his sister's funeral and being very aware of how he should play the scene, i.e., how he should move his hands, how he should appear, etc. This "confession" was meant to indicate that he is an inveterate actor who, even at this time of grief, remained sufficiently aware of the dramaturgical requirements of the situation to put on a good act.

Katherine Hepburn has also commented in her autobiography, *Me*, how she burst into tears upon hearing the news of the death of her brother. The tears, however, came only because,

> "this was what I thought I should do. . . . People die—you cry—but inside I was frozen" (Hepburn, 47).

The accounts of Cronyn and Hepburn are part of autobiographies that one might dismiss as merely following the confessional requirements of this particular genre of writing. Although this may be true, their comments nonetheless indicate the importance that we social actors attribute to the real existence of an honestly-felt emotion. When Ms. Dotty West, the well-known country singer, died last year, other entertainers eulogized her with comments concerning her authenticity. Kenny Rogers, a colleague of Ms. West, said, for example, that "While some people sang words, she sang emotions. What made Dottie West unique is that when she sang about pain, she felt pain; when she sang about love, she felt love; and when she sang about beauty, she felt that beauty." Implicit in such comments is the understanding that most entertainers, regardless of their demeanor during the course of a performance, do not—could not—actually develop an internal, emotional state consistent with the outward signs of the performance. For Kenny Rogers to compliment Dottie West in this way only serves to underscore the dramaturgical properties of all public performance, Ms. West's most likely included.

My sense of these accounts is that Snyder, Cronyn, Hepburn and Rogers each underestimate the degree to which this acute sensitivity to the details of one's performance, even in situations of grief, occurs generally throughout the population. Indeed, this has been one of Goffman's central themes, namely, that behavior in public is a performance. Impression management is a general requirement and not one that is limited to certain groups under certain circumstances. So, whereas Snyder presumes that only the high self-monitor will take the trouble of keeping his or her various audiences separated (low self-monitors presumably have "little resistance to mixing their audiences") (Snyder, 1987: 63), Goffman discusses this re-quirement as one that applies under most conditions to all social actors.

A related question concerns the status of emotions in social intercourse, that is, whether emotions are actually experienced or are merely another aspect of one's performance. Following the incidents reported in the memoirs by Cronyn and Hepburn, it seems certain that neither Cronyn nor Hepburn apparently "felt" a spontaneous sense of sorrow or grief during the particular episodes recounted above. Nonetheless, one must acknowledge the fact that human beings, by virtue of the fact we *are* social animals, are both impression managers and emotional beings. Sometimes it is true that we attempt to disguise our actual emotional state; this does not mean, however, that we never do feel "genuine" or real emotion. One (not completely reliable) marker of one's emotional state is whether one "feels" the dramatic change of bodily state that is associated with the onset of a particular emotion. Anger and fear are signalled by a rush of adrenaline and a pounding heart; embarrassment is indicated by the rush of blood to the face; joy and grief are often accompanied by uncontrollable sobbing. The link of emotions with a certain physiological symptom(s) allows one to appreciate the distinction between anger, that is associated with a symptom, and envy or jealousy, which are not. As a final note to this digression on emotions, I must add that emotions, however real in the sense that we have just discussed them, will quickly and inevitably come to the conscious attention of the individual and thereby come under his or her dramaturgical scrutiny. As we become aware of our tears streaming down our cheeks, we pause to consider the possible reactions of those who may be witness to the scene. Occasionally, as with embarrassment, this consciousness only serves to heighten the embarrassment, as when our consciousness of our red face redoubles our sense of embarrassment. With other emotions, however, something different occurs. We revel in the spectacle that our righteous anger creates and the privileged loss of control that our anger allows us. Grief is similar.

Although Snyder and his colleagues are aware of the possibility that the behavior of the low self-monitors may itself be understood in dramaturgical terms (Snyder acknowledges that their behavior may have "a self-presentational element to it"), the process of self-monitoring is conducted without the degree of autonomy or the uncertainty of outcome that many sociologists, particularly symbolic interactionists, view as intrinsic to social interaction of all kinds. Furthermore, being rooted and transmitted in the genes, self-monitoring behavior is quite distinct (it is claimed) from the performance of Goffman's impression manager "whose main business is fabricating an identity" (from an obituary on Goffman in *The New York Times*, cited by Snyder, 1987).

The psycho-biological nature of self-monitoring theory is further evident in Snyder's claims that self-monitoring is not correlated with social class. As plausible as such a link would be to a sociologist, Snyder (1987: 131) contends that "repeated efforts, using surveys and questionnaires, to implicate demographic variables as predictors of self-monitoring have come up empty-handed . . ." It is this lack of connection with social class that leads Snyder to suspect the presence of biological-genetic causes. He avers repeatedly that "people are born to be either high or low in self-monitoring . . ." (1987: 139), or that "People appear to be born with a biological-genetic predisposition to be high or low in self-monitoring" (153). And, since this belief suggests the possibility that people are either one or the other (high or low self-monitors), Snyder goes on to write that "at a genotypic level there may exist one latent causal entity that is discretely distributed into two types" (high and low self-monitoring) (159). High self-monitors, he argues, are born and, through the reinforcement of lived experience, are then made. In opposition to this viewpoint, sociologists have long held that the self cannot be adequately understood merely as an outcome preordained from childhood or as a reflection of some deeply-etched internal construction, such as character or personality. The adult self is the product of conscious choices that one makes given limitations of the body and one's social and psychological circumstances.

Precursor to Postmodernism: The Work of Erving Goffman

The second source of writings on the self that I will analyze is the work of the late Erving Goffman. From the appearance of *Presentation of Self in Everyday Life* in the 1950s to his posthumous Presidential Address on the interaction order given to the American Sociological Association (1983), Goffman scrutinized the strategies and tactics employed by social actors in everyday life. Our understanding of social encounters, or what Goffman referred to as "behavior in public," has been forever transformed as a result of his dramaturgical analyses. Goffman's views on the self contradicted not only the conventional lay wisdom of a "true self" that presumably lies at the core of human personality, but also the standard social psychological treatment in which the self is stabilized either through balancing mechanisms (the cognitive tradition of Festinger, Heider, et al.) or through the internalization of role requirements (the role theory perspective of Stryker, Kuhn, and many others). The traditional, and still dominant, view of the self in sociology is of an entity that is created through the socialization processes of childhood and adolescence and which remains malleable throughout life in response to the vicissitudes of one's life. However malleable the self might be, there is little doubt that a self of sorts exists. The sociologist may locate the source of the real self in social roles, primary among which are the occupational and familial roles (the spheres of work and love that Freud cites as well as for their pivotal contributions to human health and happiness), whereas the individual subject may feel his real self shining through only when all role requirements are lifted, which is to say, when he or she is alone. Neither the sociologist nor the social actor, however, would likely agree with Trilling's point that sincerity and authenticity are no longer particularly useful categories to apply to human social behavior.

There is little doubt, however, that Goffman would side with Trilling. With his view of social action as, at root, a presentation or performance, Goffman's theory of the self prods us to reconsider the meaning of sincerity and authenticity when applied to behavior in public. Ultimately, Goffman's dramaturgical insights must be applied to our own behavior and to that of even the most revered public figures. By its emphasis on behavior as performance and image rather than as a reflection of a deeper structure or underlying essence, his work causes us to consider not only whether society (or social groups) are real, but also whether, or in what sense, the individual may be said to be real.

Postmodernism and Self-Imaging

Postmodernism complements Goffman's dramaturgical approach by providing an account of the larger societal transformation beneath the disappearance of the autonomous subject. It is
not claimed that Goffman's impression manager is the direct
product of post-war transformations within capitalism; as Riesman (1950) observed concerning the transformation from inner-
directedness to other-directedness, however, impression management is a concern that has been selectively reinforced during
late capitalism and has become widespread. With the intrusion
of mass culture into the various regions and subcultures that
comprise contemporary society, the idea of individuality (and
the individual self) as the natural byproduct of exposure to a
unique matrix of experience becomes, ineluctably, more difficult
to sustain. Variations in experience or reinforcement history,
those facts that in the past were considered to be the source of
personality and group differences, remain highly significant yet
are tempered by the massive intrusion into private life since the
late 1940s of the mass media. The effect of this development has
been to transform personality from a congeries of lived experience into a form of style. That is, the self is now as much conditioned by the behavior of models in advertisements and of characters appearing in television serials as it is by routines of daily
living. Indeed, the mass media have so insinuated themselves
into the routines of daily living as to make the lives of the characters in the media not only more interesting than our own but
also, somehow, more real.[1]

Many unanswered questions remain about the contemporary, postmodern self, not the least of which is the approximate
time and place of its origination. Society's current preoccupation
with sincerity and authenticity seems to be a recent phenomenon
(Gergen, 1991). Of course, deceit and dissembling have quite
likely been a part of social interaction throughout the entire history of humankind. It is language that gives humans the ability
to be self-aware; consequently, it is certainly true that self-consciousness or self-awareness is not a unique characteristic of life
in the 20th century. One might argue, however, that in previous
epochs, only a few people were manipulative schemers and

these folk were thought of as deviants and shunned by other community members. Alternatively, one might hypothesize that, then, as now, people schemed and manipulated as it suited their interests but such behavior could only become widespread with increased social complexity and greater opportunities for social mobility (Finkelstein, 1991).

The latter hypothesis is, I would argue, the more compelling. The contemporary period, the era commencing with the end of the Second World War, is not only vastly different from previous eras but is different in ways that tend to reward the impression manager and self-monitor. During the latter part of the twentieth century, we have witnessed, for example, a continued trend toward increased specialization and social complexity, with an accompanying proliferation of roles; faster and more accessible modes of long-distance transportation, particularly air transportation; the continued expansion of the human lifespan, such that most inhabitants of the More Developed Regions (and increasingly more inhabitants of the Lesser Developed Regions) live long enough to experience a multiplicity of roles as well as to experience life itself from the vantage point of different generations; and, perhaps most important, a revolution in the communications-electronics industry that has had the most profound impact on the manner in which we understand and experience the world. Television is clearly the most significant of these new forms of material culture, although the importance of the "3C's" (cameras, computers, and camcorders) can hardly be gainsaid. McCrone (1991: 252) has come to a similar conclusion:

> "With the increasing complexity and specialization of modern culture, this need has probably led to a sharper sense of self than ever before. We are so aware of having to keep up a mask in public that our own inner world of private thoughts is thrown into sharp relief. Just as a tight pair of shoes can make us uncomfortably aware of our feet, the way that society forces us to wear a mask seems to have inadvertently made us more aware of the inner self we are masking."

The reality of life in the present is that, with the increased opportunity and motivation for doing so, we have become expert in the art of impression management. Freud wrote of civilization as entering the individual's mind (in the form of the superego) surreptitiously, much like the Trojan horse in Virgil's story. Just as the superego is ever-vigilant, relaxing only in sleep, our awareness of our selves is constant. For other species of primates, the state of being awake and alert denotes a condition of watchfulness and vigilance, especially with regard to conditions in the surrounding physical environment. For human beings, to be awake and alert carries the additional sense of awareness of one's own presence in the setting and the apprehension of others of this presence. The state of being "wide-awake," involving as it does continual apprehensiveness and surveillance, is difficult mental labor, a fact that explains our pleasure during the blissful moments of mindlessness, ecstasy, or flow (Csikszentmihalyi, 1990).

By the end of the 20th century, then, the nature of human self-consciousness has become more intense and more inward. Assisted now not only by mirrors but also by cameras, camcorders and computers, we undergo more continual public surveillance and private scrutiny than at any other time in history. Secondly, however, the object of our scrutiny has changed. Burdened with the knowledge of contingency, we recognize that it is not a faithful representation of our "true self" that motivates our self-consciousness but, rather, the image of our self that we have crafted to provide the socially necessary account of the being that resides within the physical body.

It would be a mistake were one to conclude, after reading Goffman or other postmodern writers, such as Baudrillard, that the anxiety of the self is, fundamentally, a symptom of narcissistic self-absorption. Social interaction, as Durkheim recognized was true in his day, is an arena in which the very important, but fragile, qualities of reputation and social honor are at stake. Dignity and self-esteem are the weighty concerns that remain the primary motivation for impression management even in the present era of postmodernity.[2]

But what is it about the present era that has served to transform the self from a real autonomous entity to an image? At the root of the perception of the loss of authenticity in human behavior and the corresponding need to maintain a sense of dignity is the revolution in communications that resulted from the post-WWII developments in the electronics industry. To understand the displacement of the social identity by the self-image, we must appreciate, for example, that in approximately 14 million American households (15 percent), there is a camcorder (Dullea, 1991). Next to the videotaped version, the actual events of our lives seem to have a certain ephemeral, unreal quality about them. They have become, according to one commentator, "a kind of shadow life, just material for televising and recording" (Dullea 1991: B4). Ironically, as the technology capable of capturing the individual essence of human lives grows more sophisticated seemingly with each day, there seem to be fewer authentic, or idiosyncratic, moments to capture.

Due to the increased possibility of surveillance, of being caught in a candid, unguarded moment, *privacy* (and its more sinister relation, *secrecy*) has assumed increased importance in the present age. Privacy allows individuals to have a *secret* self, which may be a sphere of behavior that is engaged in behind closed doors, out-of-view, and which the actor would prefer to keep separate from the public sphere. We want to maintain our private moments in order to relax but also because of fear of embarrassment or concern for the impression disclosure of the secret self might produce. To the extent that this is true, and I would argue that it is widely the case, it strongly indicates that the reflexive attention paid to the self is due not only to the necessity of having to present a consistent self to the public but to protect the disclosure of damaging evidence that one has constructed a self on an inherently flawed individual foundation.

The role of surveillance is highly significant here in that, because we are aware that we may be unknowingly under the surveillance of a hidden camera, microphone, or human being, we often take precautions to be always in a presentable or otherwise irreproachable state. The heightened awareness of the possibility of surveillance that has produced a defensive reaction among individuals that is manifest in their displaying front-stage behavior even in their back-stage regions is interesting in that it points to the frequent error that people make in presuming that the behavior that is observed in backstage regions is closer to the observed person's actual or true self than the behavior observed frontstage. The error seems to be rooted in the unexamined belief

that the pressures of surveillance that causes ego to change behavior are not similarly experienced by others.

Becoming One's Self: An Act Made Perfect in Habit

In considering the effects of postmodernism on the self, two
questions come immediately to mind. First, given the influence
of the communications media in the current age of postmodernism, does the traditional sociological conception of the self
remain a viable one? And, second, is the self a universal concept,
or are there sociological and historical variations in the nature of
selfhood? In addressing these questions, I have attempted to
make the case for considering the possibility that the self has become rationalized to the point where personalities may still exist
but only as images. Because of the importance of image for up-
ward social mobility, we have to remove any objectionable sign
of personal idiosyncrasy, unless it is interpretable as quaint or
charming, in which case we are encouraged to cultivate it. Such
signs are what people talk about and are, therefore, elements that
are entered into the social evaluation process. From our particular skills, hobbies, and avocations we derive a "personality" that
we hope will distinguish us from others. Some take flying
lessons, others climb mountains, an increasing number take yoga
and become vegetarians, others do karate or run, or read mystery novels, or take season tickets to the Braves, or read poetry,
or lift weights, or so on. In the unfolding of new relationships,
friends and lovers seek to identify certain signs of personality in
their friends and partners and will tend to take such signs as evidence of some significant long-term disposition that identifies
the person.

In addition to such behaviors, however, the most readily
available source of information about one's self is *appearance*, two
central indicators of which are clothing and hair. The interesting
sociological aspect of appearance is that, while we all *must* wear
something and *must* arrange our hair in some manner (or else
run the risk of being considered socially, even mentally, incom-

petent), we each have considerable control over the details of how we accomplish this minimal social requirement. Yet, even so, it cannot be gainsaid that styles of clothing and hair are not neutral indicators. Fashion serves as a marker of social opposition, generation and, most relevant for present purposes, one's choice of self. Susan Kaiser (1991) has recognized something very important when she describes the critical significance of appearances. "Experimentation with appearance management," she writes, "not only serves as a means for negotiating a sense of style but also as a mechanism for constructing and reconstructing a sense of self" (1991: 167). With a consideration of fashion, one is able to appreciate the critical importance of such apparently minor realms of autonomy to an individual's sense of self. It is true that our tastes in fashion are compelled into fairly narrow channels through the persuasive power of advertising. Yet, Kaiser and her colleagues make an important point when they argue (1991: 168) that ". . . to focus only on the [culture] industry's tendencies toward commodification and co-optation is to regress into a mood of capitulation, to ignore agency on the part of consumers, and to follow a path, ultimately, toward a dead end."

Thus we confront the question of whether, and to what degree, human autonomy exists. Recognizing that much has occurred in the twentieth century to reduce the sphere of human control, we still must acknowledge that individuals in the industrial democracies of the West experience everyday life as a continuous confrontation with the necessity to choose. More important than the choices of which cigarette to smoke or which brand of shaving lotion to purchase is the more self-defining decisions of whether to forego the pleasure of tobacco altogether or whether to grow a beard. This sphere of agency has levels which, although of varying degrees of relevance for the self, are frequently ignored by the critical theorist and others who ascribe to the "end of the individual" thesis. Clothing, hairstyle, and how one decorates one's work area (Harris, 1991) are integral to one's sense of self and so, too, are religious beliefs, ethnic identification, political viewpoint, tolerance of human differences, intellectual curiosity, and so on. That such characteristics are associated with social attributes such as social class, educational level, and gender must not blind us to the fact that these characteristics are, at some point in the individual's life, consciously selected and incorporated into the self that each of us continually reproduces. As Baudrillard (1975: 19) has written, "It is no longer a question of 'being' oneself but of 'producing' oneself."

Three additional points must be clarified in this view of the self. The *first* point is that the need to construct a self (the importance of having a self, any self) takes precedence over the actual content or quality of the self (its quality or social desirability). We must settle in other words for selves that either no one else seems to want or that many others devalue. Even given this fact, however, it is interesting to note that individuals will valorize both the chosen self and the cultural tradition from which that self sprung and in which it is grounded. More than mere rationalization is involved in this process of valorizing one's chosen self. The self, in order to be recognized as such, must be part of some cultural tradition. Selves, as cultural products, do not materialize from the ether or sprout forth, so to speak, from the head of Zeus. We may, with a postmodern disregard for genre or historical boundaries, introduce our chosen selves into settings where such selves are rarely, if ever, seen but one must not be surprised or take it personally when the reaction of the habitues is more outre than indifferent. Regardless of whether boundary-crossers are welcomed or shunned, the main point is that the self is recognizable as a certain type by virtue of the fact that it is apprehended as a carrier of a certain cultural tradition or habitus. The self is more than just a self; it is the embodiment of a particular (and valued) cultural experience. We may choose to valorize our ethnic identity, for example, or our Boston Brahmin ancestors, or our Southern Belle Gone-with-the-Wind heritage, or our feminist Susan B. Anthony roots, or any of a large number of other such cultural traditions that may be used both as a source of recognizable selves and as a source of legitimation for those selves. This is part of the reason why "working class kids get working class jobs." As Willis (1981) recognized, working class kids do not merely settle for working class jobs but may indeed aspire to a job in the factory because of the association of such work with the cultural values of the working class. A millhand does not deceive himself about the costs (and limited rewards) associated with his work; he is still able to valorize his identity as a "working man," however, by selecting for special emphasis those aspects of the work that require a particular skill or are otherwise estimable (Halle 1985). He may also actively screen cultural images concerning workers for those with positive content (such as the remembered images of barrel-chested laborers depicted in post office murals). The point here is that selves are indeed constructed but are not pure invention. We work with the physical material at hand and with whatever positive images pertaining to "people like us" that may be contained in the wider culture.

Our "selves," then, are as much group projects as they are the constructions of individuals. This is true in two important senses. The first is that the individual is aided in the work of the self by many others, such as spouses, partners, coworkers, parents, and children or other individuals with whom we come into daily, significant contact. Others who contribute to this project may exist only in memory or in one's imagination. It is interesting to consider that after we die our selves live on, if not in the form of an incorporeal soul at least in the form of the stories that are told about us by those who aided in the earlier construction of our selves. We are no longer present to direct the story onto paths that appeal to us but just the same our selves continue to be arranged from the bits and pieces of memories that others have. One might, following Goffman, consider the self to be, at least in part, a story or a discourse that we construct. It is, in other words, a role that we write and direct with ourselves as the key players. The play goes on after we depart; the remaining players can continue to refer to us as previous acts continue to impinge upon the action in the present. Though departed, our selves are continually invoked to further the plans or wishes of those who remain.

The second sense in which the self's construction is a group process stems from the idea of *frameworks*, or the manner in which social and cultural locations (Mannheim's *Lagerung*) serve as a realistic grounding for the self. The notion of frameworks is developed with great insight by Taylor (1989) who has convincingly argued that the status characteristics of ethnicity, class, regional ties, and so on, provide the background for our moral judgments and intuitions. Taylor dismisses the contention that since the solidity attributed to frameworks of the past has dissolved, social location no longer has the same relationship to "actual lives and judgements" that they once did. Taylor (1989: 27) reasons as follows:

> "I want to defend the strong thesis that doing without frameworks is utterly impossible for us; . . . stepping outside these limits would be tantamount to stepping outside what we would recognize as integral, that is, undamaged human personhood. . . . People may see their identity as defined partly by some moral or spiritual commitment, say as a Catholic, or an anarchist. Or they may define it in part by the nation or tradition they belong to, as an Armenian, say, or a Quebecoiis. What they are saying by this is not just that they are strongly attached to this spiritual view or background; rather it is that this provides the frame within which they can determine where they stand on questions of what is good, or worthwhile, or admirable, or of value. Put counterfactually, they are saying that were they to lose this commitment or identification, they would be at sea, as it were; they wouldn't know anymore, for an important range of questions, what the significance of things was for them."

Recognizing the central truth to Taylor's argument should not blind one to the sociological truth that, for many individuals living today, the traditional frames have lost their resonance. For these individuals, identity is framed through active participation in the consumer culture of contemporary society. The *second* point relevant to this discussion of the self is that choice and the capacity for self-production have a definite life cycle pattern, which is itself a historically variable phenomenon. Late adolescence and early adulthood constitutes a period of considerable fluctuation and lack of definition in the self. Different images are tried on, as it were, and almost as quickly taken off. We eschew any pretense of intellectuality one moment, yet embrace the world of ideas the very next. As with most things in life, the willingness (indeed, the necessity) to experiment with fashion is greatest when the self is least defined, namely, in adolescence and young adulthood.

As the life-defining matters of work and love are decided, however, the willingness (and, again, the need) to experiment declines. Our self takes on a more settled quality if only for the reason that George Herbert Mead (1910) articulated long ago, namely, the self becomes an "act made perfect in habit." By midlife, if not before, we have grown accustomed to the choices that we have made and have incorporated them into our total conception of our "self." The various components of the self, including appearance, ethnicity, gender, occupation, and family relationships among others, become so thoroughly integrated into our understanding of who we are as to become unremarkable (at least for us).

The degree to which this is true varies, of course, according to a number of factors. For minority group members in a strictly segregated society, one's status qua minority group member is continually brought to consciousness and made problematic. A woman amidst men or an old person in a college classroom with young adults is likely to have a heightened sense of the degree to which their self is constituted by their gender or age. So, too, depending upon the presence of physical traits that may be unusual or stigmatizing, one's understanding of one's self as bald, short, or light-skinned, for example, may never recede completely from conscious awareness. This point is well-known and need not be discussed at length here. I only wish to note that, even given the constraints on the self imposed by such ascribed status characteristics as ethnicity and gender, there remains a dimension of the self that must be selected, produced, and reproduced by the individual. This is the sphere of the self for which few, if any, scripts have been written.

Finally, the *third* point of clarification concerns the existence of disconfirming or exceptional cases. Cultural change occurs slowly and not all members of a culture are equally affected by whatever change, however significant, is occurring at the time. Clearly there exist groups today either (a) for whom the withering away of the self has not occurred or (b) for whom the self has been newly discovered.

In the first group, there are two subcategories. In the first part, I would place those whose lives are isolated, for the most part, from the world at large and who have been able to sustain a certain style of life across the decades regardless of the changes in the world at large. In this group, I would include individuals sentenced to long periods of incarceration; high-ranking military officers whose contact with others follows a script dictated by rank differences; and certain religious groups or other cloistered groups who intentionally restrict contact with the world. In the second part, I would include those engaged in occupations that involve life-sustaining work (farmers, fishermen and, perhaps doctors, particularly those engaged in life and death matters). Not coincidentally, most of those in the categories just mentioned are distinguished by their clothing, that is, by a specialized uniform. Army generals and prison inmates, for example, wear a uniform day-in and day-out with little room for personal embellishment or deviation. It is true that general officers are allowed some leeway in the design of their uniform but this is rarely, if ever, done. Cloistered religious orders and those in medical professions also are similarly garbed.

In the second group, those for whom the self is newly discovered or rediscovered, there are also two subcategories. In the first are those whose newly established sense of self is primarily a social or group-anchored identity. I would include AIDS sufferers, actively-engaged feminists and others committed to particular social movements, either progressive or reactionary, and those whose ethnicity places them on one or another side in a regional hostility, such as, for example, the gang warfare between Asian and Hispanic residents of Long Beach, California (Mydans, 1991), or between Korean and Black residents of New York City and Los Angeles. In each of these cases, an understanding of one's identity, one's self, becomes crystallized and paramount. In this sense, Andrea Dworkin, the feminist writer intent upon destroying the pornography industry, Randall Terry, the leader of Operation Rescue, and David Chum, a 17-year-old member of the Asian Boyz gang in Long Beach, share at least one essential characteristic in common: they possess a strong and mature sense of self.

The second subcategory of those who have a newly discovered sense of self include those whose newly-shaped identity stems not from a social identity but from a personal experience or encounter. I am thinking here of those who, following a religious conversion, brush with death, or other life redefining experience, come to think of their life as now infused with meaning or purpose.

Conclusions

Any strong conception of human agency or autonomy must be reassessed in the wake of postmodernism's emergence. This is not to say that the idea of an autonomous self has heretofore been unproblematic for social theorists. Indeed, one of the enduring and most fundamental claims of sociology concerning the self has been the degree to which the individual is a social product. It is a truism of the sociological perspective that environments shape individuals; consequently, it is believed that a change in environment (either the outer physical environment or the cultural environment or a change in role) will result in a change in certain properties of the self. There is, in other words, no constant self over the duration of one's biography, presuming that the individual did not spend his or her entire life in the same village.

A slightly different gloss on this idea of the social animal has been offered by critical theorists. In this view, the self may have at one time been able to carve out a niche of autonomous behavior from the wooden framework of basic socialization processes (or what Marcuse has identified as "basic repression"). The advancement of capitalism, however, brings with it additional constraints on behavior ("surplus repression") that, when coupled with the additional capacity for social control and surveillance enabled by the relentless refinements and breakthroughs in technology, may indeed have brought about an "end of the individual." This process of deindividuation is part of the rationalization of the modern world that Weber understood with remarkable prescience.

The loss of the self in the postmodern age may be discerned primarily in the perceived loss of *real* emotion, *real* feelings, and *real* opinions. We want to have values and ideas but cannot dismiss the suspicion that what we claim as expressions of a true inner state are merely sounds we make in order to create the desired impression. Those of us less agile with words content ourselves to assert our competence as social actors through an appropriate use of cliche and matching body posture. We no longer expect our interaction partners to display authentic emotion; a sense of mot juste, however, is much admired.

It is this sense of selflessness, what the writer Bernard Malamud (1961) described as being "weatherless," that accounts for our fascination with telecasts of catastrophic occurrences and significant athletic events. We scrutinize the euphoria of the players romping on the infield immediately following the final pitch of the culminating World Series game or the dazed expression of the homeowners sifting through the littered remnants of their home following a tornado in the hope of witnessing individuals in unscripted situations who may present us with an authentic depiction of spontaneous behavior. We suspect our own displays of happiness, sadness, anger and so on of a certain bogus quality. Even our tears, as Kundera (1984) has observed, become objects of our wonder and, ultimately, a source of pride as we consider how sensitive we must appear to others at the very moment the glistening tear becomes visible.

The changes in the self that have evolved during the postwar period have been problematic for social psychology generally and, in particular, for symbolic interactionism. The theoretical premise underlying much social psychological research, particularly that done by sociologists, is that of a role-making, world-shaping individual. The problem that postmodernism presents for those social psychologists who, like symbolic interactionists, generally take a very strong position on human autonomy and social agency, is the logical difficulty of sustaining commitments to science and the self, too. Denzin (1990: 148) gets to the heart of the matter when he writes of Blumer that, like Weber, he sought

> "an objective, interpretive science that is both subjective and rigorously objective, and valid and in conformity with the canons of a natural, empirical, science. They want it both ways. Herein lies their problem, for an interpretive discipline must reject the canons of positivism (of whatever form), and wholeheartedly embrace a fully interpretive, hermeneutic [sic] perspective."

But, more than this, the problem for social psychologists is that the world has changed. Through the palimpsest of cultural traces that remain available from earlier periods, one may learn of former social worlds. From impressionist paintings of the late 19th century, for example, we obtain a glimpse of the everyday lives of the confident, self-assured, middle classes of Europe and North America. As a theoretical account of the self in such a milieu, the social behaviorism of Mead and Cooley must surely be judged to be a success, on both empirical and aesthetic grounds. Yet one must wonder, along with Denzin, how the developers of symbolic interactionism would see the self now, as the twentieth century comes to a close. According to Denzin (1990: 151),

> "If Blumer were writing today he would tell us to confront the world that we live in. This is a postmodern world, and it was not the world Blumer initially confronted when he did his critique of Thomas and Znaniecki. . . . It is time to go beyond Blumer."

NOTES

1. One apparent outcome of the penetration of media images into our daily lives has been the decline of the self as a responsible moral agent. Although much has been written concerning this development, it is extremely difficult to evaluate both for the fact that much evidence exists of highly principled behavior that would seemingly contradict the basic contention and, second, for the reason that postmodernism has largely been silent on issues relating to the moral underpinnings of human actions. Whether such a decline has actually occurred is far from obvious. For a further discussion of this topic, please see Eagleton (1985); and Johnston (1990).

2. In his highly regarded work on the self, Taylor (1989: 15) comments on the human concern with self-presentation and dignity. He writes that,

> "Our 'dignity,' in the particular sense I am using it here, is our sense of ourselves as commanding (attitudinal) respect . . . our dignity is so much woven into our very com-

portment. The very way we walk, move, gesture, speak is shaped from the earliest moments by our awareness that we appear before others, that we stand in public space, and that this space is potentially one of respect or contempt, of pride or shame. Our style of movement expresses how we see ourselves as enjoying respect or lacking it, as commanding it or failing to do so."

Contributors

Lawrence J. Biskowski is the author of articles on Hannah Arendt and practical judgment (*Journal of Politics*), and of numerous articles on environmental issues, including "Eco-justice," "Environmental Defense Fund," "Marine Mammals Protection Act," "Greenpeace," "Earth Island Institute," and others. He is Assistant Professor of Political Science at the University of Georgia, where he teaches contemporary political theory.

Linda Marie Brooks is the author of the forthcoming *The Negative Sublime: Autobiography and Self-Annihilation in Schiller and Coleridge*, editorial consultant for Philippe Lacoue-Labarthe's *Typography: Mimesis, Philosophy, Politics* (Harvard) and *The Subject of Philosophy* (Minnesota) and is currently coediting and contributing to a book-length collection of articles on Eastern and Western concepts of the self titled "Re-Imagining the Self: Agency, Representation, and Identity Politics." She has published on Romanticism, the postmodern sublime, fascist semiotics, and on contemporary art, theater, and independent film. She is Assistant Professor of Comparative Literature at the University of Georgia.

Bernard P. Dauenhauer is University Professor of Philosophy and until recently, Director of the Humanities Center at the University of Georgia. He is the author of *Silence: The Phenomenon and Its Ontological Interpretation*, *The Politics of Hope*, *Elements of a Responsible Politics*, and numerous articles including a number on the self, especially as it relates to Husserl, Heidegger, and Merleau Ponty. He is the editor of *At the Nexus of Philosophy and History* and *Textual Fidelity and Textual Disregard*.

He is currently working on a book-length study tentatively titled *Citizenship: A Politico-Moral Study*.

Victoria Davion is the author of articles on ethics and feminist philosophy (*Hypatia: A Journal of Feminist Philosophy*), and on political philosophy (*Social Theory and Practice*). She is Assistant Professor of Philosophy at the University of Georgia. She teaches applied ethics, including contemporary moral issues, business ethics, and environmental ethics.

Margaret Dickie is the Helen H. Lanier Distinguished Professor of English at the University of Georgia. She is the author of *Hart Crane: The Patterns of His Poetry* (published under the name Magaret Uroff), *Sylvia Plath and Ted Hughes*, *On the Modernist Long Poem*, *Lyric Contingencies: Emily Dickinson and Wallace Stevens*, and numerous articles. She is currently editing a collection of essays on twentieth-century American women poets and the canon, and is at work on a book-length study on Gertrude Stein, Elizabeth Bishop, and Adrienne Rich.

James J. Dowd is the author of *Stratification Among the Aged*, the co-author of *The Primary Group: Its Rediscovery in Contemporary Sociology*, and of numerous articles, including a number of studies on the self. He is currently completing a book-length study titled "Rationalism and Reaction," a study on cultural theory and the construction of self-identity over the life course, including the concept of the self in film and media and in old age. He is also currently at work on a project focusing on the relation of personal and social identity as manifested in army generals and in other military elite. He is Professor of Sociology at the University of Georgia.

R. Baxter Miller is Professor of English and Director of the Institute of African American Studies at the University of Georgia. He is the author of *The Art and Imagination of Langston Hughes* for which he won the 1991 American Book Award, *The Reference Guide to Langston Hughes and Gwendolyn Brooks*, and is the editor of *Black American Literature and Humanism* and *Black American Poets Between Worlds, 1940-1960*. He is one of five co-editors of the McGraw Hill series *African American Tradition in Literature*, with a volume on the Harlem Renaissance, 1915–1945, and guest editor for a special issue on Langston Hughes for *Black American Literature Forum*. He is currently at work on a book-length study entitled "New Chicago Renaissance from Wright to Kent."

David D. Roberts is the author of *The Syndicalist Tradition and Italian Fascism* and *Benedetto Croce and the Uses of Historicism*; and the forthcoming Italian translation *Florence: La Nuova Italia*, as well as numerous articles and reviews. He has recently completed a book-length study entitled "Nothing But History: Theme and Variation in the Search for a Post-Metaphysical Culture." He is professor of Modern European History at the University of Georgia.

Sarah Spence is the author of *The Rhetorics of Reason and Desire: Vergil, Augustine, and the Troubadours, The French Chansons of Charles d'Orleans*, and has just completed a book-length study titled "Corpus: Body, Text and Self in Twelfth-Century France." She is Associate Professor of Comparative Literature and adjunct member of the Classics Department at the University of Georgia. She is currently at work on a book titled "The Feminine Voice in Vergil's Aeneid."

James A. Winders is the author of *Gender, Theory, and the Canon*, co-author of *Reading for Difference: Texts on Gender, Race, and Class*, and has published numerous articles on Postmodern Theory, Feminist Theory, Marxism, French Literature, and Popular Music. He is currently at work on a book-length study on African music in contemporary Paris. He is Professor of History at Appalachian State University.

Bibliography

Alexander, Jeffrey. "Symbolic interactionism: Individualism and the Work of Blumer and Goffman." In *Twenty Lectures: Sociological Theory since World War II*. New York: Columbia University Press, 1987.

Alexander, Marguerite. *Flights From Realism: Themes and Strategies in Postmodernist British and American Fiction*. London: Edward Arnold, 1990.

Althusser, Louis. *For Marx*. Tr. Ben Brewster. London: Penguin, 1969.

Anderson, Perry. *Arguments Within English Marxism*. London: Verso/NLB, 1980.

——. *Considerations on Western Marxism*. London: Verso/NLB, 1976.

Arendt, Hannah. "What Is *Existenz* Philosophy?" *Partisan Review* 1946, 13: 34–56.

——. "Social Science Techniques and the Study of Concentration Camps." *Jewish Social Studies* 12/1 (1950): 49–64.

——. *The Human Condition*. Chicago: University of Chicago Press, 1958.

——. *On Revolution*. Harmondsworth: Penguin, 1963.

——. *Men in Dark Times*. San Diego: Harcourt Brace Jovanovich, 1968.

——. "Thinking and Moral Considerations: A Lecture." *Social Research* 38/3 (1971): 417–46.

——. *The Origins of Totalitarianism*. New York: Harcourt Brace Jovanovich, 1973.

——. *Between Past and Future*. Harmondsworth: Penguin, 1977.

——. *The Life of the Mind*. New York: Harcourt Brace Jovanovich, 1978.

——. "Labor, Work, Action." In *Amor Mundi: Explorations in the Faith and Thought of Hannah Arendt*. Ed. James Bernauer. Dordrecht: Martinus Nijhoff, 1987.

Aristotle. *The Nichomachean Ethics*. Tr. David Ross. London: Oxford University Press, 1980.

Baker, Houston A., Jr. *The Journey Back: Issues in Black Literature*. Chicago: University of Chicago Press, 1980.

Bakhtin, Mikhail. *Rabelais and His World*. Tr. Helen Iswolsky. Cambridge: MIT Press, 1968.

Balsamo, Anne. "Imagining Cyborgs: Postmodernism and Symbolic Interactionism." *Studies in Symbolic Interaction* 10 (Pt. B) (1989): 369–381.

Barash, Jeffrey Andrew. *Martin Heidegger and the Problem of Historical Meaning*. Dordrecht: Martinus Nijhoff, 1988.

Barber, Benjamin. "Cultural Conservatism and Democratic Education." *Salmagundi* 81 (1989): 159–173.

Barthes, Roland. "The Death of the Author." In *Image-Music-Text*. Ed. & Tr. Stephen Heath. New York: Hill and Wang, 1977.

———. *The Empire of Signs*. Tr. Richard Howard. New York: Hill & Wang, 1982.

———. *Camera Lucida: Reflections on Photography*. Tr. Richard Howard. New York: Hill & Wang, 1981.

Baudelaire, Charles. *Les Fleurs du mal*. Tr. Richard Howard. Boston: David R. Godine, 1982.

Baudrillard, Jean. *The Mirror of Production.* Tr. Mark Poster. St. Louis: Telos Press, 1975.

———. *De la seduction*. Paris: Editions Galilee, 1979.

Bauman, Zygmunt. *Modernity and Ambivalence*. Ithaca: Cornell University Press, 1991.

Bec, Pierre. "Espace poétique." *Cahiers de Civilisation Médiévale* 29 (1986): 9–14.

Beckett, Samuel. *The Unnamable*. New York: Grove Press, 1970.

Bellah, Robert N., et al. *Habits of the Heart: Individualism and Commitment in American Life*. New York: Harper & Row, 1986.

Benhabib, Seyla. *Situating the Self: Gender, Community and Postmodernism in Contemporary Ethics*. New York: Routledge, 1992.

———. "Liberal Dialogue Versus a Discursive Theory of Legitimation." In *Liberalism and the Moral Life*. Ed. Nancy Rosenblum. Cambridge, Ma.: Harvard University Press, 1989.

Bennett, William J. *To Reclaim a Legacy: A Report on the Humanities in Higher Education.* Reprinted in *Chronicle of Higher Education* 28 November 1984: 16–21.

———. *Our Children and Our Country.* New York: Simon & Schuster, 1988.

Berger, Peter L. *Invitation to Sociology: A Humanistic Perspective.* New York: Anchor Press, 1963.

Berry, Faith. *Langston Hughes: Before and Beyond Harlem.* Westport: Lawrence Hill, 1983.

Black, Joel. *The Aesthetics of Murder: A Study in Romantic Literature and Contemporary Culture.* Baltimore: Johns Hopkins University Press, 1991.

Blight, David W. *Frederick Douglass' Civil War.* Baton Rouge and London: Louisiana State University Press, 1989.

Bloch, R. Howard. *Genealogies and Etymologies: A Literary Anthropology of the French Middle Ages.* Chicago: University Press, 1983.

Bloom, Allan. *The Closing of the American Mind.* New York: Simon & Schuster, 1987.

Bloom, Harold. *A Map of Misreading.* New York: Oxford University Press, 1975.

———. *The Anxiety of Influence: A Theory of Poetry.* New York: Oxford University Press, 1973.

Boswell, John. *Christianity, Homosexuality, and Social Tolerance: Gay People in the Western World from Classical Antiquity to the Fourteenth Century.* Chicago: University of Chicago Press, 1980.

Bové, Paul. "The Foucault Phenomenon: The Problematics of Style." Foreword to *Foucault*, by Gilles Deleuze. Minneapolis: University of Minnesota Press, 1988.

Brinkley, Tony and Joseph Arsenault. "The Shoah, Annihilation, with Respect to the Sublime." *The Centennial Review* 35 (Fall 1991): 479–500.

Brogan, Jacqueline. *Part of the Climate: American Cubist Poetry.* Berkeley: University of California Press, 1991.

Burgwinkle, William. *The Troubadour as Subject: Biography, Erotics and Culture* (DAI 49/12A, p. 3743).

Burke, Carolyn. "Getting Spliced: Modernism and Sexual Difference." *American Quarterly* 39:100.

Cadava, Eduardo, et al., eds. *Who Comes After the Subject?* New York: Routledge, 1991.

Caputo, John D. *Radical Hermeneutics: Repetition, Deconstruction, and the Hermeneutic Project.* Bloomington: Indiana University Press, 1987.

———. "Gadamer's Closet Essentialism: A Derridean Critique." In *Dialogue and Deconstruction: The Gadamer-Derrida Encounter.* Eds. Diane P. Michelfelder & Richard E. Palmer. Albany: State University of New York Press, 1989.

Card, Claudia. "Caring and Evil." *Hypatia: A Journal of Feminist Philosophy* 5.1 (1990): 101–108.

Chisholm, Dianne. *H. D.'s Freudian Poetics: Psychoanalysis in Translation.* Ithaca: Cornell University Press, 1992.

Chakrabarty, Dipesh. "Postcoloniality and the Artifice of History: Who Speaks for 'Indian' Pasts?" *Representations* 37 (Winter, 1992).

Chodorow, Nancy Julia. "Toward a Relational Individualism: The Meditation of Self Through Psychoanalysis." In *Reconstructing Individualism: Autonomy, Individuality, and the Self in Western Thought,* 197–207. Eds. T. V. Heller, M. Sosna & D. E. Wellbery. Stanford: Stanford University Press, 1986.

Coetzee, J.M. "On the Edge of Revelation." *The New York Review of Books* 18 (Dec. 1986): 10–12.

Cole, David. *The Theatrical Event: A Mythos, A Vocabulary, A Perspective.* Middletown: Wesleyan University Press, 1975.

Connell, R.W. "Curriculum Politics: Hegemony and Strategies for Social Change." In *Popular Culture, Schooling, and Everyday Life.* Ed. Henry Giroux et al. Granby: Bergin & Garvey, 1989.

Connolly, William E. *Identity-Difference: Democratic Negotiations of Political Paradox.* Ithaca: Cornell University Press, 1991.

Corngold, Stanley. *The Fate of the Self: German Writers and French Theory.* New York: Columbia University Press, 1986.

Costello, Bonnie. *Marianne Moore: Imaginary Possessions.* Cambridge, Ma.: Harvard University Press, 1981.

Croce, Benedetto. *Cultura e vita morale.* Bari: Laterza, 1955.

———. *Filosofia della pratica.* Bari: Laterza, 1963.

———. *Filosofia e storiografia.* Bari: Laterza, 1969.

———. *Discorsi di varia filosofia.* 2 vols. Bari: Laterza, 1959.

———. *Terze pagine sparse.* 2 vols. Bari: Laterza, 1955.

———. *History of the Kingdom of Naples.* Chicago: University of Chicago Press, 1970.

———. "Frammenti di etica," In *Etica e politica.* Bari: Laterza, 1967.

————. *Ultimi saggi*. Bari: Laterza, 1963.

————. *Conversazioni critiche*. 4th ser. Bari: Laterza, 1951.

————. *Il carattere della filosofia moderna*. Bari: Laterza, 1963.

Cronyn, Hume. *A Terrible Liar*. New York: Morrow, 1991.

Csikszentmihalyi, Mihalyi. *Flow: The Psychology of Optimal Experience*. New York: Harper & Row, 1990.

Culler, Jonathan. *Structuralist Poetics*. Ithaca and London: Cornell University Press, 1972.

Darnton, Robert. "Workers Revolt: The Great Cat Massacre of the Rue Saint-Severin." In *The Great Cat Massacre and Other Episodes in French Cultural History*. New York: Basic Books, 1984.

————. "First Steps Toward a History of Reading." In *The Kiss of Lamourette: Reflections in Cultural History*. New York: Norton, 1990.

Dauenhauer, Bernard P. *Elements of Responsible Politics*. Dordrecht: Kluwer Academic Publishers, 1991.

————. "The Ego Revisited." *Journal of the British Society for Phenomenology*. 21 (Jan. 1990): 48–52.

————. *The Politics of Hope*. New York and London: Routledge and Kegan Paul, 1986.

————. "Heidegger: Spokesman for the Dweller." *The Southern Journal of Philosophy* 15.2 (1977): 189–199.

Davion, Victoria. "Action Guides and Wrongful Intentions." *Public Affairs Quarterly* 6.4 (1992): 365–374.

————. "Do Good Feminists Compete?" *Hypatia: A Journal of Feminist Philosophy* 2.2 (1987): 55–65.

————. "How Feminist is Ecofeminism?" In *The Environmental Ethics and Policy Book*. Eds. Donald VanDeveer & Christine Pierce. California: Wadsworth Publishing Company, 1993.

————. "Integrity and Radical Change." In *Feminist Ethics*. Ed. Claudia Card. Kansas: The University of Kansas Press, 1991.

————. "Pacifism and Care." *Hypatia: A Journal of Feminist Philosophy* 5.1 (1990): 90-100.

Davis, Natalie Zemon. "Women On Top." In *Society and Culture in Early Modern France*. Stanford: Stanford University Press, 1975.

————. *The Return of Martin Guerre*. Cambridge, Ma.: Harvard University Press, 1983.

de Lauretis, Teresa. *Alice Doesn't: Feminism, Semiotics, Cinema*. Bloomington: Indiana University Press, 1984.

Deleuze, Gilles and Felix Guattari. *Anti-oedipus: Capitalism and Schizophrenia (Vol. 1)* Tr. Brian Massumi. Minneapolis: University of Minnesota Press, 1983.

———. *A Thousand Plateaus: Capitalism and Schizophrenia (Vol. 2)* Tr. Robert Hurley, Mark Seem & Helen Lang. Minneapolis: University of Minnesota Press, 1987.

DeLillo, Don. *White Noise*. New York: Viking Penguin, 1985.

Denzin, Norman K. "The Spaces of Postmodernism: Reading Plummer on Blumer." *Symbolic Interaction* 13 (1990): 145–154.

———. "Postmodern Social Theory." *Sociological Theory* 4 (1986): 194–204.

———. "Thoughts on Critique and Renewal in Symbolic Interactionism." *Studies in Symbolic Interaction* 10 (1989): 3–8.

———. "Blue Velvet: Postmodern Contradictions." *Theory, Culture and Society* 5 (1988): 461–73.

Derrida, Jacques. "Living on Borderlines." In *Deconstruction and Criticism*. New York: Seabury, 1979.

———. *Margins of Philosophy*. Tr. Alan Bass. Chicago: University of Chicago Press, 1982.

———. *Of Grammatology*. Tr. Gayatri Chakravorty Spivak. Baltimore: Johns Hopkins University Press, 1976.

———. "Eating Well." In *Who Comes After the Subject*. Ed. Eduardo Cadava, Peter Conner & Jean-Luc Nancy. New York: Routledge, 1991.

———. *Writing and Difference*. Tr. Alan Bass. Chicago: University of Chicago Press, 1978.

———. "Otobiographies." In *The Ear of the Other: Otobiography, Transference, Translation*. New York: Schocken, 1985.

———. *The Post Card: From Socrates to Freud and Beyond*. Tr. Alan Bass. Chicago: University of Chicago Press, 1987.

Dickie, Margaret. *Hart Crane: The Patterns of His Poetry*. Urbana: University of Illinois Press, 1974. (First published under the name, Uroff, M.D.)

———. *Sylvia Plath and Ted Hughes*. Urbana: University of Illinois Press, 1979.

———. *On the Modernist Long Poem*. Iowa City: University of Iowa Press, 1986.

———. *Lyric Contingencies: Emily Dickinson and Wallace Stevens*. Philadelphia: University of Pennsylvania Press, 1991.

Diehl, Joanne Feit. *Women Poets and the American Sublime*. Bloomington: Indiana University Press, 1990.

Douglass, Frederick. *Life and Times of Frederick Douglass*. New York: Collier and McMillan, 1892;1962.

———. *My Bondage and My Freedom (1855)*. Ed. William L. Andrews. Urbana and Chicago: University of Illinois Press, 1987.

———. "Narrative of the Life of Frederick Douglass." *The Classic Slave Narratives*. Ed. Henry Louis Gates, Jr. New York: Signet, 1987.

Dowd, James J. "Ever Since Durkheim: The Socialization of Human Development." *Human Development* 33 (1990): 138–159.

———. "Social Psychology in a Postmodern Age: A Discipline Without a Subject." *American Sociologist* 26 (Fall/Winter) 1991: 28–49.

Dreyfus, Hubert L. & Paul Robinow. *Michel Foucault: Beyond Structuralism and Hermeneutics*. 2nd ed. Chicago: University of Chicago Press, 1982.

Du Bois, W. E. B. *A Soliloquy on Viewing My Life from the Last Decade of Its First Century: The Autobiography of W. E. B. Du Bois*. New York: International Publishers, 1968.

Dullea, Georgia. "Camcorder! Action! Lives Become Roles." *The New York Times*. August 15, 1991: A1, B4.

Dylan, Bob. "I Shall Be Free - No. 10." *Another Side of Bob Dylan*. Columbia Records, 1964.

Eagleton, Terry. "Capitalism, Modernism and Postmodernism." *New Left Review* 152 (1985): 60-73.

———. *The Significance of Theory*. Cambridge: Blackwell, 1990.

Eliot, T.S. *Four Quartets*. San Diego: Harcourt Brace Jovanovich, 1943.

———. *Selected Prose of T.S. Eliot*. Ed. Frank Kermode. New York: Harcourt Brace Jovanovich, 1975.

Ellis, John M. *Against Deconstruction*. Princeton, N.J.: Princeton University Press, 1989.

Featherstone, Mike. "Towards a Sociology of Postmodern Culture." In *Social Structure and Culture*. Ed. Hans Haferkamp. New York: Walter de Gruyter, 1989.

———. "Lifestyle and Consumer Culture." *Theory, Culture and Society* 4 (1988): 55–70.

Finkelstein, Joanne. *The Fashioned Self*. Philadelphia: Temple University Press, 1991.

Fish, Stanley. "How To Recognize a Poem When You See One." In *Is There a Text in This Class?* Cambridge, Ma.: Harvard University Press, 1980.

Foucault, Michel. *Language, Counter-Memory, Practice: Selected Essays and Interviews*. Ed. Donald F. Bouchard. Ithaca: Cornell University Press, 1977.

———. *Power/Knowledge: Selected Interviews and Other Writings, 1972–1977*. Ed. Colin Gordon. New York: Pantheon, 1980.

———. "The Subject and Power." Afterword to *Michel Foucault: Beyond Structuralism and Hermeneutics*. Hubert L. Dreyfus and Paul Rabinow. 2nd ed. Chicago: University of Chicago Press, 1983.

———. *The History of Sexuality: Volume I: An Introduction*. Tr. Robert Hurley. New York: Vintage, 1980.

———. *The History of Sexuality: Volume II: The Use of Pleasure*. Tr. Robert Hurley. New York: Vintage, 1986.

———. *The History of Sexuality: Volume III: The Care of the Self*. Tr. Robert Hurley. New York: Vintage, 1989.

———. *The Order of Things*. Tr. A.M. Sheridan-Smith. New York: Vintage Books, 1973.

———. *The Archeology of Knowledge*. Tr. A.M. Sheridan-Smith. New York: Harper & Row, 1972.

———. *Foucault: A Critical Reader*. Ed. David Couzzens Hoy. Oxford: Blackwell, 1986.

Franchot, Jenny. "The Punishment of Esther: Frederick Douglass and the Construction of the Feminine." In *Frederick Douglass: New Literary and Historical Essays*. Ed. Eric J. Sundquist. Cambridge: Cambridge University Press, 1990.

Frank, Arthur W. "The Self at the Funeral: An Ethnography on the Limits of Postmodernism." *Studies in Symbolic Interaction*. 11 (1990): 191–206.

Freire, Paulo. *Cultural Action for Freedom*. Cambridge, Ma.: Harvard Educational Review, 1970.

———. *Pedagogy of the Oppressed*. New York: Seabury, 1970.

———. *Education for Critical Consciousness*. New York: Seabury, 1974.

Gadamer, Hans-Georg. *Reason in the Age of Science*. Cambridge: MIT Press, 1981.

———. *Truth and Method*. New York: Seabury, 1975.

———. *Philosophical Hermeneutics*. Berkeley and Los Angeles: University of California Press, 1977.

Gates, Henry Louis, Jr. *Loose Canons: Notes on the Culture Wars*. New York: Oxford University Press, 1992.

———. *The Signifying Monkey: A Theory of African-American Literary Criticism*. New York: Oxford University Press, 1988.

Geertz, Clifford. "Deep Play: Notes on the Balinese Cockfight." In *The Interpretation of Cultures: Selected Essays*. New York: Basic Books, 1973.

Gergen, Kenneth. *The Saturated Self: Dilemmas of Identity in Contemporary Life*. New York: Basic, 1991.

Gide, André. *The Immoralist*. New York: Vintage, 1970.

Gilligan, Carol. *In a Different Voice*. Cambridge, Ma.: Harvard University Press, 1982.

———. "Remapping the Moral Domain: New Images of the Self in Relationship." In *Reconstructing Individualism*, 237–252. Ed. T. Heller, et al. Stanford: Stanford University Press, 1986.

———. "Moral Orientation and Moral Development." In *Women and Moral Theory*. Eds. Eva Kittay & Diana T. Meyers. Maryland: Rowman and Littlefield Press, 1987.

Goffman, Erving. *Presentation of Self in Everyday Life*. Garden City: Doubleday, 1959.

———. "The Interaction Order." *American Sociological Review* 48 (1983): 1–17.

Goodheart, Eugene. "Some Speculations on Don DeLillo and the Cinematic Real." In *Introducing Don DeLillo*. Ed. F. Lentricchia. Durham: Duke University Press, 1991.

Greenblatt, Stephen. *Renaissance Self-Fashioning: From More to Shakespeare*. Chicago: University of Chicago Press, 1980.

Grossberg, Lawrence. "Pedagogy in the Present: Politics, Postmodernity and the Popular." In Henry Giroux, et al., eds. *Popular Culture, Schooling, and Everyday Life*. Granby: Bergin & Harvey, 1989.

Gutmann, Amy. *Democratic Education*. Princeton: Princeton University Press, 1987.

H. D. *H.D.: Collected Poems: 1912–1944*. New York: New Directions, 1983.

————. *Notes on Thought and Vision and The Wise Sappho*. San Francisco: City Lights Books, 1982.

————. *Tribute to Freud*. New York: New Directions, 1974.

Habermas, Jürgen. *Toward a Rational Society*. Boston: Beacon Press, 1970.

————. *The New Conservatism*. Cambridge: MIT Press, 1989.

Hacking, Ian. "The Archaeology of Foucault." In *Foucault: A Critical Reader*. Ed. David Couzens Hoy. Oxford: Blackwell, 1986.

Halle, David. *America's Working Man: Work, Home, and Politics Among Blue-collar Property Owners*. Chicago: University of Chicago Press, 1985.

Harris, Daniel. "What Do Office Workers Place on Their Desks and in Their Offices?" *Salmagundi* 92 (1991): 202–210.

Havel, Václav. *Disturbing the Peace: A Conversation With Karel Hvizdala*. New York: Vintage, 1991.

Hegel, Robert E. and Richard C. Hessney, eds. *Expressions of the Self in Chinese Literature*. New York: Columbia University Press, 1985.

Heidegger, Martin. *What Is Called Thinking?* New York: Harper & Row, 1968.

————. *On Time and Being*. Tr. Joan Stambaugh. New York: Harper & Row, 1972.

————. *Early Greek Thinking*. Tr. David F. Krell and Frank A. Capuzzi. San Francisco: Harper & Row, 1984.

————. *The Basic Problems of Phenomenology*. Tr. Albert Hofstadter. Bloomington: Indiana University Press, 1982.

————. *Nietzsche* Tr. Frank A. Capuzzi. San Francisco: Harper & Row, 1982.

————. "The Origin of the Work of Art." *Poetry, Language and Thought*. Tr. Albert Hofstadter. New York: Harper & Row, 1971.

————. *Being and Time*. Tr. John Macquarrie & Edward Robinson. Ed. David Farrell Krell. New York: Harper & Row, 1962.

Heller, Joseph. *Something Happened*. New York: Alfred A. Knopf, 1974.

Heller, T. V., M. Sosna & D. E. Wellbery, eds. *Reconstructing Individualism: Autonomy, Individuality, and the Self in Western Thought*. Stanford: Stanford University Press, 1986.

Hepburn, Katherine. *Me*. New York: Alfred A. Knopf, 1991.

Hewitt, John P. *Self and Society: A Symbolic Interactionist Social Psychology*. Boston: Allyn and Bacon, 1991.

Hill, Melvyn, ed. *Hannah Arendt: The Recovery of the Public World*. New York: St. Martin's Press, 1979.

Hirsch, Marianne. *The Mother / Daughter Plot: Narrative, Psychoanalysis, Feminism*. Bloomington: Indiana University Press, 1989.

Hjort, Mette. *The Strategy of Letters*. Cambridge, Ma.: Harvard University Press, 1993.

Hoagland, Sarah Lucia. "Some Concerns about Noddings." *Hypatia: A Journal of Feminist Philosophy* 5.1 (1990): 109–114.

Homans, Margaret. *Bearing the Word: Language and Female Experience in Nineteenth-Century Women's Writing*. Chicago: University of Chicago Press, 1986.

———. *Women Writers and Poetic Identity: Dorothy Wordsworth, Emily Brontë, and Emily Dickinson*. Princeton: Princeton University Press, 1980.

Hornby, Richard. *Script into Performance*. Austin: University of Texas Press, 1977.

Son House, "Louise McGhee." *Father of the Delta Blues: The Complete 1965 Sessions*. Columbia/Legacy, 1992.

Houston, Barbara. "Caring and Exploitation." *Hypatia: A Journal of Feminist Philosophy* 5.1 (1990): 155–199.

Hughes, Langston. *The Big Sea*. New York: Hill and Wang, 1986.

———. *I Wonder as I Wander: An Autobiographical Journey*. New York: Rinehardt, 1956.

Ice-T. "Escape From the Killing Fields." *O.G./Original Gangster*. Sire Records, 1991.

Irigaray, Luce. "Ce sexe qui n'en est pas un." In *New French Feminisms: An Anthology*. Eds. Elaine Marks & Isabelle de Courtivron. New York: Schocken Books, 1981.

Iser, Wolfgang. *The Implied Reader: Patterns of Communication in Prose Fiction from Bunyan to Beckett*. Baltimore: Johns Hopkins University Press, 1974.

Jacob, Margaret C. *Living the Enlightenment: Freemasonry and Politics in 18th-Century Europe*. New York: Oxford University Press, 1991.

Jacobs, Harriet A. *Incidents in the Life of a Slave Girl Written by Herself*. Cambridge, Ma.: Harvard University Press, 1987.

Jameson, Fredric. "Postmodernism and Consumer Society." In *Postmodernism and its Discontents*. Ed. E. Ann Kaplan. London: Verso, 1988.

———. "Postmodernism, or the Cultural Logic of Late Capitalism." *New Left Review* 146 (1984): 53–92.

Jardine, Alice A. *Gynesis: Configurations of Woman and Modernity*. Ithaca: Cornell University Press, 1985.

Jay, Martin. *Marxism and Totality*. Berkeley: University of California Press, 1984.

Johnson, Barbara. *A World of Difference*. Baltimore: Johns Hopkins University Press, 1987.

Johnston, John. "Ideology, Representation, Schizophrenia: Toward a Theory of the Postmodern Subject." In *After the Future: Postmodern Times and Places*. Ed. Gary Shapiro. New York: SUNY Press, 1990.

Jones, Kathleen B. "On Authority: Or, Why Women Are Not Entitled to Speak." In *Foucault & Feminism: Reflections on Resistance*. Ed. Irene Diamond & Lee Quinby. Boston: Northeastern University Press, 1988.

Jones, LeRoi. *The Dutchman*. New York: Morrow, 1964.

Jones, Quincey. *I Heard That*. 1975.

Kaiser, Susan B., Richard H. Nagasawa & Sandra S. Hutton. "Fashion, Postmodernity and Personal Appearance: A Symbolic Interactionist Formulation." *Symbolic Interaction* 14 (1991): 165–185.

Kant, Immanual. *Groundwork of the Metaphysic of Morals*. Tr. H. J. Paton. New York: Harper & Row, 1964.

Karenga, Maulana Ron. "Black Cultural Nationalism." In *The Black Aesthetic*. Ed. Addison Gayle, Jr. New York: Anchor Books, 1972.

Kateb, George. "Freedom and Worldliness in the Thought of Hannah Arendt." *Political Theory* 5/2 (1977): 141–82.

———. *The Inner Ocean*. Ithaca: Cornell, 1992.

Kay, Sarah. "Love in a Mirror." *Medium Aevum* 52 (1983): 272–285.

Kendrick, Laura. *The Game of Love: Troubadour Wordplay*. Berkeley: University of California Press, 1988.

Kimball, Charles. *Tenured Radicals: How Politics has Corrupted Higher Education*. New York: Harper & Row, 1990.

Kipnis, Laura. "Feminism: The Political Conscience of Postmodernism?" In *Universal Abandon? The Politics of Postmodernism*. Ed. Andrew Ross. Minneapolis: University of Minnesota Press, 1988.

Kolb, David. *The Critique of Pure Modernity*. Chicago: University of Chicago Press, 1986.

Kristeva, Julia. *Desire in Language: A Semiotic Approach to Literature and Art*. Ed. Leon Rodriquez. New York: Columbia University Press, 1980.

———. *Revolution in Language* Tr. Margaret Walker. New York: Columbia University Press, 1984.

———. "Stabat Mater." In *Tales of Love*. Tr. Leon Rodriquez. New York: Columbia University Press, 1987.

Krug, Gary J. and Laurel D. Graham. "Symbolic Interactionism: Pragmatism for the Postmodern Age." *Studies in Symbolic Interaction* 10 (Pt.A) (1989): 61–71.

Kundera, Milan. *The Unbearable Lightness of Being*. New York: Harper & Row, 1984.

LaCapra, Dominick. *"Madame Bovary" On Trial*. Ithaca: Cornell University Press, 1982.

Laplanche, Jean and J.-B. Pontalis. *Vocabulaire de la psychanalyse*. Paris: Presses Universitaires de France, 1967.

Lasch, Christopher. *The Culture of Narcissism: American Life in an Age of Diminishing Expectations*. New York: Norton, 1978.

Lash, Scott and Jonathan Friedman, eds. *Modernity and Identity*. Oxford: Blackwell, 1992.

Laslett, Peter. *The World We Have Lost: England Before the Industrial Age*. New York: Charles Scribner's Sons, 1973.

Lears, Jackson. "The Ad Man and the Grand Inquisitor: Intimacy, Publicity and the Managed Self in America, 1880-1940." In *Constructions of the Self*. Ed. George Levine. New Brunswick: Rutgers University Press, 1992.

Levin, David Michael. *The Listening Self: Personal Growth, Social Change and the Closure of Metaphysics*. New York: Routledge, 1989.

Levine, George, ed. *Constructions of the Self*. New Brunswick: Rutgers University Press, 1992.

Liebersohn, Harry. *Fate and Utopia in German Sociology, 1870-1923*. Cambridge: MIT Press, 1988.

Lindesmith, Alfred R., Anselm L. Strauss and Norman K. Denzin. *Social Psychology*. Englewood Cliffs: Prentice-Hall, 1988.

Longenbach, James. *Modernist Poetics of History: Pound, Eliot, and the Sense of the Past*. Princeton: Princeton University Press, 1987.

Löwith, Karl. *Nature, History, and Existentialism, and Other Essays in the Philosophy of History*. Ed. Arnold Levison. Evanston: Northwestern University Press, 1966.

Lukács, Georg. *The Meaning of Contemporary Realism*. London: Merlin, 1963.

Lyotard, Jean-François and Jean-Loup Thébaud. *Just Gaming*. Tr. Wlad Godzich. Minneapolis: University of Minnesota Press, 1985.

MacIntyre, Alasdair. *Whose Justice? Which Rationality?* Notre Dame: University of Notre Dame Press, 1988.

——. *After Virtue: A Study in Moral Theory*. Notre Dame: Notre Dame University Press, 1984.

Malamud, Bernard. *A New Life*. New York: Farrar, Straus, and Cudahy, 1961.

Mandel, Ernst. "The Role of the Individual in History: The Case of WW II." *New Left Review* 157 (1986): 61–77.

Marcel, Gabriel. *Creative Fidelity*. Tr. Robert Rosthal. New York: Farrar, Straus and Co., 1964.

Marshall, J.H. "On the Text and the Interpretation of a Poem of Raimbaut d'Orange (*Cars, douz*; ed. Pattison, I)." *Medium Aevum* 37 (1968): 12–36.

Martin, Waldo E., Jr. "Images of Frederick Douglass in the Afro-American Mind: The Recent Black Freedom Struggle." In *Frederick Douglass: New Literary and Historical Essays*. Ed. William L. Andrews. Cambridge: Cambridge University Press, 1990.

——. *The Mind of Frederick Douglass*. Chapel Hill: University of North Carolina Press, 1984.

Mayhew, Bruce. "Structuralism Versus Individualism: Pt. 1, Shadowboxing in the Dark." *Social Forces* 59 (1980): 335–75.

McCrone, John. *The Ape That Spoke: Language and the Evolution of the Human Mind*. New York: William Morrow, 1991.

McDowell, Deborah E. "In the First Place: Making Frederick Douglass and the Afro-American Narrative Tradition." In *Critical Essays on Frederick Douglass*. Ed. William L. Andrews. Boston: G.K. Hall, 1991.

Mead, George H. "Social Consciousness and the Consciousness of Meaning." *Psychological Bulletin* 7 (1910): 397–405.

Melville, Herman. *Billy Budd and Other Stories*. New York: New American Library, 1961.

Merleau-Ponty, Maurice. *The Visible and the Invisible*. Tr. Alphonso Lingis. Evanston: Northwestern University Press, 1968.

Meyers, Diana T. "The Socialized Self and Individual Autonomy: An Intersection Between Philosophy and Psychology." In *Women and Moral Theory*. Eds. Eva Kittay & Diana T. Meyers. Maryland: Rowman and Littlefield Press, 1987.

Miller, Nancy K. *Getting Personal: Feminist Occasions and Other Autobiographical Acts*. New York: Routledge, 1991.

Miller, R. Baxter. *The Art and Imagination of Langston Hughes*. Lexington: University Press of Kentucky, 1989.

———. *Black American Literature and Humanism*. Lexington: University Press of Kentucky, 1981.

Minnich, Elizabeth Kamarck. "From Ivory Tower to Tower of Babel?" *South Atlantic Quarterly* 89;1 (Winter, 1990).

Mitzman, Arthur. "Roads, Vulgarity, Rebellion, and Pure Art: The Inner Space in Flaubert and French Culture." *Journal of Modern History* 51, no. 3 (September 1979): 504–24.

Moore, Marianne. *The Complete Poems of Marianne Moore*. New York: Viking Press, 1967.

———. *The Complete Prose of Marianne Moore*. New York: Viking Press, 1986.

Morse, Carl and Joan Larkin, eds. *Gay & Lesbian Poetry in Our Time*. New York: St. Martin's Press, 1988.

Moses, Wilson J. "Writing Freely? Frederick Douglass and the Constraints of Racialized Writing." In *Frederick Douglass: New Literary and Historical Essays*. Ed. Eric J. Sundquist. Cambridge: Cambridge University Press, 1990.

Musil, Robert. *The Man Without Qualities*. London: Picador, 1979.

Nagel, Thomas and Bernard Williams. "Symposium on Moral Luck." *Proceedings of the American Aristotelean Society* 1 (1976): 115–151.

Nehamas, Alexander. *Nietzsche: Life as Literature*. Cambridge, Ma.: Harvard University Press, 1985.

Neitzsche, Friedrich. *The Will To Power*. Tr. Walter Kaufmann & R.J. Hollingdale. New York: Random House, 1967.

———. *Twilight of the Idols*. In *The Portable Nietzsche*. Ed. & Tr. Walter Kaufmann. New York: Viking, 1954.

———. *Thus Spoke Zarathustra*. In *The Portable Nietzsche*.

———. "On the Uses and Disadvantages of History for Life." In *Untimely Meditations*. Cambridge: Cambridge University Press, 1983.

Nitchie, George. *Marianne Moore: An Introduction to the Poetry*. New York: Columbia University Press, 1969.

Noddings, Nel. "A Response." *Hypatia: A Journal of Feminist Philosophy* 5.1 (1990): 120–27.

———. *Caring: A Feminine Approach to Moral Education*. Berkeley: University of California Press, 1984.

Norris, Christopher. *The Contest of Faculties*. London: Methuen, 1985.

———. *Derrida*. Cambridge, Ma.: Harvard University Press, 1987.

Norton, Anne. *Reflections on Political Identity*. Baltimore: Johns Hopkins University Press, 1988.

Ostriker, Alicia. *Stealing the Language: The Emergence of Women's Poetry in America*. Boston: Beacon Press, 1986.

Pattison, Walter T. *The Life and Works of the Troubadour Raimbaut D'Orange*. Minneapolis: University of Minnesota Press, 1952.

Pizzorno, Alessandro. "Foucault and the Liberal View of the Individual." In *Michel Foucault: Philosopher*. Ed. and Tr. Timothy J. Armstrong. New York: Routledge, 1992.

Plummer, Ken. "Staying in the Empirical World: Symbolic Interactionism." *Symbolic Interaction* 13 (1990): 155–160.

Poster, Mark. *The Mode of Information: Poststructuralism and Social Context*. Chicago: University of Chicago Press, 1990.

Rampersad, Arnold. *The Art and Imagination of W. E. B. Du Bois*. Cambridge, Ma.: Harvard University Press, 1976.

———. *The Life of Langston Hughes*. 2 vols. New York: Oxford University Press, 1986;1988.

Ricardou, Jean. *Le théatre des métamorphoses.* Paris: Seuil, 1982.

———. *Pour Une Théorie Du Nouveau Roman*. Paris: Éditions du Seuil, 1971.

Ricoeur, Paul. "The Hermeneutical Function of Distanciation." In *Hermeneutics and the Human Sciences: Essays on Language, Action, and Interpretation*. Tr. John B. Thompson. New York: Cambridge University Press, 1981.

———. "Ethique et politique." *Esprit* 101 mai (1985): 1–11.

———. "The Tasks of the Political Educator." *Philosophy Today* 17.2 (1973): 134–147.

————. *Soi-même comme un autre*. Paris: Editions du Seuil, 1990.

————. *Oneself as Another*. Tr. Kathleen Blamey. Chicago: University of Chicago Press, 1992.

————. *Time and Narrative*. 3 Vols. Tr. Kathleen McLaughlin & David Pellauer. Chicago: University of Chicago Press, 1984–88.

Riesman, David. *The Lonely Crowd*. New Haven: Yale University Press, 1950.

Riley, Matilda W. "Age Strata in Social Systems." In *Handbook of Aging and the Social Sciences*. Eds. Robert Binstock & Ethel Shanas. New York: Van Nostrand Rinehold, 1985.

Rilke, Rainer Maria. *The Selected Poetry of Rainer Maria Rilke*. Ed. and Tr. Stephen Mitchell. New York: Vintage Books, 1984.

Roberts, David D. "Frustrated Liberals: De Ruggiero, Gobetti, and the Challenge of Socialism." *The Canadian Journal of History* 17 (April 1982): 59–86.

————. *The Syndicalist Tradition and Italian Fascism*. Chapel Hill: University of North Carolina Press, 1979.

————. "Petty Bourgeois Fascism in Italy: Form and Content." In *Who Were the Fascists: Social Roots of European Fascism*. Ed. Stein Ugelvik Larsen et al. Bergen and Oslo: Universitetsforlaget (Norwegian Universities Press), 1980.

————. "Straight Stories, Crooked Histories, and Vichian Possibilities." *New Vico Studies* 8 (1990): 79–88.

————. "Croce and Beyond: Italian Intellectuals and the First World War." *The International History Review* 3 (April 1981): 201–35.

————. *Benedetto Croce and the Uses of Historicism*. Berkeley and Los Angeles: University of California Press, 1987.

————. "Benedetto Croce and the Dilemmas of Liberal Restoration." *The Review of Politics* 44 (April 1982): 214–41.

Rorty, Richard. "Habermas and Lyotard on Postmodernity." In *Habermas and Modernity*. Ed. Richard J. Bernstein. Cambridge: MIT Press, 1985.

————. *Essays on Heidegger and Others*. Cambridge: Cambridge University Press, 1991.

————. *Contingency, Irony, and Solidarity*. Cambridge: Cambridge University Press, 1989.

————. *Consequences of Pragmatism (Essays: 1972–1980)*. Minneapolis: University of Minnesota Press, 1982.

———. *Philosophy and the Mirror of Nature*. Princeton: Princeton University Press, 1979.

Rossi, Pietro. "Max Weber and Benedetto Croce." In *Max Weber and His Contemporaries*. Eds. Wolfgang J. Mommsen & Jürgen Osterhammel. London: Allen and Unwin, 1987.

Ruddick, Lisa. *Reading Gertrude Stein: Body, Text, Gnosis*. Ithaca: Cornell University Press, 1990.

Ruddick, Sara. "Maternal Thinking." In *Feminist Studies*. 6;2 (1980): 342–67.

———. *Maternal Thinking: Toward a Politics of Peace*. Boston: Beacon Press, 1989.

Ryan, Michael. *Marxism and Deconstruction: A Critical Articulation*. Baltimore: Johns Hopkins University Press, 1982.

Salinger, J. D. *The Catcher in the Rye*. Boston: Little, Brown, 1951.

Sansom, William. *A Contest of Ladies*. New York: Reynal, 1956.

Saunders, Ian. "The Concept Discourse." *Textual Practice* 2 (1988): 221–232.

Schrag, Calvin. *Communicative Praxis*. Bloomington: Indiana University Press, 1986.

Schulman, Grace. *Marianne Moore: The Poetry of Engagement*. New York: Paragon House, 1989.

Searle, John. "An Exchange on Deconstruction." *The New York Review of Books* 2 (Feb. 1984): 47–48.

Segal, Jerome M. *Agency and Alienation: A Theory of Human Presence*. Savage: Rowman and Littlefield, 1991.

Sewell, William H. Jr. *Work and Revolution in France: The Language of Labor From the Old Regime to 1848*. Cambridge: Cambridge University Press, 1980.

Shils, Edward. "In the Grip of the Past." In *Tradition*. Chicago: University of Chicago Press, 1981.

Silber, John. *Straight Shooting: What's Wrong with America and How to Fix It*. New York: Harper & Row, 1989.

Sloterdijk, Peter. *Critique of Cynical Reason*. Tr. Michael Eldred. Minneapolis: University of Minnesota Press, 1987.

Smalley, Beryl. *The Study of the Bible in the Middle Ages*. Notre Dame: University of Notre Dame Press, 1964.

Smith, Paul. *Discerning the Subject*. Minneapolis: University of Minnesota Press, 1988.

Snyder, Mark and William B. Swann. "When Actions Reflect Attitudes: The Politics of Impression Management." *Journal of Personality and Social Psychology* 36 (1976): 1202–1212.

———. "The Self-monitoring of Expressive Behavior." *Journal of Personality and Social Behavior* 30 (1974): 526–537.

———. "Self-monitoring Processes." In *Advances in Experimental Social Psychology*. Vol. 12. Ed. L. Berkowitz. New York: Academic Press, 1979.

———. *Public Appearances, Private Realities*. New York: W.H. Freeman, 1987.

Sokolowski, Robert. *Moral Action*. Bloomington: Indiana University Press, 1985.

Solomon, Robert C. *Continental Philosophy Since 1750: The Rise and Fall of the Self*. Oxford: Oxford University Press, 1988.

Spanos, William V. "Breaking the Circle: Hermeneutics as Dis-Closure." In *Boundary* 2 (1977) 5:421–457.

Spence, Sarah. "Reg(u)arding the Text: The Role of Vision in the Chansons of Charles d'Orleans." *Chaucer's French Contemporaries: The Poetry/Poetics of Self and Tradition*. Ed. R. Barton Palmer. New York: AMS, forthcoming.

Sprengnether, Madelon. *The Spectral Mother: Freud, Feminism, and Psychoanalysis*. Ithaca: Cornell University Press, 1990.

Stein, Gertrude. *The Autobiography of Alice B. Toklas*. New York: Vintage, 1960.

———. *Lectures in America*. Boston: Beacon Press, 1985.

———. *Selected Writings of Gertrude Stein*. Ed. Carl Van Vechten. New York: Vintage, 1972.

———. *The Yale Gertrude Stein*. New Haven: Yale University Press, 1980.

Stepto, Robert Jr. *From Behind the Veil: A Study of Afro-American Narrative*. Urbana: University of Illinois Press, 1979.

Stock, Brian. *Implications of Literacy: Written Language and Models of Interpretation in the Eleventh and Twelfth Centuries*. Princeton: Princeton University Press, 1982.

Stone, Lawrence. "The Growth of Affective Individualism." *The Family, Sex and Marriage in England 1500-1800*. New York: Harper & Row, 1979.

Suleiman, Susan Rubin. *Subversive Intent: Gender, Politics and the Avant-Garde*. Cambridge, Ma.: Harvard University Press, 1990.

Sundquist, Eric J. "Frederick Douglass' Literacy and Paternalism." In *Critical Essays on Frederick Douglass*. Ed. William L. Andrews. Boston: G. K. Hall, 1991.

Sykes, Charles J. *Profscam: Professors and the Demise of Higher Education*. New York: St. Martin's Press, 1988.

Taylor, Charles. *Sources of the Self: The Making of Modern Identity*. Cambridge, Ma.: Harvard University Press, 1989.

―――. *The Ethics of Authenticity*. Cambridge, Ma.: Harvard University Press, 1992.

―――. *Multiculturalism and "The Politics of Recognition."* Princeton: Princeton University Press, 1992.

―――. "Cross-Purposes: The Liberal-Communitarian Debate." In *Liberalism and the Moral Life*. Ed. Nancy L. Rosenblum. Cambridge, Ma.: Harvard University Press, 1989.

―――. *Philosophy and the Human Sciences*. Cambridge: Cambridge University Press, 1985.

―――. "Foucault on Freedom and Truth." In *Foucault: A Critical Reader*. Ed. David Couzens Hoy. Oxford: Basil Blackwell, 1986.

Taylor, Mark C. *Journeys to Selfhood: Hegel and Kierkegaard*. Berkeley and Los Angeles: University of California Press, 1980.

Tennyson, Alfred. *Selected Poetry*. Ed. Douglass Bush. New York: Modern Library, 1951.

Trilling, Lionel. *Sincerity and Authenticity*. New York: Harcourt, Brace, Jovanovich, 1980.

Tu Wei-ming. *Confucian Thought: Selfhood as Creative Transformation*. New York: SUNY Press, 1991.

Tucker, Charles W. and Robert L. Stewart. "Science, Self, and Symbolic Interaction." *Studies in Symbolic Interaction* 10 (1989): 45–60.

Turner, Ralph. "The Real Self: From Institution to Impulse." *American Journal of Sociology* 81 (1976): 989–1016.

Vijlstecke, Marc. "*Cars, Douz e Fenhz* de Raimbaud d'Orange." In *Etudes de Philologie Romane e d'Histoire Litteraire Offertes a Jules Horrent*. Eds. Jean Marie d'Heur and Nicoletta Cherubini. Liege, 1980.

Wahl, Jean. *Du Role de l'Idée de l'Instant dans le Philosophie de Descartes*. Paris: Librairie Felix Alcan, 1920.

Warnke, Georgia. *Gadamer: Hermeneutics, Tradition and Reason*. Stanford: Stanford University Press, 1987.

West, Cornel. "The New Cultural Politics of Difference." *October* 53 (Summer 1990).

Weeks, Jeffrey. *Sexuality and Its Discontents: Modern Meanings, Myths, Sexualities*. London: Routledge & Kegan Paul, 1985.

Whitman, Walt. *Song of Myself. Leaves of Grass*. Ed. John Hollander. New York: Vintage, 1992.

Williams, Bernard. *Problems of the Self: Philosophical Papers 1956–1972*. Cambridge: Cambridge University Press, 1991.

Willis, Paul. *Learning to Labor: How Working Class Kids Get Working Class Jobs*. New York: Columbia University Press, 1981.

Winders, James. *Gender, Theory and the Canon*. Madison: University of Wisconsin Press, 1991.

———. "Writing Like a Man (?): Descartes, Science, and Madness." In *Rereading the Canon: Descartes*. Ed. Susan R. Bordo. University Park: Pennsylvania State University Press, forthcoming.

———. "Baudrillard, the Masses and Hyperreality: The Limits of Postmodern French Cultural Theory," *Proceedings of the Annual Meeting of the Western Society for French History* 18 (1991).

———. *Reading for Difference: Texts on Gender, Race, and Class*. Eds. Melissa E. Barth, Thomas McLaughlin and James A. Winders. Fort Worth: Harcourt Brace Jovanovich College Publishers, 1993.

Wittig, Monique. *The Lesbian Body*. Tr. David Le Vay. Boston: Beacon Press, 1986.

Wolfe, Tom. *The Bonfire of the Vanities*. New York: Farrar, Straus & Giroux, 1987.

Wolin, Sheldon. "Hannah Arendt and the Ordinance of Time." In *Social Research* 44/1 (1977): 91–105.

Young, Iris Marion. *Justice and the Politics of Difference*. Princeton: Princeton University Press, 1990.

Ziolkowski, Thad. "Antithesis: The Dialectic of Violence and Literacy in Frederick Douglass' Narrative of 1845." In *Critical Essays on Frederick Douglass*. Ed. William L. Andrews. Boston: G. K. Hall, 1990.

Ziolkowski, Theodore. *Dimensions of the Modern Novel: German Texts and European Contexts*. Princeton: Princeton University Press, 1969.

Index